W9-CZI-814

# WASHINGTON, D.C., with Kids 2002-2003

**SANDRA BURT**
**LINDA PERLIS**

PRIMA PUBLISHING

With love to our favorite traveling companions,
nine terrific men: our husbands, Jeff and Barry; our sons,
Stephen, Roy, Jonathan, Daniel, Cliff, Andrew, and Aaron; and
our two wonderful daughters-in-law, Jessie and Debbie.

© 2001 by Random House, Inc.

All rights reserved. No part of this book may be reproduced or transmitted in any form or by any means, electronic or mechanical, including photocopying, recording, or by any information storage or retrieval system, without written permission from Random House, Inc., except for the inclusion of brief quotations in a review.

Published by Prima Publishing, Roseville, California. Member of the Crown Publishing Group, a division of Random House, Inc.

Random House, Inc. New York, Toronto, London, Sydney, Auckland

PRIMA PUBLISHING and colophon are trademarks of Random House, Inc., registered with the United States Patent and Trademark Office.

All products mentioned in this book are trademarks of their respective companies.

Every effort has been made to make this book complete and accurate as of the date of publication. In a time of rapid change, however, it is difficult to ensure that all information is entirely up-to-date. Although the publisher and author cannot be liable for any inaccuracies or omissions in this book, they are always grateful for corrections and suggestions for improvement. Please feel free to send your comments and corrections to parentsper@aol.com and visit http://i.am/parentsperspective.com.

*Illustrations and maps by Nathaniel Levine*

*Interior photos © Russ Finley (pages 44, 58, 69, 90, 196, 227, 325, 327); © The White House Historical Association (page 93);© RWC-A-1 (pages 117, 301);© 1998 Parks and History Association, photo by Carol M. Highsmith (page 120);© Finley-Holiday Films (pages 203, 292, 319); © Impact, photo by John Wagner (page 33);© PhotoDisc (pages 9, 23, 114, 130); photos by John Wagner (pages 122, 295); photos by Barry R. Perlis (pages 223, 234, 342, 344); photo by Maury Sullivan (page 167); photo provided by the Textile Museum (page 166)*

**Library of Congress Cataloging-in-Publication Data on File**

ISBN 0-7615-2920-9

01 02 03 04 DD 10 9 8 7 6 5 4 3 2 1

Printed in the United States of America

First Edition

**Visit us online at www.primapublishing.com**

# Contents

## Chapter 3  The National Mall          53

## Chapter 4  White House/Foggy Bottom          83

## Chapter 5  Tidal Basin                                   109

## Chapter 6  Georgetown/Embassy Row                       135

## Chapter 7  Dupont Circle/Adams Morgan        157

## Chapter 8  Chinatown/Gallery Place        183

# List of Maps

# List of Quick Guides

# Icons

Every chapter contains symbols to help locate specific tips:

 Smart Stuff

 Helpful Hint

 Money-Saving Tip

 Time-Saving Tip

 Parents/Teachers Take Note

★ Major Site

Watch for Smart Stuff questions throughout the book. Answers appear at the end of each chapter.

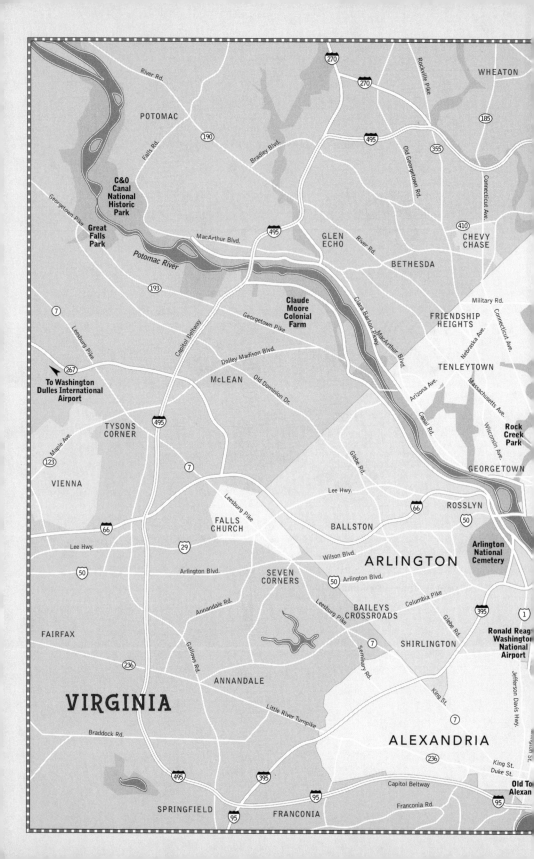

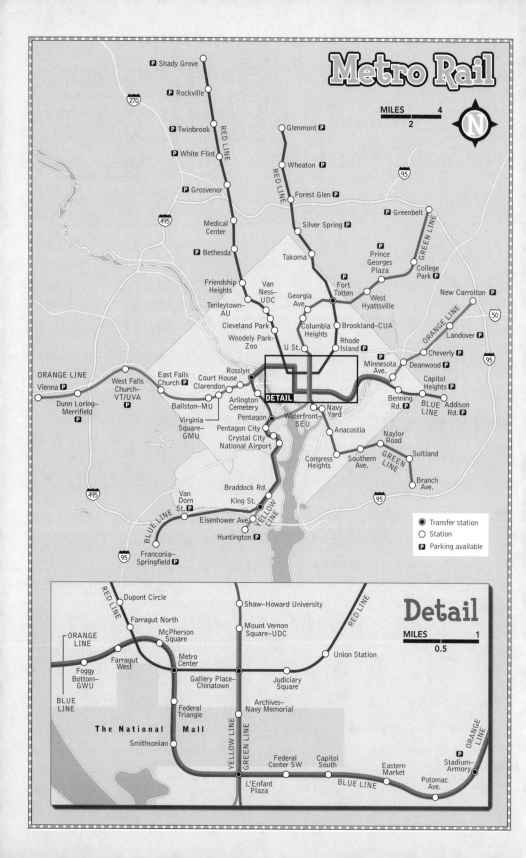

# Metro Rail

MILES
4
2

N

**Red Line stations:**
- Shady Grove (P)
- Rockville (P)
- Twinbrook (P)
- White Flint (P)
- Grosvenor (P)
- Medical Center
- Bethesda (P)
- Friendship Heights
- Tenleytown–AU
- Cleveland Park
- Woodely Park-Zoo
- Glenmont (P)
- Wheaton (P)
- Forest Glen (P)
- Silver Spring (P)
- Takoma
- Van Ness–UDC
- Georgia Ave.
- Fort Totten (P)
- Columbia Heights
- U St.
- Brookland–CUA
- Rhode Island (P)

I-270
I-495
I-95
I-50

- Greenbelt (P)
- Prince Georges Plaza (P)
- College Park (P)
- West Hyattsville
- New Carrolton (P)
- Landover (P)
- Cheverly (P)
- Deanwood (P)
- Minnesota Ave.
- Capitol Heights (P)
- Benning Rd. (P)
- Addison Rd. (P)

**Orange Line:**
- Vienna (P)
- Dunn Loring–Merrifield (P)
- West Falls Church–VT/UVA (P)
- East Falls Church
- Court House
- Clarendon
- Virginia Square–GMU
- Ballston–MU
- Rosslyn
- Arlington Cemetery
- Pentagon

- Pentagon City
- Crystal City
- National Airport
- Waterfront-SEU
- Navy Yard
- Anacostia
- Congress Heights
- Southern Ave.
- Naylor Road
- Suitland
- Branch Ave.

**Blue/Yellow Line:**
- Van Dorn St. (P)
- Braddock Rd.
- King St.
- Eisenhower Ave.
- Huntington (P)
- Franconia–Springfield (P)

Transfer station
Station
(P) Parking available

# Detail

MILES
1
0.5

- Dupont Circle
- Farragut North
- McPherson Square
- Shaw–Howard University
- Mount Vernon Square–UDC
- Union Station

ORANGE LINE
RED LINE
BLUE LINE

- Foggy Bottom–GWU
- Farragut West
- Metro Center
- Gallery Place–Chinatown
- Judiciary Square
- Federal Triangle
- Archives–Navy Memorial
- Smithsonian

The National Mall

- L'Enfant Plaza
- Federal Center SW
- Capitol South
- Eastern Market
- Potomac Ave.
- Stadium–Armory

YELLOW LINE
GREEN LINE
BLUE LINE
ORANGE LINE

# Acknowledgments

Little did we suspect that our journey rediscovering our hometown of Washington, D.C., would become a genuine expedition. The suggestions and support of numerous people have made this book a reality. And along the way, we have been the fortunate recipients of much encouragement.

As chief scout, our agent and dear friend, Sara Camilli, has kept us on course, all the while making us feel cared for and empowered. Our editor, Jamie Miller, has given us the gift of her belief in our work. She and Ben Dominitz had a vision for this book long before we did. We are grateful for their faith in us. Michelle Filippini, Nathaniel Levine, and Brenda Ginty have lent us their professionalism as well as their energy, and, as always, the Prima staff members involved have used their impressive talents to enhance our project.

The Washington, D.C., Convention and Visitors Association, the Alexandria Convention and Visitors Association, and the Hirschhorn Museum Education Department, as well as museum educators, librarians, and other specialists, including Julia Neubauer (Textile Museum), Sheila Brennan (Navy Museum), Evelyn Espinueva (National Law Enforcement Officers Memorial), Suzanne Wright (Phillips Collection), Sallie E. Altizer (National Museum of Women in the Arts), Dee Hoffman (Children's Concierge), Michelle Shuster, Suzanne Carbone (Montgomery County Public Libraries), and Sari Hornstein (historian) have kindly shared their materials and expertise.

Both teachers and students across the country gave us the benefit of their experiences visiting Washington, D.C. Alex Cutler, Diana Epstein, Patricia Lambert, Michael Moore, and Joreta Speck were particularly generous with their time and suggestions. To Tami Ishaeik and Julie Gasway, for their superlative people-finding, Linda and Jon Goldman, for their dependable information-gathering, and Peggy Waitt, for her thoughtfulness, go our special thanks.

Especially appreciated for their enthusiastic contributions to this project, Millard and Ruth Cass and Barry Perlis kept us constantly supplied with clippings, books, suggestions, and ideas. We are grateful for the efforts of such a caring "research department." Jessica Bennett, Jonathan Burt, Stephen Burt, and Nell Minow weighed in with guidance on appropriate movies and books to recommend; two thumbs-up for their kind assistance. Jeff Burt generously gave us the benefit of his legal skill and personal concern in our contract negotiations. The continued patience and support of both of our families throughout this enterprise have been invaluable.

Together we have weathered yet another adventure, a trip neither of us could or would have taken alone. And for all the bumps along the road, we've discovered that each of us is the other's best shock absorber. Hope you enjoy your own journey of discovery in our nation's capital.

# Introduction

Thinking about a trip to Washington, D.C.? What a great idea!

## Why Visit Washington, D.C.?

Visitors to Washington, D.C., arrive from all over the world, all year 'round. They come with their families, with their classes, with their Scout troops, with their youth groups, with 4-H clubs, and with their friends. Washington, D.C., is the capital of the United States of America, the capital of the free world, and the capital of our modern world's first democracy.

Washington visitors can both watch and participate in activities that only happen in the United States. They can see representatives debate bills and craft laws; they can sit in on Congressional committee hearings on subjects they read about in the daily newspapers; and they can hear arguments before the Supreme Court. In contrast to many other governments, both American citizens and foreign visitors are welcomed alike.

**Smart Stuff**

Why is Washington called the District of Columbia? (A.)

Unlike many other capital cities, Washington, D.C., is not famous for elaborate or ancient architecture. Instead, its buildings represent a variety of styles, many quite simple, reflecting our early colonial heritage and the indelible influence of ancient Greece and Rome.

## Take Note

Journals are wonderful learning tools and mementos of travels. It is fun for kids and teachers/parents to keep separate journals of what they see and think about. They can write down adventures that are funny or of special interest; they can also save brochures, postcards, and so forth in the journal. After the trip, comparing different people's versions of the same places and experiences will be fun!

Washington, D.C. (or the District, as some locals call it, for District of Columbia) also owes a debt to Frenchman Pierre L'Enfant, a brilliant engineer who envisioned a city of grand boulevards radiating out from a central Capitol building. Like his beloved Paris, Washington has green spaces, parks, and beautiful trees throughout the city. From Japan came a major contribution to the city's beauty—the cherry blossom trees that draw thousands of tourists every spring.

## Smart Stuff

For Tikes... Washington is a city of statues of famous (and not-so-famous) people. If you could choose a statue to put in your school, whom would it commemorate? Draw (or sculpt from clay) your design for a statue.

Washington is a city built on a human scale. The maximum height allowed for buildings within city limits was set at 110 feet, to keep the Capitol visible from everywhere in the city. Downtown Washington is pedestrian-friendly. The broad expanse of the Mall, stretching from the west front of the Capitol all the way to the Lincoln Memorial on the Potomac River, is designed for walking. It is lined with major sites and beautiful areas for recreation and relaxation, where numerous festivals and fairs take place throughout the year.

For any American, coming to Washington is like coming home—it is your city, no matter where you actually live. It is a city whose builders represented much of the diversity of our country. Geographer Andrew Ellicott, whose family founded Ellicott City, Maryland; African American astronomer Benjamin Banneker; physician William Thornton; Irishman James Hoban; and architect Benjamin Latrobe all contributed to the planning, design, and building of this capital city created by a newborn nation. Visitors also appreciate learning that Washington, D.C., is a bargain: There are more free attractions here than in any other U.S. city! In fact, unless otherwise specified, all sites described in *Washington, D.C., with Kids* are free.

**Smart Stuff**

**For Tweens and Teens...**
Which Native American nations populated the area where Washington, D.C., is now? What was their frightening prophecy? (B.)

# What Can This Trip Do for You?

Travel exposes everyone to experiences beyond the familiar. Kids particularly respond to new places and events, integrating them into their developing view of themselves and the world. When they physically encounter sites they have read or heard about, they can better understand their connection to a new ingredient in their environment.

Sharing experiences and adventures with their peers promotes camaraderie among young people. Coming from the same base (hometown, school, or group), kids can more easily help each other interpret their experiences. They enjoy what they are discovering even more when they share. Each member enriches the group with his or her individual contributions.

Adults can help children focus their attention and can help them interpret what they see and hear into a context they can more easily understand. Adults provide responsible guidance, support, and safety. An extra bonus for adults who travel with children is the benefit of their youthful perspective and energy.

As anyone who deals with kids knows, we need to be flexible, and that is especially true with travel. Things don't always go according to plan. We recently heard a story about a class who came to Washington for two days (probably in February!) and awoke to a major snowstorm on the first morning. Even the museums were closed—a rarity in Washington. Via television, students and their chaperones learned that D.C. hospitals were requesting volunteers to make up for staff who couldn't reach their workplaces. So, being right in the city, students eagerly filled in. Their experiences at the hospital made them feel much more important than a day of cruising the monuments would have. It proved to be an unexpected but treasured highlight of their trip. We wish you better weather, of course, but similar satisfaction. (By the way, we could always use leaf-rakers, yard-workers, or garage cleaner-outers, if you're hard up for activities!)

## Brief Historic Background

The earliest white visitors arrived here by boat, when Captain John Smith led the first expedition up the Potomac River. For more than a hundred years, this area was a quiet backwater until the new nation needed a capital. How appropriate that Washington, a city of political give and take, was established through a compromise. Shepherded through the Congress of 1790 by Alexander Hamilton and Thomas Jefferson, the Residence Act, establishing the capital city at its present location, was passed. Both the North and the South had wanted the capital in their own jurisdictions; they were also divided on whether the federal government should assume payment of individual states' Revolutionary War debts. The North agreed to establishment of the capital in a southern location when the South agreed that Congress should assume the states' war debts. President George Washington chose the site, and the U.S. Geographer General, Andrew Ellicott, drew the boundaries.

The city of Washington is grateful to a daughter of Virginia Quaker parents, who rescued the portrait of our first Commander-in-Chief from the burning White House. On August 23, 1814, when the British invaded and burned Washington, Dolley Madison, wife of President James Madison, decided to remain in the White House until the last possible moment; she took Gilbert Stuart's famous portrait of Washington, along with the most important state documents and works of art, to safety.

**Smart Stuff**

For Tweens and Teens... In which eight cities did the U.S. government meet before the capital was established in the District of Columbia? (C.)

During the Civil War, Washington became a city ringed with forts. To reduce the city's vulnerability to Confederate troops, the Union built 68 forts, one of which was visited by President Abraham Lincoln, who came to view the conflict. Standing over six feet tall and wearing his stovepipe hat, he made a notable target on the ramparts of Fort Stephens. Accordingly, an army officer next to him shouted impulsively, "Get down, you fool!" Fortunately, he did. The army officer turned out to be a pretty sharp fellow; his name was Lieutenant Colonel Oliver Wendell Holmes, later a justice of the U. S. Supreme Court. Lincoln had government buildings converted into barracks, and fields in the city became pastures for grazing animals. The forts and batteries have been maintained by the National Park Service; children at play can climb up on the mounds that once served to protect the capital city.

Following the Civil War, a construction boom modernized much of Washington with paved streets, sidewalks, streetlights, and a sewer system. Over the ensuing years, such notables as Frederick Law Olmsted, Augustus Saint-Gaudens, and Lady Bird Johnson became involved in the beautification of the city. These are all interesting people to read about; check your library or the Web.

Between 1910 and 1935, Washington saw the birth of many new museums, galleries, and concert halls, including the Smithsonian's Natural History Museum, the Folger Shakespeare Library and

Theater, the Freer Gallery, the National Theater, and the Lincoln Memorial.

Beginning with World War I and the Wilson era, Washington's voice in world affairs became more powerful. Government began an expansion that increased dramatically by World War II. Buildings proliferated in several areas of the city to accommodate living and working space for the ever-increasing federal work force. The new Pentagon Building, across the river in Arlington, Virginia, accommodated 40,000 employees.

## Smart Stuff

**For Tweens and Teens...**
What famous lady was responsible for obtaining the cherry blossom trees for Washington, D.C.?
(D.)

Washington again became the focus for thousands of people during the 1960s. Marches to end hunger, promote civil rights, and conclude the war in Vietnam, were all staged in the nation's capital. Emotion-filled events such as Marion Anderson's performances in 1939 and 1952, and Dr. Martin Luther King Jr.'s famous speech ("I have a dream. . .") in 1963, took place on the steps of the Lincoln Memorial.

From the Bonus Marchers of World War I, to the occupants of the "Poor People's tent city" on the Mall, to the Million Mom March for gun safety, citizens of the United States look to their nation's capital as the place where their voices can be heard. Continuing national rituals, such as the Inauguration on the steps of the Capitol building and the ensuing parade, funerals of presidents and national leaders, and ceremonies for visiting heads of state, take place in Washington, D.C. Sites like Arlington National Cemetery and the Vietnam Memorial Wall continue to evoke emotional responses.

## What's in This Book and How to Use It

*Washington, D.C., with Kids* is divided into twelve geographic chapters, followed by sections on entertainment, tours, and follow-up.

Each section includes maps of city areas, lists of recommended sites and the appropriate information for visiting them, along with ideas and activities to enhance children's learning about the city. Child-friendly accommodations and restaurants are included in each section as well. In every chapter, icons identify money-saving tips, time-saving tips, smart stuff, etc. Age-appropriateness for each site is indicated by the terms *Tikes* (children under 6), *Tweens* (ages 7–12), or *Teens* (ages 13–19). A glossary list of icons is also included.

# Especially for Foreign Visitors and the Physically Challenged

The new Visitor Information Center is located at 1300 Pennsylvania Avenue, NW, in the Ronald Reagan Building and International Trade Center. Up-to-date information is available here, with brochures, maps, souvenirs, assistance with hotel and restaurant reservations, a food court, public phones, and public rest rooms. Open Monday through Saturday from 8 A.M. to 6 P.M., and Sunday, noon to 5 P.M., this center is a valuable resource, no matter where you are coming from. Telephone: 202-DC VISIT. Two very helpful Washington, D.C., Web sites are: www.washington.org and www.washingtonpost.com. The National Park Service also has a useful Web site: www.nps.gov/ncro/parklist.htm, as does the Smithsonian Institution: www.si.edu.

The Meridian International Center (1624 and 1630 Crescent Place, NW) offers services specifically for international visitors. At Dulles International Airport, Meridian International has an information desk, where it offers multilingual services, and where a telephone language bank is available. The Center can also tailor programs for groups. Telephone: 202-939-5568 or 202-667-6800. Web site: www.Meridian.org. A new Internet site designed to help tourists visiting the U.S. from other countries is www.usawelcome .com. Adams Morgan, an eclectic neighborhood of multicultural eateries and shops, is on Eighteenth Street, only two blocks away from the Meridian International Center. (We do not suggest walking alone in this area at night.)

Washington, D.C., is one of the most accessible and welcoming cities in the world for the physically challenged. Most government buildings, museums, galleries, hotels, restaurants, and shopping areas have wheelchair ramps and accessible restrooms and water fountains. There are also Braille menus, telephones for the hearing-impaired, and large-print brochures. A free flyer detailing accessibility in the capital city is available; phone 202-789-7000 or FAX 202-789-7037.

# What if You Get Sick While You're Here?

Getting sick or having an accident when away from home can be alarming. Be sure everyone brings all prescription medications, extra eyeglasses or contact lenses, health insurance information, and over-the-counter medications frequently used (such as for motion sickness or upset stomach). A hotel concierge is a good source for finding a doctor. The Washington Hospital Center (202-877-DOCS) offers a referral service during the week, 8 A.M.–4 P.M., and can help you locate a doctor as close as possible to where you are staying. However, visitors often have to go to the nearest hospital for help. Some emergency rooms have walk-in clinics for non-life-threatening problems, and service there is much less expensive than in the emergency room itself. Four local hospitals are: Children's Hospital National Medical Center (111 Michigan Avenue, NW, 202-884-5000; Emergency Room: 202-884-5200); George Washington University Hospital (901 23rd Street, NW, 202-994-3211; Emergency Room: 202-715-4911); Georgetown University Hospital (3800 Reservoir Road, NW, 202-784-2118; Emergency Room: 202-784-3111); and Howard University Hospital (2041 Georgia Avenue, NW, 202-865-6100; Emergency Room: 202-865-1131). There are several 24-hour CVS pharmacies: at 14th Street and Vermont Avenue (Thomas Circle), 202-628-0720, and at 67 Dupont Circle, 202-785-1466.

## Helpful Hint

The White House, Smithsonian Institution, Kennedy Center, Library of Congress, and some other attractions offer brochures in a number of different languages. All foreign embassies and legations offer information and assistance to visitors from their countries. Advance contact is especially helpful, and telephone numbers are listed in the District of Columbia telephone directory's Yellow Pages under Embassies and Legations. You can access Yellow Pages at any library (in your hometown) and on the Internet at www.YellowPages.com.

All airports serving the Washington, D.C., area, and Union Station (trains), offer information desks for arriving visitors.

# Some Suggestions for Reading

There are many books, movies, and games about Washington, D.C., and specific places and people here: *Underground Train,* by Mary Quattlebaum (tikes); *A Visit to Washington, D.C.,* by Jill Kremetz (tikes); *The Inside-Outside Book of Washington, D.C.,* by R. Munro (tikes); *Washington City is Burning,* by Harriette G. Robinet (tweens); *Look Out, Washington, D.C.!* by Patricia Reilly Giff (tweens); *Washington, D.C. (Cities of the World series),* by R. Conrad Stein (tweens); *Washington, D.C. (From Sea to Shining Sea),* by Dennis B. Fradin (tweens); *Lives of the Presidents, Fame, Shame (and What the Neighbors Thought),* by Kathleen Krull, a book about the lives of presidents as husbands, fathers, pet owners, and neighbors (tweens); *Eyewitness to Power: The Essence of Leadership, Nixon to Clinton,* by David R. Gergen (teens); and *Anything Goes!: What I've Learned from Pundits, Politicians, and Presidents,* by Larry King.

An international chain of hotels, food, and hospitality services was begun inauspiciously with a root beer stand at 14th Street and Park Road, NW, in 1927. The young entrepreneurs did quite well in the end; their names were Alice and J. W. Marriott.

*Just the Facts: Fun Facts of American History* (tweens and teens) is a video about the evolution of the United States, its customs, origins of its symbols, and even new inventions. A 1,000-piece puzzle for tweens and teens, United States Presidents Jigsaw Puzzle, makes it fun to put together a 24" × 30" composite of colored pictures of the U.S. presidents. Run-Off Presidential Game is a board game (tweens and teens) enabling players to collect electoral votes with their knowledge of U.S. politics, history, and geography. A game of humor and politics, power and prestige, Democracy would also be fun for teens to play.

Have a safe and happy visit!

Oh, and by the way, please keep in touch. To help us update our suggestions and information, we need to hear from our readers. Visit our Web site at http://i.am/parentsperspective or send an e-mail to parentsper@aol.com.

# Answers to Smart Stuff Questions

**A.** In 1871, Congress passed a law, making Washington a federal territory. Since 1802, it had been a city simply called Washington, with a mayor appointed by the president, and a city council. After the Civil War, corruption was rampant in city governments across the country, and Washington was no exception. In an attempt to keep the capital from being moved to a different part of the country, Congress instituted territorial status (no more local government). Because the U.S. was popularly known as "Columbia" (in honor of Christopher Columbus), the new capital was named the District of Columbia.

**B.** Algonquin and Iroquois. The prophecy they believed in held that strangers from across the ocean would come and destroy their people.

**C.** Philadelphia, Pennsylvania; Baltimore, Maryland; Lancaster, Pennsylvania; York, Pennsylvania; Princeton, New Jersey; Annapolis, Maryland; Trenton, New Jersey; and New York, New York

**D.** Helen Herron (Mrs. William Howard) Taft received the ornamental cherry trees as a gift to the United States from Japan.

# About the Authors

**Sandra Burt** and **Linda Perlis,** authors of *Parents as Mentors,* produce and host the weekly public service radio program  *Parents' Perspective.* Both grew up in the Washington, D.C., area, and they have been working together for more than twenty years. Between them, they have raised seven sons.

CHAPTER
1

Preparing
to Come

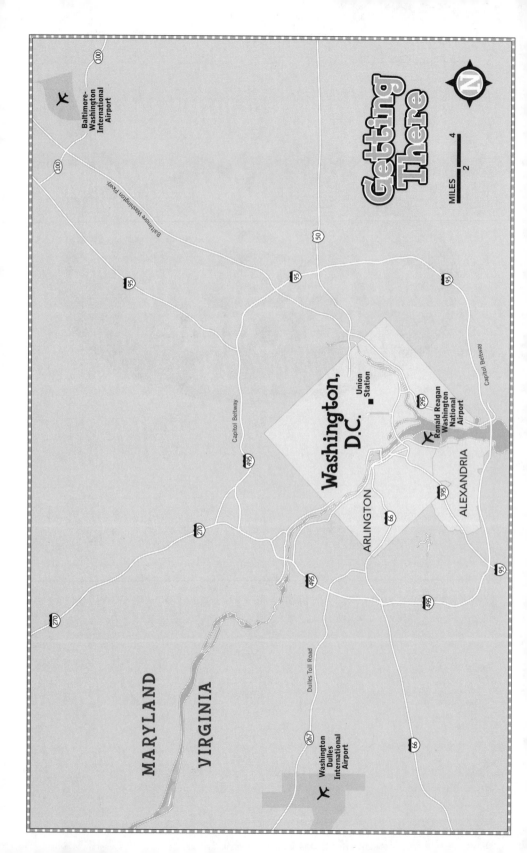

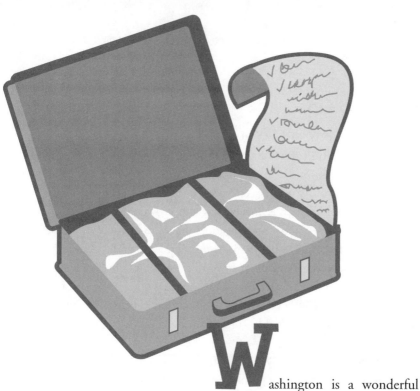

**W**ashington is a wonderful city for visitors at all times of the year. In the spring, its famous cherry blossoms festoon the Tidal Basin and adjoining Potomac Park in ribbons of pastel pink. In the summer, visitors can enjoy the annual Smithsonian Folklife Festival spread out across the Mall. Thousands come to sit under the stars on the grounds of the Washington Monument every Independence Day, and marvel at the canopy of fireworks crackling in magnificent displays overhead. In addition to the beauty of leaves changing color in a city filled with trees, fall brings the opening of the United States Supreme Court and the return of Congress from its August recess. Winter is always a season of surprises, from the glittery frost and snow that greeted the Kennedy inauguration, to bright, clear days when the white marble buildings reflect the sunlight against a deep blue sky. Winters are normally mild and not crowded with tourists; a short subway, bus, or taxi ride can still get you quickly to almost any destination in the city.

# When to Go

Speaking of tourists, they crowd into all of Washington's most popular attractions and forms of transportation at cherry blossom time and in the hot, humid summer months when school is out. The best times to avoid a mob scene are late spring—May and early June, when the weather is lovely and the crowds are lighter—or after Labor Day, when most schools have re-opened and the weather is more comfortable than in summer. Weekends can still be a challenge, however. November brings lighter numbers of travelers and welcome fall temperatures. Winter, while unpredictable weather-wise, is the least crowded season of all and brings the added bonus of a full and accessible cultural scene. Daytime spring temperatures average from the low 60s to the mid-70s; summer sizzles with temperatures regularly in the 80s and sometimes into the 90s (don't forget about Washington's famous humidity); fall begins in the 70s and ends in the 50s; and winter temperatures hover normally in the 40s. But there *can* be stretches of bone-chilling weather and snow.

The winter holiday season in Washington is popular because of the many colorful events open to the public, but this does mean long waits for some activities. Saturdays bring peak numbers of visitors all year long, and Mondays through Wednesdays are the least crowded times at most sites.

# Planning Your Itinerary

The logical question is whether or not to pull children out of school to visit Washington, D.C. What more educational city could a child visit? Whether for a family trip or a school trip, parents and teachers together need to facilitate a workable plan, so that a child doesn't return home to enormous loads of make-up work, and can use his travel experience productively. A creative teacher might make up a list of questions as a framework for the child's written response (see *A Capital Scavenger Hunt* at the end of this chapter).

## Parents/Teachers Take Note

### Scrapbook

Everywhere you go in Washington, D.C., there will be pictures and papers to collect, so it's a good idea for each young person to prepare a scrapbook to save these items after the trip. Some people might choose to select a specific theme for a scrapbook, such as architecture, monuments and/or statues, or maps and charts. Gallon-size plastic zip-lock bags make good storage containers for these treasured items. Pack a few in backpacks and label each with a sticker.

Needless to say, everything that pertains to children and trips needs a name and address label (except, perhaps, the child!). Three-dimensional objects that cannot be pasted in a scrapbook can be saved in a memory box, a container specifically purchased or made by the child to showcase these items.

And don't forget about those *journals*.

Autograph collectors, bring your *autograph books*. In addition to collecting signatures, you might also want to preserve a meaningful name from the Vietnam Veterans Wall, for example. You can hold a page up against the name and rub the side of a pencil or crayon over it; the name will appear on your page.

Every monument, gallery, and museum has free (or inexpensive) informative guides and brochures to enhance the visit. Encourage students to collect information and reflect on and discuss what they see and hear. (Journals come in handy here.)

If possible, arrange in advance with your Congressional representative's or senator's office to obtain passes to watch Congress in session; students can often meet these people at their offices when picking up the passes.

To call the Capitol to ask for VIP tickets, phone 202-225-6827. The daily newspapers in Washington, D.C., publish lists of which subcommittee meetings and congressional hearings are open to the public; high school students and adults might find such events especially interesting. These hands-on experiences can be more revealing and memorable teachers than any class in (or lecture on) U.S. government. Come see how your tax dollars are spent.

Call the Smithsonian Information Center (202-357-2700) to request a free copy of "Planning Your Smithsonian Visit." And several helpful telephone numbers to keep with you on the trip are: Dial-a-Museum, 202-357-2020; Dial-a-Phenomenon, 202-357-2000; Dial-A-Park, 202-619-7275; National Park Service, 202-619-7222; and Recreation and Parks Department (D.C., not federal), 202-673-7660, when you need information you can't find in your other materials. Another excellent source for D.C. information is the Travel Books and Language Center (4437 Wisconsin Avenue, NW); call to ask for their catalog (202-237-1322 or 1-800-220-2665).

All three major airports that serve Washington, D.C., provide trained staff members to help with the kinds of problems travelers might encounter on arrival. The National Park Service has two kiosks—on the Ellipse and near the Vietnam Veterans Memorial—open all year to help visitors; other kiosks around the city open seasonally.

The Guide Service of Washington, Inc. offers a variety of planned tour options as well as private tours led by licensed guides; there are also guides who can offer tours for foreign visitors in their native languages (202-628-2842). The Service can meet and greet airport arrivals, and provide shuttle buses for groups to get to their hotels.

The Children's Concierge designs itineraries for groups and families, offering ways to involve kids interactively in Washington's cultural and historical sights (301-948-3312).

## Helpful Hint

When it comes to finding out about Washington, D.C., resources abound. Internet sources list all kinds of references you can explore (keyword: Washington, D.C.), and Web sites offer details about what to see, when, where, and how. The "official Web site" for the capital city is: www.washington.org; event calendars and travel tips are generally kept up to date. This site also enables you to make hotel reservations online. Another helpful site is www.digitalcity.com, where you can click onto a Visitor's Guide or find tips on entertainment, shopping, news, and "best of the city." The Washington, D.C., Convention and Visitors Association publishes "The American Experience," a helpful pamphlet, as well as seasonal calendars of events and a clear, helpful Visitor Map (with Metro map). Phone: 202-789-7000.

An evergreen in the resource department is, of course, the always-dependable AAA Mid-Atlantic Tour Book (Web site: www.aaa.com). AAA issues the most comprehensive highway and city maps we have found; these are free for AAA members. Other books we have found helpful are listed in the bibliography.

## Media Resources

The *Washington Post*, a favorite with local news junkies, is especially valuable for its Friday edition, which includes the "Weekend" section. Here's where to find tips for what's hot during the time you're in town. The *Washington Times* (conservative name, conservative paper) offers "Washington Daybook," a daily listing of all the meetings around town and guests on local and national talk shows. *City Paper*, a free "Generation-X"-friendly alternative paper, is a good source for information on arts, theaters, clubs, popular music, and

reviews of current movies. *Washington Afro-American* provides coverage of black D.C. events and citizens. *Washington Jewish Week* lists synagogues and kosher dining information, in addition to community news and editorials. The *Washingtonian* is a monthly magazine with all sorts of events listings, restaurant write-ups, and special features. Hotel desks provide the ubiquitous, free *Go* and *Where* brochures that list what's going on around town.

On the airwaves, Washingtonians have a variety of choices. Newsaholics (of which there are many here) can watch or listen to C-SPAN 24 hours a day, broadcasting coverage of Congressional events (on the radio, it's 90.1 FM; check with your hotel for all Washington, D.C., TV channels). Local news here is often national news; you might see yourselves on a local station if you've spent the day visiting a government event or congressional hearing. Several radio stations focus on news, talk, and sports programming; these include 630 AM, 930 AM, and 1500 AM. Everyone's musical tastes can be satisfied by at least one D.C. area radio station; check the *Washington Post* for listings. Parents and teachers enjoy "Parents' Perspective," an encouraging and enlightening parenting program on WPFW 89.3 FM every Friday morning at 11:30 A.M. Listeners who catch this show in their own hometowns will be happy to find it here in Washington, D.C.

# Preparing Can Be Fun: Movies, Books, and Games

Heat up the popcorn; watch a film. Some good movies with a "Washington, D.C., connection" are: *Advise and Consent* (a classic; moral issues, set in a Senate confirmation hearing; teens), *All the President's Men* (a gripping whodunit that just happens to be a real-life story; kids need to be reminded that the work two reporters began resulted in the only resignation of a president in U.S. history; appropriate for older tweens and teens), *Mr. Smith Goes to Washington* (patriotism and civic duty set in familiar sites, the Lincoln Memorial and the U.S. Capitol; this film made Jimmy Stewart, playing a naïve congressman, a star; teens), *The American President*

(Michael Douglas plays a U.S. president whose wife has died. In familiar Washington surroundings, he resumes dating; lighthearted and enjoyable for teens), and *Dave* (a presidential look-alike is manipulated by unscrupulous staff as a puppet stand-in, but turns out to have scruples of his own; teens can relate to this one).

Book lovers will especially enjoy delving through the rich selection of works on Washington, D.C. Here is a quick overview to get started: *The Mystery in Washington, D.C. (Boxcar Children),* by Gertrude Chandler Warner (a mystery for tweens, with visits to many Washington, D.C., sites); *The Case of Capital Intrigue (Nancy Drew),* by Carolyn Keene (another exciting mystery, this time about a theft in the nation's capital; tweens and young teens); *Undercover Washington: Touring the Sites Where Infamous Spies Lived, Worked, and Loved,* by Pamela Kessler (a guide to places in and around D.C. complete with true stories about dastardly deeds; for older teens); *Private Washington: Residences in the Nation's Capital,* by Jan Cigliano, Walter Smalling, and Sally Quinn (a real insider's guide to twenty-six of the District's famous official residences and private homes—a special treat for the grown-ups!); *Murder in Foggy Bottom,* by Margaret Truman (another in her well-received Capital Crimes Series set in and around D.C.; she should know the territory—she's former President Harry Truman's daughter; older teens); *Murder in the Executive Mansion* and *Murder in the West Wing: An Eleanor Roosevelt Mystery,* by Elliott Roosevelt (two popular titles in a series of such

*A good map is essential. Do you know if your destination is NW or NE?*

mysteries, set in the capital city by Eleanor and Franklin Roosevelt's son; teens); *The Incumbent: A Washington Thriller,* by Brian McGrory (a Boston journalist gets involved in a political thriller that begins with a presidential assassination attempt; older teens); *The Street Lawyer,* by John Grisham (the famous mystery writer does it again, this time taking his hero from the plush offices of his high-priced firm to the gritty world of the homeless; teens); and *Washington, D.C.: A Novel,* by Gore Vidal (a searing look at politics, politicians, and others from the New Deal to the McCarthy era; older teens). For those interested in Washington's natural world, two suggestions are *Spring in Washington,* by Louis J. Halle (teens); and *Specimen Days,* by Walt Whitman (teens), describing the District and its surrounding areas during the Civil War era. And one of the funniest we've come across is *Hail to the Chiefs: How to Tell Your Polks from Your Tylers,* by Barbara Holland; it's a hilarious romp through presidential politics (older tweens and teens), and, though out of print, very much worth a library or used book store search.

And if you're just feeling like sitting on the floor together for hours, you can indulge in *Washington, D.C., Monopoly.* Here you really *can* own the Treasury!

## Expense Planning

What will a trip to Washington, D.C., cost? There are certain built-in expenses like transportation, lodging, meals, souvenirs (if you indulge), and entertainment. The good news, however, is that in this city, most tourist attractions are free. Well, not exactly: you've already paid for them with your tax money. Remember: unless otherwise noted, all museums and galleries we describe charge no admission fees.

Rates for everything change according to season, except for local transportation. Your best ammunition is to ask questions. As with the "rack rates" for hotels, there are always alternatives, but you have to learn what the options are. Check out special rates for students, seniors, tours, groups, AAA members, AARP members, union members, and any other group you've ever been associated

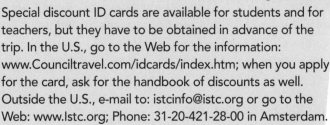

## Money-Saving Tip
### International Student/Teacher Identity Cards
Special discount ID cards are available for students and for teachers, but they have to be obtained in advance of the trip. In the U.S., go to the Web for the information: www.Counciltravel.com/idcards/index.htm; when you apply for the card, ask for the handbook of discounts as well. Outside the U.S., e-mail to: istcinfo@istc.org or go to the Web: www.Istc.org; Phone: 31-20-421-28-00 in Amsterdam.

with! Ask: "But do you have anything for *less?*" Another thought: some universities make dormitory space available for their students who come to work or study in Washington, so you might contact your local university to see if they have vacancies in their facilities here; check on the fees.

Most travelers already know it is not wise to carry wads of cash. Depending on your preferences and the snacking habits of your traveling companions, it's a good idea to plan generously and end up with cash for last-minute, take-home items. Since traveler's checks are fast becoming an anachronism, some advance planning is in order. ATMs offer the convenience of picking up only the money you need when you need it—as long as you plan ahead and know which of your cards is acceptable to the most machines. Check in advance with your hotel, because it is always safer to use an ATM inside your hotel, or inside any building, than to stop out in the open and let the world all around know you are filling your pockets with a fresh supply of cash. Credit cards, of course, are wonderful and generally safe, but it is wise to copy the 800# for emergencies off the card and put it somewhere separate from the card. If your credit card is lost or stolen, you will have the necessary number to call and cancel it immediately.

It might be reassuring to know some basic price ranges in Washington, D.C. To take a taxi from Ronald Reagan Washington

National Airport to downtown D.C. runs about $15; from Dulles Airport in northern Virginia, taxi fare is about $45. There are several shuttle services to and from these and BWI as well, all of which run about $10 to $28 to downtown; the second person's rate is substantially reduced. Within the city, taxis run $4 and up; the system is confusing because there are eight zones plus add-ons. Prices are posted in each taxi. Metro (D.C.'s subway system) runs $1.10 to $3.25; there's a fare card system with clear instructions on easily accessible dispensers at each station. Prices vary according to day, distance, and time of day (i.e., weekends or rush hours); there are some special discount deals for fare cards, also clearly posted.

## Money-Saving Tip

Telephone calls from hotel rooms can be quite pricey; most hotels tack on extra fees beyond the $.35 you would pay on a local pay phone. Come prepared with quarters and dimes!

Local pay phone calls are $.35. Tips for bellhops and porters generally are $1/bag; checkroom attendants expect $1/garment; parking lot attendants and doormen (who hail a taxi for you) expect $1. Restaurants, depending on the service and formality, anticipate 15 to 20 percent tips for employees, and cabdrivers, about 15 percent of the fare.

## Money-Saving Tip

Food is everywhere and at every price. You can sit on a park bench and gobble a hotdog and soda from a street vendor for just a few dollars, and you can look for the early bird specials or prix fixe menus at the fancier restaurants. Eating your big meal at lunchtime can save money, too. For each section of the city, we offer suggestions for a variety of places to chow down.

Hotels can run anywhere from the five-star variety at megabucks to the inexpensive suburban chains and city youth hostels. Convenience to what you want to visit will have to be meshed with your budget to come up with a satisfactory compromise. Currently, the hotel tax in the District is 14.5 percent, a not insignificant sum when tacked onto room rates. More on this as we move along—stick with us. Every chapter will have helpful suggestions for its particular area of the city.

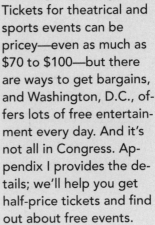

**Money-Saving Tip**
Tickets for theatrical and sports events can be pricey—even as much as $70 to $100—but there are ways to get bargains, and Washington, D.C., offers lots of free entertainment every day. And it's not all in Congress. Appendix I provides the details; we'll help you get half-price tickets and find out about free events.

## Where to Stay

Ah, the glories of room service and telephones in your bathroom. But when you're planning where to stay in downtown Washington, D.C., you need to consider even more essential ingredients. If you're going to be exploring the downtown D.C. area on foot, as you should (cars are impossible to park, and some older lots cannot accommodate large cars at all!), you will want to stay within easy walking distance of a Metro station. Don't worry—*Washington, D.C., with Kids* comes with its own Metro map—and we're here to tell you what accommodations are near which stops. The

**Helpful Hint**
Be absolutely sure to have *reservations* for accommodations before you come to Washington, D.C.

size of your group will also dictate your choices; some places are delighted with tour busloads of teenagers, while others are too small, and cater instead to adults or families. Count on a really good travel agent if you can find one; they often know more places and get better deals than you can find otherwise. Several telephone numbers you will find useful while planning this part of the trip include:

Accommodations Express, 1-800-906-4685

Central Reservation Service Corporation, 407-740-6442 or 1-800-555-7555

Hotel Reservations Network, 1-800-964-6835

U.S.A. Groups, Inc., 1-800-872-4777

Washington, D.C., Accommodations, 1-800-554-2220

Capital Reservations, 1-800-323-2149 or www.hotelsdc.com

One caveat for anyone taking groups of students: Absolutely avoid hotel rooms with balconies!

## Smart Stuff

Game time! A wonderful way to introduce kids to the layout of Washington, D.C., is to have them work in groups with a large city map and a colored map of the Metro (subway) system. These are available free of charge from the Washington, D.C., Convention and Visitors Association; 202-789-7000 or via the Internet: www.washington.org.

Give each group six to eight places to locate on their street maps and then have them identify which subway stops they would use to get there. The difficulty of locations and number of assignments can be geared to the ages of the participants, whether fifth graders or tenth graders. This can be a race among the groups; Washington, D.C., T-shirts would make wonderful prizes.

# What to Bring

In contrast to travelers who need a truck just to get their luggage to the airport, savvy travelers to Washington, D.C., come with as little baggage as practical. (Everyone does bring political preferences, but these don't take up space.) Summer packing is the easiest, because no coats or boots are needed ever (but don't forget these if you are coming in late fall through early spring). You might want to pack a little personal fan (a tiny machine, not a groupie); the hot, sticky weather will require coping with sweat (yours and everyone else's). No matter when you visit D.C., raincoats and/or umbrellas are wise choices. Almost everywhere you go will welcome "casual" attire; however, this means clothing that will not embarrass adult chaperones. Shoes are required. They should be the most comfortable pair you've ever worn, as you could even wear them out on this trip. A travel tip we have found useful is to pack an extra pair of spongy insoles you can insert into any pair. Happy feet make happy travelers. Any season could surprise you—a sweater or lightweight jacket to use as a layer can stave off early morning or late evening chill. Layers, in fact, are always a good idea. In the summer, many buildings have thermostats set to arctic temperatures. Even the teen who packs two shirts and announces, "I'm ready to go!" needs to be convinced that he might have to change some of his clothes more than once a day. One dressier outfit is a safe bet—a jacket, slacks, dress shirt, tie, dress or skirt, and change of shoes should suffice for any special dinner, religious service, or event.

Especially for kids, backpacks or fanny packs offer space to stow a whole day's worth of supplies: jacket, camera, notepad/pen, small game or toy, snacks, and box drinks. We have found that when traveling with children, *snack* is the most valuable word in our vocabulary, because it is the key to a child's stamina and an adult's patience. Teens also require frequent infusions of energy, and might need a reminder to be prepared.

A small notebook or bound blank book, or a set of small note cards, can serve as a journal for each traveler. Teachers and parents need to allow time each day for kids to jot their own personal notes.

Where they go, what they see, whom they meet, jokes they want to remember, and thoughts, ideas, or brilliant revelations that occur to them in their travels are all worth saving in journal form. And what fun it is afterward for everyone, adults and kids alike, to share and compare their versions of the trip. Of course, every traveler should bring a camera; the little disposable versions work fine. A wonderful (but pricier) little invention, the Polaroid camera that produces sticky-backed tiny photos, can deliver treasured mementos of the visit.

If you want your group's members to stay together, plan for everyone to wear something identifiable. Sun visors, baseball caps, or bandannas—all matching—are easy to recognize; they're also helpful to tour guides and entrance staff so they can recognize who's in your group. Some people use T-shirts for this purpose, but, teenagers' habits notwithstanding, the shirts do need to be washed, and therefore can't be counted on for daily wear. They do make nice souvenirs, though.

# Transportation

No matter where you are coming from, the most important thing to remember when you arrive in Washington, D.C., is that the time it will take to get to your specific destination depends absolutely on the time of day you are traveling. Tuned to the traffic reports on their radios for hours at the beginning and end of each working day, most Washingtonians are more worried about transportation gridlock than they are about legislation gridlock. Rush hours are impossible, so plan accordingly. From 6:30 to 9:30 A.M. and from 3:30 to 7:00 P.M. (we are *not* making this up!) traffic snarls are everywhere, and you will have to plan at least an extra hour to go *anywhere*. In fact, if you are caught in this jumble, you will probably get to know the occupants of cars, trucks, or buses on both sides, and possibly behind and in front, of you, better than you had planned to.

## How to Get Here

Years ago, wise planners thought they had the solution: a highway encircling the city. The Capital Beltway, which consists of interstates I-495 and I-95, can come to a complete standstill if there is an accident anywhere along the way. Connecting to the Beltway are four major highways that go off in different directions: Route 66 goes west in Virginia; Interstate 50 heads east toward Annapolis, the Chesapeake Bay, and the beaches; Interstate 95 is a north–south route that overlaps the Beltway for awhile; and Interstate 270 goes northwest through Frederick, Maryland, and beyond. Exits are clearly marked, but wherever you are heading, be sure to get specific directions, *including* exit numbers. Bridges that cross the Potomac to and from Virginia and the Anacostia River in D.C. itself also become bottlenecks at rush hours. (We've heard rumors that people have met and become engaged while caught in D.C. bridge traffic.)

Buses connect Washington with cities all over the United States. The downtown bus terminal is in northeast Washington, D.C. (an area you would not want to walk in alone at night) at 1005 First Street, NE. To reach Greyhound and Peter Pan–Trailways for detailed schedules, call 1-800-343-9999 or 202-289-5154.

Train travel brings you right into the heart of Washington, D.C. Union Station (400 North Capitol Street, NW, Washington, D.C. 20001) is right across the street from Congress. AMTRAK (1-800-USA-RAIL), America's only national railroad passenger system, arrives and departs many times daily. The Metro (subway system) has a stop right inside Union Station. From here, a traveler can easily head for any part of the city, either through Metro or the lines of taxis waiting in front of the station. The many shops and restaurants inside this huge and beautiful building afford families with cranky or hungry children places to relax and fill up. The MARC Train (1-888-218-2267), a separate line, goes from Union Station to Baltimore and other places in Maryland.

Washington's three airports are busy at all hours. BWI (Baltimore/Washington International Airport), Washington–Dulles International Airport, and Ronald Reagan Washington National Airport all serve the Washington, D.C., traveler. Taxis, shuttle buses (some are door-to-door, some are for hotel drop-offs), and limousine services are available at all three locations, and there are information desks for travelers who need assistance. For information about BWI,

phone 1-800-I-FLY-BWI or 301-261-1000; write P.O. Box 8766, BWI Airport, MD 21240. To find out more about Washington-Dulles International Airport, phone 703-572-2700. For Ronald Reagan Washington National Airport, phone 703-417-8000.

If you ever doubt that Washington, D.C., is an international city, a ride in a D.C. area cab will be a quick reminder; your driver will be from anywhere *but* Washington, D.C., and most likely even from outside the United States. Conversations with these people can be especially interesting; one cab driver told us of his distress when he arrived in the United States and the authorities took away his monkey!

Washington, D.C., operates nominally on Eastern Standard Time (Eastern Daylight Time in the summer), but in reality everyone is on "fast-forward." Plan your travel so that you won't be a member of the frantic masses. (For example, a 4:00 P.M. arrival at Dulles does not match well with a 6:00 P.M. appointment *anywhere*.) Welcome to Washington, D.C. Drivers, start your engines.

## Getting Around

Washington, D.C., actually does have a basic plan, and once you understand it, getting around is a lot less mysterious. Even taxi drivers might rely on your knowing how to get to your destination. The city is divided into four basic sections: NW, NE, SE, and SW, with the United States Capitol building in the center. Washington, D.C., is all on the east side of the Potomac River; Virginia is on the west and south side. The quadrants are in no way equal in size; NW is much larger than any other area of the city. Anything south of the Capitol is SE and south of the Mall is SW. North Capitol Street separates NW and NE; East Capitol Street separates NE and SE, and South Capitol Street separates the two southern quadrants. When visiting anywhere in the seventy square miles that make up the city, you will need to know which section you are heading for; the same address, for example 500 C Street can be found in all four. Numbered streets run north-south; lettered streets run east-west. Avenues (named for states), run diagonally, and often pass through traffic circles and squares (navigating these is an interesting outdoor sport for natives and visitors alike).

Metrorail (the subway system) and Metro bus are safe, clean, and efficient; for route details, phone 202-636-3425. We've learned from folks we've interviewed that, for many travelers, our Metro is their first experience with subways; most find it an exciting adventure, in addition to convenient. Buses crisscross the city all day and into the evening, with more frequent stops during morning and evening rush hours. Metrorail lines have color names: red, yellow, orange, blue, and green, and each station is marked with the letter "M" at street level. In addition to clear route maps posted at every station, there is a kiosk with an attendant who can answer your questions. There are farecard vending machines inside each station; the farecard is used both entering *and leaving* the subway platforms, so hang onto your farecard even after you board! For special farecard discount rates, contact the Washington Metropolitan Area Transit Authority (600 5th Street, NW #6G04, Washington, DC 20001; 202-962-1122). And keep in mind: NO EATING is allowed on the subway; just ask the local middle-school student who was handcuffed by police for this unsavory crime. Taxi fares are based on travel among eight zones; cabs have zone maps inside. You can usually hail a taxi in front of any hotel, subway or bus station, or major site.

By the way, those colorful brochures vendors will hawk on the streets are available in most buildings and museums for *free*. Some bargains aren't really bargains at all.

## Touring

Teachers and students we've interviewed have made touring suggestions you might find helpful. In most cases, when teachers bring large groups of students, they work with tour companies well in advance of their trip. Several they have had good experiences with are:

**World Strides**
www.worldstrides.com
281-647-7000

**American Student Travel (now part of World Strides)**
www.astravel.com

**EF Educational Tours**
1-800-775-4040
www.edtours.com

**Educational Travel Adventures**
704-663-4070 or 336-983-3421
www.educationaltraveladv.com

**USA Consolidated Travel**
www.usastudenttravel.com

**USA Educational Adventures**
1-800-949-0650
www.usaeducationaladventures.com

If you contact a tour company, you will want to know what these folks can do for you; do they pick up at your school and take your group to (and bring back from) the airport, for example? Do they transport you to all the sites you will visit? Do they provide guide service or just a driver? Do they arrange for accommodations, meals, etc.? Ask to receive all details in writing and discuss all your questions with one contact person; of course, ask for references, and call and grill them. Most companies offer three-, four-, and five-day plans for Washington, D.C. Some school groups from far-off places do plan tours spending, say, three days in Washington, D.C., two in Philadelphia, and two or three in New York City. Ask about these plans, if that's of interest. Other teachers plan independently, some bringing groups on an early flight one morning and returning late evening of the next day, spending two very full days in D.C. Teachers stress that if you use a tour organization, you will want to thoroughly research the choice of guide (and driver) for your group.

Another wonderful source to consider is the Close Up Foundation, a "citizenship education organization," founded in 1970. Close Up offers a selection of civic education activities for middle school and high school students. Billed as an "innovative, experiential learning program," each is a short, participatory course in U.S. history, quite different from a sightseeing tour. Students who have come to Washington for a week or so of Close Up have described their experiences to us with much enthusiasm. Many books and videos are also published by Close Up on topics relevant to this kind of study.

**Close Up Foundation**
703-706-3300
www.closeup.org

From our teachers and students, here are "the big eight" suggestions:

1. Be prepared; figure out your optimum itinerary in advance, taking into account *your* group's needs and requirements.

2. Be flexible. If one site is unexpectedly off-limits, have a "B" list to substitute from.

3. Take advantage of "specials." These might be time of year, specific "visiting" shows or performances—anything you know about in advance can become a treasured extra for your visit.

4. If possible, try to connect with at least one other student tour. Kids love to meet students from other areas of the country than their own.

5. Use what the city has to offer. Have lunch in a public park (if the weather cooperates) or use the Metro; walk when you can—you'll see more.

6. Fit the sites to the curriculum; students are not enthusiastic about visiting memorials to folks they've never studied.

7. Choose your chaperones (whether teachers or parents) wisely. Responsible and understanding adults can make or break a trip.

8. Separation can reduce anxiety. For some age groups, putting boys and girls (and appropriate chaperones) on separate floors (of the hotel) gives everyone a better night's sleep.

# Keeping Safe

As in any city, tourists need to be cautious in Washington, D.C. Adults traveling with children should talk with them before the trip about safety issues. Washington is a city made for tourists; safety of visitors is a major priority in a place that is so dependent on income from travelers. The main visitor areas, the Mall, Georgetown, upper Northwest, Dupont Circle, Adams Morgan, and downtown have a strong police presence. Additional agencies are also involved in your protection, including the U.S. Park Police, the U.S. Capitol Police, the Secret Service, Metro police, and even the Smithsonian Institution's own police force. Visitors can spot officers on foot, on horseback, on bicycles, on motorcycles, and in cars. While monuments are open daily 24 hours, National Park Service Rangers are on duty at each from 8 A.M. until midnight.

Smart is safe. (Being smart keeps you safe.) All kids need to be able to recognize security people on the streets and in buildings. Whenever you enter a new place, designate a *specific* meeting spot that everyone can easily find; someone just might get lost or separated, and all need to know where to go in that situation.

The crime statistics you hear about most frequently are rarely random shootings; they are usually connected with the drug trade, which is centered in non-tourist areas. The parts of Washington, D.C., that tend to have the highest crime rates are parts of Northeast and Southeast not regularly frequented by tourists. If you are visiting a site in one of those areas, go as a group and go in the daytime.

The best protection—anywhere—is always self-protection. Walk purposefully and with a group; *look* like you *know* where you are going, even when you don't. If you have to pull out a map, go into a store or museum. Women should keep purses close to their bodies, even under a coat if you are wearing one. Men should keep wallets in *front* pants pockets, *not* an easily-accessible-to-anyone back pocket. It's a good idea to have small bills readily available to pull out, instead of a big wad or wallet packed full of twenties.

If you should ever face a crime situation, your mouth is your best weapon. Shout very loudly for help and move quickly away.

*The United States
Capitol Building*

Shouting "FIRE!" gets more attention than "Stop, thief!" The last thing a criminal wants is for anyone to notice. If you are asked to turn over your wallet, *throw* it and run the *other* way; the robber will be much more interested in going after the money than going after you.

If you need to catch a taxi at the train or bus stations, or at an airport, always use the taxi line, where properly licensed and regulated drivers and vehicles are lined up for your safety. Offers for taxi or limo rides from people on the street or in the terminals could result in major overcharges or personal harm. If you are driving, and become lost at night, *do not* stop the car to ask for directions; keep driving until you find a hotel, gas station, police station, or fire station, where you can ask for assistance.

After dark, do not travel *alone* anywhere in the city. Even teenagers, who, of course, feel indestructible, need to remember that there is safety in numbers. Although in a group, under no circumstances should young people interact with suspicious-looking strangers. This is advice appropriate for *all* travelers. People on street corners or in front of restaurants asking for money *do* have resources for food and shelter funded by the city; your response is your personal choice.

# A Capital Scavenger Hunt

One enjoyable way to keep kids' attention throughout a visit is to offer a game, and *you* get to come up with an appropriate prize (how about a D.C. souvenir—a sweatshirt or T-shirt?). We suggest a scavenger hunt, perhaps in teams, and here is a list of items to search for during a Washington, D.C., visit:

1. Huge bronze doors depicting the life of Christopher Columbus

2. Figure of a blindfolded lady holding scales

3. A statue topped with two graceful cranes side-by-side

4. Statue of A. Philip Randolph

5. A large clock with IIII instead of the traditional IV for 4

6. Washington's only round museum

7. The *Enola Gay*

8. Bronze statue of the Messenger of the Gods

9. A baseball autographed by Babe Ruth

10. Statue of Alexander Hamilton

11. Statue of famous scientist seated on a bench in a grove of elm and holly trees

12. Around the top of the Lincoln Memorial are the names of the 48 states in the Union at the time the memorial was dedicated. Where are the names of Alaska and Hawaii?

13. Corn and tobacco peeking out from the coat on a sculpture of a president

14. A $100,000 bill

15. Statue of Gandhi

16. Where can you find these words: "The Government of the United States. . . gives to bigotry no sanction and to persecution no assistance. . . ."? Who was the author?

17. The Congress Bells (Hint: They are *not* on Capitol Hill.)

18. Quote: "What is past is prologue."

19. Statue of a lion protecting its cubs

20. A piece of moon rock that is *not* in the Air and Space Museum

21. Twenty-two tall free-standing columns in a park setting

22. America's earliest submarine

23. An exhibit featuring an important escape vessel used by a young naval officer who later became president

24. "The Growlery"

25. The mast of the USS *Maine*

26. A traffic-stopping monument featuring a Confederate soldier

(**ANSWERS** at end of Appendix III)

CHAPTER

2

Capitol
Hill

he most important land elevation in the free world, Capitol Hill is actually much more than a collection of buildings. It is a neighborhood of historic homes, restaurants, shops, hotels, and bars, where residents who are blue collar or white collar workers mingle with Congressmen, legislative aides, and lobbyists. The heart of Capitol Hill is still the main tourist attraction: the **U.S. Capitol Building,** with its neighbors, the **Supreme Court,** the **Library of Congress,** the **House and Senate Office Buildings,** and **Union Station.** This area is well worth a full day: the combination of history and current events packed into this real estate demands your time and attention. Be cautious here at night, however.

## U.S. Botanic Garden

**For All Ages...** A fun place for children is the U.S. Botanic Garden, with **Bartholdi Park** across the street on Independence Avenue. Frederic Auguste Bartholdi designed the fountain in this park; he is perhaps more well-known as the designer of the Statue of Liberty in New York harbor.

More exciting than reading about exotic plants is seeing, smelling, and touching them in the U.S. Botanic Garden. Chocolate and vanilla trees, a coffee tree, and a pineapple plant are all there for the sniffing. More economical than airline tickets to some exotic place, a visit to the Australian bunya bunya tree, the Brazilian tapioca plant, and the Chinese lychee tree doesn't even require a passport. Don't forget to look for the "living fossil," the 200-million-year-old plant species called the cycad. Orchids, azaleas, and other beautiful and rare flowering plants elicit wide-eyed pleasure and a furtive attempt to snatch a souvenir. *Don't!*

Note: The magnificent Victorian Conservatory might still be undergoing its multiyear renovation, but the park, with its rock

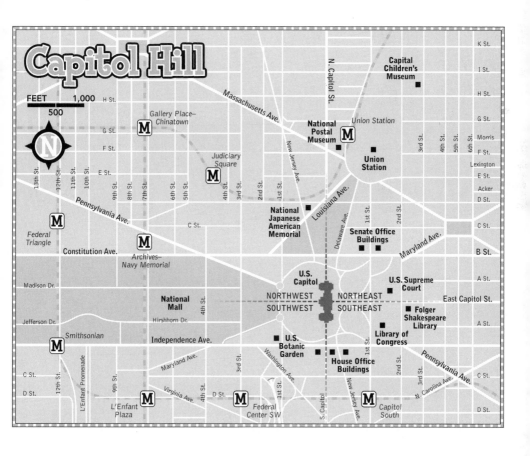

# Quick Guide to

| Attraction | Location |
|---|---|
| U.S. Botanic Garden | West side of the Capitol, First Street and Maryland Avenue, SW |
| ★The United States Capitol Building | On Capitol Hill, at the east end of the Mall |
| ★Library of Congress | First Street and Independence Avenue, SE, across from the Capitol |
| Folger Shakespeare Library | 201 E. Capitol Street, SE, east of the Library of Congress |
| ★Supreme Court Building | First Street and Maryland Avenue, NE, facing the Capitol |
| National Japanese American Memorial | In a triangular park, bounded by New Jersey and Louisiana Avenues and D Street, NW |
| National Postal Museum | 2 Massachusetts Avenue, NE |
| ★Union Station | 50 Massachusetts Avenue, NE |
| Capital Children's Museum | 800 3rd Street (at H Street, NE) |

# Capitol Hill Attractions

| Age Range | Hours | Details on |
| --- | --- | --- |
| All Ages | 9 A.M.–5 P.M. daily | Page 28 |
| Tweens and Teens | 9 A.M.–8 P.M. daily (March–Aug.); 9 A.M.–4:30 P.M. daily (Sept.–Feb.) | Page 33 |
| Teens | Jefferson Building: Mon.–Sat. 10 A.M.–5:30 P.M.; American Treasures: Mon.–Sat. 10 A.M.–5 P.M.; Madison Building: Mon.–Fri. 8:30 A.M.–9:30 P.M., Sat. 8:30 A.M.–6 P.M. | Page 39 |
| Tweens and Teens | Mon.–Sat. 10 A.M.–4 P.M. | Page 42 |
| Tweens and Teens | Mon.–Fri. 9 A.M.–4:30 P.M. | Page 43 |
| All Ages | 24 hours, daily | Page 46 |
| All Ages | 10 A.M.–5:30 P.M. daily | Page 47 |
| All Ages | Shops open Mon.–Sat. 10 A.M.–9 P.M., Sun. 10 A.M.–6 P.M. | Page 48 |
| Tikes and Tweens | 10 A.M.–6 P.M. daily (Memorial Day–Labor Day); 10 A.M.–5 P.M. (rest of year) | Page 50 |

garden, changing seasonal displays, and Bartholdi Fountain (from the Centennial Exposition of 1876 in Philadelphia) remain open.

Metro: Federal Center Southwest
West side of the Capitol, First Street and Maryland Avenue, SW
Garden open 9 A.M.–5 P.M. daily.
202-225-8333 or 202-225-7099

Located on opposite sides of the Capitol Plaza, the **Senate and House of Representatives Office Buildings** are important for two reasons (besides the fact that actual *work* sometimes gets done there). First, this is where to pick up your passes to the House or Senate galleries or for VIP tours of the Capitol; and second, there are some good eats to be found within some of these marble walls.

## Helpful Hint

To ensure availability, it is an especially good idea to request passes/tickets for the House and Senate galleries well in advance of your visit to Washington, D.C. (No passes are needed when Congress is *not* in session.) The names of your senators and representatives should be listed in the front of your local telephone directory, along with a local contact number; to reach your legislator while visiting Washington, D.C., call the main congressional switchboard at 202-224-3121, and ask to be connected to your legislator's office. Only five tickets can be issued under one visitor's name; because of various ceremonies and unscheduled events, tickets can be reserved no more than three months in advance. The most recent run on tickets came for the impeachment hearings of President Bill Clinton. (Talk about watching your government at work!) Senate offices (on Constitution Avenue between Delaware Avenue and 2nd Street, NE) are open Monday through Friday 8 A.M.–6 P.M., Saturday 9 A.M.–1 P.M. House offices (Independence Avenue between First Street, SW and First Street, SE, and corner C Street/New Jersey Avenue) are open Monday through Friday 8 A.M.–6 P.M., Saturday 8 A.M.–1 P.M.

Next to the Hart Senate Office Building, on the northeast side of the Capitol, is the **Sewall–Belmont House,** since 1929 the head-quarters of the National Woman's Party, founded by Alice Paul in 1913. Paul authored the first version of the Equal Rights Amendment to the Constitution; she lived in this house from 1929 to 1972. For students and adults interested in the women's suffrage movement, there are party memorabilia, portraits, and even antique furniture. Look for the small sculpture of Sybil Ludington, a heroine of the Revolutionary War who, in true feminist style, made a ride similar to Paul Revere's, only four times longer! A 28-minute videotape, "We Were Arrested of Course," chronicles the history of how women got the vote. Some books of interest are: *Susan B. Anthony (American Women of Achievement),* by Barbara Weisberg (tweens); and *Amazing Women in American History: Roles and Achievements of Women in America from Pre-history to the End of the Twentieth Century,* by New York Public Library (tweens and teens). (144 Constitution Avenue, NE; donations; 202-546-3989).

# ★The United States Capitol Building

**For Teens and Tweens...** Who says our Capitol doesn't respond to hot air? Its cast iron dome even expands and contracts as much as four inches under extreme temperatures. And to help heal the body politic, its first architect was a physician, Dr. William Thornton. A domed central Rotunda is

*U.S. Capitol Building*

## Smart Stuff

**For Tweens...** Kids might enjoy writing their own letters from the viewpoint of a youngster encountering a famous person in a historic period.

## Smart Stuff

**For Tweens and Teens...** In the continental United States, there is one geographic location that has no voting representatives in Congress. Its residents, however, are U.S. citizens and pay federal taxes. Can you name this place?

(A.)

flanked by wings on each side, the Senate and House chambers. The original Supreme Court and Senate met in the central section; Statuary Hall, where the House originally met, is a great place for youngsters to explore and try to identify the likenesses of famous people. During the Civil War, one part of it, the Rotunda, was used for the not-so-famous, as a soldiers' barracks and then as a hospital. Don't let the simplicity of the Capitol's design fool you. The building is a labyrinth of rooms and corridors (some say there are 550 rooms!), and it is easy to get lost. Large groups work best here with a guided tour (arranged for in advance), but small groups can use self-guiding materials.

Stories about this building are legion. Evidently, John Quincy Adams was the beneficiary of a fascinating architectural quirk: a spot in the Rotunda where he had his desk echoed sounds, even whispered from the other side, so he was able to respond to his op-

## Parents/Teachers Take Note

Kids will enjoy trying to find the VIP from their own state in Statuary Hall. These range from Utah's Philo Farnsworth, the father of TV, to King Kamehameha of Hawaii.

ponents' arguments even before they made them! Students love to stand on the designated spot (a guide can point this out) and whisper, to see if a friend across the room can hear them.

The wonderful fresco in the Capitol dome, *The Apotheosis of Washington,* was painted by Italian immigrant artist Constantino Brumidi, who lay on his back on scaffolding for eleven months to create this work. The thirteen angels (representing the original thirteen states) welcoming George Washington into heaven are said to have been painted using local prostitutes as models. (Aren't we taught that in a democracy, every citizen can become involved?) An enthusiastic patriot, Brumidi often signed his paintings "C. Brumidi, artist. Citizen of the United States."

**Smart Stuff**

**For Teens...** What is a fresco? Students can research the method and see if they can find other famous artists who employed this technique. (B.)

Outside, the sculpture atop the Capitol dome (no, it is not Pocahontas or Sacajawea) is *Freedom.* Originally, she was supposed to be free of clothing, but that was too daring for the mid-1800s. So, appropriately draped and crowned with feathers, she weighs an astonishing seven tons and had to be raised and lowered by helicopter in recent years for cleaning and restoration (after 130 years wouldn't *you* want a bath?).

Committee hearings, often the pulse of Congress, can offer an exciting glimpse of the give and take of power. Each weekday the *Washington Post* has a "Today In Congress" column, with details on the times of House and Senate sessions and committee hearings. Here you will also find which hearings are open to the public, so you can choose what is of interest. If you'd like to know

**Smart Stuff**

How can you tell whether the House or Senate is in session from looking at the outside of the Capitol building? What about at night? (C.)

what already happened in these hallowed halls, you might browse through the *Congressional Record;* you can find it on the Web at http://Thomas.loc.gov.

In addition to the regular movers and shakers toiling on Capitol Hill, young people might notice another important but less visible group: teenagers who are the Capitol Pages. They work in the House of Representatives, the Senate, and the Supreme Court. While spending a high school semester in Washington, these students live in a dormitory and attend the Capitol Page School at the Library of Congress. Their school day begins every morning at 6:45 A.M., so their classes do not conflict with their work. They wear navy jackets and gray pants (or skirts), white dress shirts with uniform ties (provided for them), and black shoes. The Pages receive a small salary, out of which federal and state taxes, Social Security, and their residence hall fees are deducted. Basically, the Pages run errands and answer phones, but regulations still stipulate that they are to "keep the Senate snuff boxes filled." The very first Capitol Page was appointed by Daniel Webster and Henry Clay in 1829. There were no child labor laws at that time; he was only nine years old.

## Smart Stuff

What is the shortest subway in the United States? (D.)

A great place to celebrity-watch, and go somewhere besides, are the congressional subways. *Not* the D.C. Metro, they are located in the basement of the Capitol, and run by electromagnets. They take Congress people, staff assistants, and *you* to and from the **Rayburn House Office Building** and the House side of the Capitol; between the **Hart Senate Office Building** and the Senate side of the Capitol (stopping at the **Dirksen Senate Office Building**); and between the **Russell Senate Office Building** and the Senate side of the Capitol. Although they are not on the train routes, the **Cannon** and **Longworth House Office Buildings** are reachable by walking at street level or continuing along an underground passageway. Ask any Capitol guide how to get to these trains; just don't call them the Metro!

In addition to making the newspapers every day, doings in the Capitol make for some very good books, plays, and movies. *Jefferson: Character in Time: The U.S. Presidents,* a play by R. David Cox, is a fun way for tweens and teens to explore the legislative process with all its warts. *Letters from Vinnie,* by Maureen Stack Sappey, uses a wonderful fictional framework to tell the true story of the teenaged sculptress (Vinnie Ream) who created the statue of Abraham Lincoln gracing the Rotunda of the Capitol building (tweens). A book that will prove interesting and enjoyable to tweens and teens is *In Praise of Public Life,* by Senator Joseph I. Lieberman. Teens might explore *Democracy Is a Discussion: Civic Engagement in Old and New Democracies,* edited by Sondra Myers. Also worth a read are *All the King's Men* (based on the story of Congressman Huey Long), by Robert Penn Warren (teens) and *Lord of the Flies,* by William Golding (teens); there are also films of both. The most famous movie about Congress is *Advise and Consent* (teens), with Henry Fonda; others to take a look at are: *State of the Union* (tweens and teens), with Spencer Tracy and Katherine Hepburn; *The Best Man* (teens); *Close Up Conversations: The Role of Congress* (teens), by Close Up Publishing; and *The Great McGinty* (teens). Teens can learn about the budget—budgeting!—from a game by Close Up Publishing: *Slicing the Pie: A Federal Budget Game;* kids learn about issues and strategies while acting as members of Congress, lobbyists, and citizens. We don't guarantee this will improve their personal spending habits, however.

Hungry? The Capitol subways can take you to convenient and inexpensive lunch spots. The favorite seems to be the **Dirksen Senate Office Building South Buffet Room** (1st and C Streets, NE). Kids and

## Money-Saving Tip

While lunch here costs more than just a sandwich or a pizza slice, this is a real bargain for a full meal. It's not a bad idea to be like our neighbor nations to the south: have your big meal in the middle of the day today.

adults alike will love this generous all-you-can-eat buffet. In an art-deco room with white linen-covered tables and floral centerpieces, diners can indulge themselves in their big meal of the day. Choices include numerous meats and other hot entrees, vegetables, pasta, rice, potatoes, a fruit and salad bar, a create-your-own sundae bar, tea, coffee, milk, and sodas. If your group consists of six or more, reservations are recommended; 202-224-4249 (Monday through Friday 11:30 A.M.–2:30 P.M.).

If your sleepy teenagers are overwhelmed just putting on clothes before they leave the hotel, and arrive at their Capitol Hill destination starving, you're in luck: the Longworth and Rayburn Buildings offer food as early as 7:30 A.M. The **Longworth Building Cafeteria** (Independence and S. Capitol Streets, NE) offers an inexpensive breakfast and a wide selection of lunch entrees, with pies and cakes for dessert. The **Rayburn Building Cafeteria** (next door) also has breakfasts; for lunch, in addition to entrees and vegetable side dishes, servers will make salads to order here. Try the cheesecake for dessert. Also, the adjoining **Pizza Plus** is open Monday through Friday from 11 A.M.–7 P.M., with lighter fare.

If your goal is to see rather than be seen, there are two restaurants frequented by senators and representatives. At the far end of the House side of the Capitol (room H118) is the elegant royal blue **Bennett Dining Room** (ask a guard for directions—you might want to leave a trail of breadcrumbs on the floor for finding your way back). In contrast to the opulent surroundings, the prices are extremely reasonable. Salads, entrees, and sandwiches are all good *and* bargains. Tip-free, there's no required dress code, but you'll find that most men are in jackets and ties (9 A.M.–2:30 P.M.; closed to the public from 11 A.M. to 1:30 P.M. when Congress is in session; 202-225-6300).

On the Senate side, is the **Senators' Dining Room,** for which you will need a note from your senator, sort of like a school hall pass only better. Proper attire: jacket and tie for men, no jeans for anyone, as this is the most elegant of the Capitol's restaurants. (Note: You can eat the same food—and in jeans!—on the Senate side's first floor, for less money, in **The Refectory.**) Speaking of money, *yours* is supporting all these eateries, so enjoy, and enter like you own the place. After all, you *do*.

Metro: Capitol South

On Capitol Hill, at the east end of the Mall

Open daily 9 A.M.–8 P.M., March through August; September through February, 9 A.M.–4:30 P.M.

Closed January 1, Thanksgiving, and December 25. No guided tours on Sundays.

202-225-6827 (Ask about VIP tours; for information on guided tours and details for visiting; to make *advance reservations* for groups of 15 or more, call 202-244-4910.)

www.dcpages.com/ttwdc/capitol.html

Among the largest equestrian sculptural groupings in the world, the **statue of President Ulysses S. Grant on his horse,** Cincinnatus, is an imposing sight in front of the U.S. Capitol (First Street, NW, between Maryland and Pennsylvania Avenues, on the Capitol's west side). Presented as a Civil War hero rather than a less than effective politician, Grant is shown as a brave commander leading his troops into battle. This dramatic monument is often a hit with youngsters, like the little guy whose father spent a lengthy period pointing out the significance of the statues and the importance of Ulysses S. Grant in American history. The little boy was awed by the sculptures, but finally asked, as they were leaving, "Dad, who was that *riding* on General Grant?"

Frederick Law Olmstead didn't only design landscapes; he also created a delightful little **Summer House** in the shadow of the West Front of the Capitol. A hexagonal brick building built around a small fountain, the Summer House is partially secluded by foliage. It is reached by a small descending stairway. Stone benches and beckoning archways invite the fortunate visitor to relax and unwind.

# ★Library of Congress

**For Teens...** Thomas Jefferson made his mark here; the Library of Congress began with the books from his personal library. My, how we've grown. One hundred thirteen million items, including 26 million books in 460 languages live on 532 *miles* of shelves in three different buildings in this one collection. Nevertheless, neither you nor anyone else, even a senator or representative, can check out a book to take home! But anyone over high school age may browse here and do research.

The main building, the **Thomas Jefferson Building,** is the jewel in the crown. Standing at the base of the majestic staircases, looking at the gilt ornamentation on the walls and ceiling, we can imagine what European palaces must look like. Rising 75 feet from its marble floor to its stained-glass ceiling, the **Great Hall** graces our most elegant government building. The **Main Reading Room,** a throwback to an earlier era of dark paneling and ornate decoration, is still in use today. High on the walls are the seals of the forty-eight contiguous states, set in stained glass windows. You can gaze down at legislative aides, college students, and government officials doing research side by side.

Start with the American Treasures exhibit, a permanent collection of more than 200 historic items. Among them are: Thomas Jefferson's rough draft of the Declaration of Independence, letters written by George Washington, and Abraham Lincoln's Gettysburg Address. Even younger visitors will be fascinated by the display of the contents of Lincoln's pockets the night he was assassinated. Magic-lovers will enjoy the scrapbooks of master magician Harry Houdini.

In the Jefferson Building, rotating exhibits are arranged by themes: Memory (history), Reason (philosophy, law, science, and geography), and Imagination (fine arts, architecture, music, literature, and sports). You can view them at www.loc.gov/ exhibits. The Visitors' Center inside the west front entrance provides brochures and information. A 90-seat theater offers a short movie about the Library, and the gift shop, also on the ground floor, stocks an appealing collection of reproductions, books, and souvenirs. A self-guiding audiotape tour of "Treasures of America" is available for $2.50.

Puritanical John Adams would have raised his eyebrow at the décor of the library building bearing his name: 1939 Art Deco. This

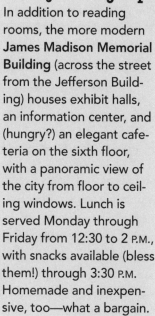

second building of the Library of Congress, just behind the Jefferson Building, contains a number of reading rooms devoted to specialized material.

Metro: Capitol South First Street and Independence Avenue, SE, across from the Capitol Jefferson Building, Monday through Saturday 10 A.M.– 5:30 P.M. (guided tours 11:30 A.M., 1 P.M., 2:30 P.M., 4 P.M.); American Treasures, Monday through Saturday 10 A.M.–5 P.M.; Madison Building,

## Money-Saving Tip

In addition to reading rooms, the more modern **James Madison Memorial Building** (across the street from the Jefferson Building) houses exhibit halls, an information center, and (hungry?) an elegant cafeteria on the sixth floor, with a panoramic view of the city from floor to ceiling windows. Lunch is served Monday through Friday from 12:30 to 2 P.M., with snacks available (bless them!) through 3:30 P.M. Homemade and inexpensive, too—what a bargain.

## Smart Stuff

**For Teens...** At the Library of Congress, you can look up any book published in the United States by its title, author, or call number. (For Library of Congress research, you will need a special pass. Go to Room 140 in the Independence Avenue entrance of the Madison Building; present a photo ID with your name and address to get a User ID Card. Entering the main entrance of the Jefferson (main) Building, go to the computer catalogue center on the first floor. A reference librarian will assist you.)

Try this one: HQ769.B823. Who are the authors? Who's the publisher? (E.)

Monday through Friday 8:30 A.M.–9:30 P.M., Saturday
8:30 A.M.–6 P.M. Closed holidays.
Special tours can be tailored to children. Phone 202-707-
5458.
Fee for audiotape tours.
202-707-8000 or 202-707-5000
For information on poetry and other literary readings, phone
202-707-5394.

## Folger Shakespeare Library

**For Tweens and Teens...** More than a library, this classic white marble building houses a research facility, a Tudor-style Great Hall, and
an Elizabethan theater (modeled after the Blackfriars Theater, where
many of Shakespeare's plays were produced). The world's largest collection of Shakespearean works and artifacts lives here, but unless
you're doing graduate-level research, you'll have to take our word for
it; it's off-limits to the rest of us. *Except* on one April weekend a year
(the Saturday closest to April 26), the research areas are opened to
the masses, in celebration of Shakespeare's birthday. Music, theatrical
productions, special children's events, and food enliven the festivities.

Docent-led guided tours of the Great Hall can explain the
changing exhibits of Renaissance and Shakespeare-related items, such
as rare books and manuscripts, memorabilia, and paintings. From
productions of Shakespearean plays to concerts to lectures and readings of poetry and fiction, the Folger (as it is known around town) is
an important part of the Washington cultural scene. Evening events
usually require an admission fee, and, sometimes, an invitation.

## Parents/Teachers Take Note

The Education Department of the Folger sponsors festivals for high school students each spring, complete with
sword-fighting demonstrations, slide presentations, and
other activities. Call 202-544-4600; ask for the Education Department.

Of course, there are endless lists of books to read, both by and about Shakespeare. We know you can find any of Shakespeare's plays on your own. Here are a few other suggestions: *All the World's A Stage: A Pop-up Biography of William Shakespeare,* by Michael Bender (tweens); *Tales from Shakespeare (Children's Classics),* by Charles Lamb (tweens and teens); *Twisted Tales from Shakespeare,* by Richard Armour (tweens and teens—this one is out of print but *very funny,* so check your library); *Stories from Shakespeare: The Complete Plays of William Shakespeare,* by Marchette Chute (teens); and *Acting Shakespeare,* by John Gielgud and John Miller (teens and adults). An interesting game, useful as a dramatic introduction to Shakespeare, is *The Play's the Thing* (teens).

Metro: Capitol South
201 E. Capitol Street, SE, east of the Library of Congress
Open Monday through Saturday 10 A.M.–4 P.M.; closed federal holidays
Free guided tours: Monday through Saturday at 11 A.M. and Saturday at 1 P.M.
202-544-7077

# ★Supreme Court Building

**For Tweens and Teens...** It is not by accident that the Supreme Court was designed to look like a Greek temple. This temple of American democracy has its motto over the door: *Equal Justice Under Law.*

All court sessions are open to the public, but seating is on a first-come, first-served basis. You will need to arrive by 9 A.M. to get in line; actually, there are two lines: one if you wish to hear an entire argument (about an hour), and one for people who just want to stay and watch for a few minutes. Also, you will need quarters for the lockers where backpacks, cameras, etc. must be stored for security purposes.

Visit the exhibit hall featuring the history of the Court and the building on the ground floor (near the Maryland Avenue entrance). Nearby on this floor, in the small theater, you can view a

## The Supreme Court

20-minute film that explains the judicial process through interviews with a number of justices.

Books that help demystify the judicial process and personalities include: *Sandra Day O'Connor: First Woman on the Supreme Court,* by Carol Greene (tweens); *The Supreme Court,* by Carol Greene (tweens); *To Kill A Mockingbird,* by Harper Lee (tweens and teens); *The Supreme Court,* by Ann E. Weiss (teens); *Night of January 16th,* by Ayn Rand (teens), which is actually a play script, an informative and fun way to explore the courtroom (it even has a choice of endings); *The Autobiography of William O. Douglas: The Early Years; Go East, Young Man* (teens); *Thurgood Marshal, American Revolutionary,* by Juan Williams (teens); and *Pursuit of Justices: Presidential Politics in the Selection of Supreme Court Nominees,* by David Alistair Yalof (teens). Movies can also enrich this visit for tweens and teens. Such classics as *Twelve Angry Men, Inherit the Wind,* and *To Kill A Mockingbird* bring home in dynamic fashion the importance of the judicial branch of our legislative system. Teens would also enjoy *Gideon's Trumpet.*

A small museum, a gift shop, a snack bar, and a cafeteria are all on the ground floor.

A nearby restaurant with a hybrid name, **Thai Roma,** at 313 Pennsylvania Avenue, SE, was formerly an Italian restaurant but found its Thai menu getting raves, so forget the Italian part and enjoy Thai delicacies like pork satay, calamari with lemongrass,

## Money-Saving Tip

The **Supreme Court Cafeteria** is a supreme bargain among government buildings' food offerings. Fresh-baked goods are featured at breakfast, and soups, salads, sandwiches, entrees, and pies, cakes, and ice cream are all offered for lunchtime. Wednesdays are ethnic cuisine days here—with a different one each week. The snack bar sells inexpensive homemade desserts. Breakfast is served Monday through Friday 7:30–10:30 A.M.; lunch is 11:30 A.M.–2 P.M. Snack Bar hours are Monday through Friday 10:30 A.M.–3:30 P.M., when the Court is in session.

## Parents/Teachers Take Note

Middle school and high school students especially would enjoy presenting their own versions of courtroom dramas like the movies listed.

## Parents/Teachers Take Note

The movie *Gideon's Trumpet* (Henry Fonda played the lead) deals with the case of an imprisoned itinerant worker, Clarence Earl Gideon, whose poverty prevented him from hiring legal counsel. His case was taken on by an attorney named Abe Fortas, who brought it to the Supreme Court. The case was a landmark decision affirming the right of *everyone* to legal representation. Later, Abe Fortas served as a Supreme Court Justice.

curry dishes, and seafood; 202-544-2338. For the vegetarian-inclined, there's a wide selection, including Chinese eggplant and mixed vegetables in a curry coconut sauce, or tofu with cashews. Need plainer fare? Try the pastas. Buon appetito!

> Metro: Capitol South
> First Street and Maryland Avenue, NE, facing the Capitol
> Open Monday through Friday 9 A.M.–4:30 P.M.; closed holidays and sometimes for cleaning!
> Free lectures when court is not in session: every hour on the half-hour 9:30 A.M.–3:30 P.M.
> 202-479-3000
> 202-479-3211, an automated public information line for information on when arguments are presented and when opinions are delivered.
> www.law.cornell.edu/supct/justices/fullcourt.html

# National Japanese American Memorial

**For All Ages...** Dedicated in November 2000, the National Japanese American Memorial commemorates the patriotism, heroism, and sacrifice of the Japanese American veterans of World War II. The beauty of this memorial is in stark contrast to the injustice that it represents. Although more than 120,000 persons of Japanese ancestry were interned with their families in detention camps during World War II, 3,000 Japanese Americans served proudly in the uniform of the United States. The all-Japanese American 442nd Regimental Combat Team became one of the most decorated military units in the war. Awards included 18,143 personal decorations, seven Presidential Unit Citations, 52 Distinguished Service Crosses, 588 Silver Stars, 22 Legions of Merit, 5,200 Bronze Stars, 12 Croix de Guerre, 9,486 Purple Hearts, one Medal of Honor, and one Distinguished Service Medal.

Bordered by ornamental cherry trees, and softened by the water of a cascading pool as it reflects the daylight, stands a pink granite wall. On it are cited the ten internment camps, their locations, their populations, and the names of the 800 Japanese Americans who lost their lives in U.S. military service during World War II. Rising fourteen feet and visible above the wall, is a green Vermont marble column, crowned with a bronze statue of two cranes side-by-side, their left wings extended upward together. Their right (outside) wings are pinioned to their sides by a strand of barbed wire, the ends of which are held in their beaks. They symbolize both individual effort and communal support, while dramatically depicting the attempt of peoples to break free from the bonds of prejudice. This eloquent cry from the Japanese American community reminds us that what they endured should never again happen to *any* group of people.

Japanese legend holds that if a person who is ill makes a thousand paper cranes, the gods will grant that person's wish to be well again. *Sadako,* by Eleanor Coerr and Ed Young (tweens), tells the story of a twelve-year-old who develops leukemia ten years after the bomb was dropped on her native Hiroshima. *Come See the Paradise* is a film older teens might want to see, about a soldier who falls in love with a girl whose family is interned in a camp.

Metro: Union Station
In a triangular park, bounded by New Jersey and Louisiana
     Avenues and D Street, NW
Daily, 24 hours

# National Postal Museum

**For All Ages...** With three antique mail planes hanging from the ceiling, early mail trucks, holography, 3-D movies, interactive computers, and lasers, the National Postal Museum has a little something for everyone. This beaux-arts building (the City Post Office, not to be confused with the Old Post Office Pavilion, closer to the Mall) houses the world's largest philatelic collection. Kids will especially enjoy designing a piece of direct (junk) mail, and having it "sent" to themselves. Imagine you are a Pony Express rider; an exhibit takes you through a virtual journey. The Civil War section chronicles a most extraordinary piece of mail: a slave named Henry "Box" Brown mailed himself from Richmond, Virginia, to an abolitionist in Pennsylvania in 1856. Created to house and display the Smithsonian's collection of stamps and postal history memorabilia, The National Postal Museum offers America's 20 million stamp collectors a unique opportunity. Changing exhibits highlight the art and history of stamps. In the gift shop, you can find banks made from old mailboxes, books and workbooks on stamps and postal history for children, stamp jewelry, and an assortment of writing paper and postcards.

## Smart Stuff

**For Tweens and Teens...** "The Lone Eagle" was the nickname for our country's most famous airmail pilot. Who was he? What made him famous? (F.)

> Metro: Union Station
> 2 Massachusetts Avenue, NE
> Daily 10 A.M.–5:30 P.M.; closed December 25. Special tours for student groups available; phone Monday through Friday 10 A.M.–3 P.M.: 202-357-2991.
> Library Research Center open by appointment only
> 202-357-2700 for museum information.

# ★ Union Station

**For All Ages...** In a departure from the profusion of Greek temple designs for government buildings, Union Station was modeled on the Baths of Diocletian and the Arch of Constantine in Rome. Clearly, this is no small place. When it was completed in 1907, it was the largest train station in the world, and it certainly remains one of the most elegant. This spectacular building houses not only a major train station, commuter trains, and a subway station in the basement, but also two levels of eating places, two wings of shops, and a nine-screen movie theater complex. You can't live here, but you can certainly spend at least a day entertaining yourself; this is a terrific change when you are suffering from museum fatigue or need a dry haven from the rain. Younger travelers will enjoy identifying the large figure in front of the building (Christopher Columbus). Teens will relish trying to figure out why the thirty-six Roman legionnaires on the balcony of the Great Hall all carry shields in the same position. (Answer: since they didn't have any other clothing, the powers-that-were thought the shields were moral necessities.)

This most visited attraction in Washington, D.C. (the National Air and Space Museum is second) also has a long history of famous travelers. When General Pershing returned from World War I in 1918, he was welcomed here by President Wilson; Rear Admiral Richard Byrd (the South Pole explorer) had his homecoming here as well. In 1945, thousands of mourners congregated here to meet President Franklin D. Roosevelt's casket, borne on his funeral train. More recently, this grand palace of a building has hosted presidential inaugural balls.

Shops range from the mall types, including **Foot Locker, Nine West,** and **Structure,** to unique places like **Made In America,** where you can find government agency baseball caps (CIA, for example) along with "White House" guest towels; **Political Americana,** selling the obvious; **Flights of Fancy,** offering books, toys, games, and amusements; and—wouldn't you expect this?—**The Great Train Store,** with everything about trains, naturally.

Eating choices here run from the everyday to the truly exotic, from food courts to regular restaurants. On the lower level, a large eatery offers numerous ethnic as well as more traditional American fare. On the first and second floors, restaurants as well as fast food places give diners a variety of tasty choices.

Metro: Union Station
50 Massachusetts Avenue, NE
Tour with Officer Choo-Choo, 202-906-3103
Shops open Monday through Saturday 10 A.M.–9 P.M.,
      Sunday 10 A.M.–6 P.M.
202-371-9441

# Capital Children's Museum

**For Tikes and Tweens...** Imagine a whole museum inviting children to *touch and play with* its exhibits. Participation is the rule here, and children learn by firsthand experience. From grinding Mexican chocolate beans or making paper flowers, to taping a television commercial, to learning by hearing in the interactive exhibit about sound and deafness, to typing on a Braille typewriter, children enjoy a raft of rich experiences. Recently, the museum added a whole new permanent display: "Japan: Through the Eyes of a Child," which enables children to discover Japanese technology (even the computerized toilet!—with its heated seat and spray of water), groceries, kites, language, and daily life, including schools where instead of janitorial help, the children do the cleaning. As you're dragging them away, don't tell them it was educational. There is no mention of *food* here, because there *isn't* any; plan ahead.

> Metro: Union Station
> The museum is not in the best area of the city, so take a taxi from the Metro stop.
> 800 3rd Street (at H St., NE)
> Daily 10 A.M.–6 P.M., Memorial Day through Labor Day; 10 A.M.–5 P.M. rest of year
> Closed January 1, Easter, Thanksgiving, and December 25
> Admission fee
> 202-675-4120
> www.ccm.org

# Where to Stay in the Capitol Hill Area

Capitol Hill can be pricey, but as in any other real estate deal, you are paying for location. Don't forget to ask for every possible bargain category (group, corporate, preferred rates, etc.). Some suggestions to check out:

### Capitol Hill Suites
200 C Street, SE
202-543-6000
Metro: Capitol South

### Holiday Inn on the Hill
415 New Jersey Avenue, NW
202-638-1616 or 1-800-638-1116
Metro: Union Station

### Hyatt Regency Washington on Capitol Hill
400 New Jersey Avenue, NW
202-737-1234 or 1-800-233-1234
Metro: Union Station

# Answers to Smart Stuff Questions

**A.** Washington, D.C.

The city's license plates now read: "Taxation without Representation." (Does this phrase sound familiar?)

**B.** Fresco: The name comes from the application of mineral colors diluted in water onto fresh mortar, usually just put upon a wall. This technique enables the mortar to absorb the color. The process is repeated in sections until the entire picture is completed. It is found in works of old masters, such as Raphael.

**C.** A flag flies over the appropriate wing of the Capitol when its occupants are in session. At night, a light in the dome indicates one group is burning the midnight oil.

**D.** The Capitol subway that runs to the Senate and the House.

**E.** The book is *Parents as Mentors*. The authors' names might sound familiar: Sandra Burt and Linda Perlis. And the publisher should sound familiar, too: Prima. Just seeing if you were paying attention.

**F.** "The Lone Eagle," Charles A. Lindbergh, flew his plane, "The Spirit of St. Louis," from Long Island to land at Le Bourget Airfield outside of Paris (May 21, 1927) in 33½ hours, making the first nonstop transatlantic flight, solo.

CHAPTER 3

# The National Mall

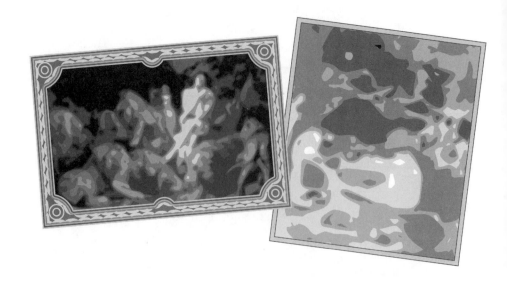

**I**f you were to stand in the middle of the green expanse of the National Mall and look in any direction, you would see some of the most significant and distinguished buildings in the world. Surrounded by frisbee-players, dog-walkers, joggers, bikers, skaters, and lunchtime picnickers, you might glimpse the **Lincoln Memorial,** beyond the stark obelisk of the **Washington Monument,** at the west end; the gleaming dome of the **U.S. Capitol** on the east end; or nine buildings of the world-famous **Smithsonian Institution** on the north and south sides. This area is one of the country's oldest federal parks, originally envisioned in L'Enfant's plan for the city. It is the center for many special Washington festivals and events, an arrival and departure point for visiting dignitaries, and, of course, the location of many of the most famous landmarks in the city. And just think: we all own this wonderful place together!

## ★Smithsonian Visitor Information Center ("The Castle")

**For All Ages...** Emblematic of America's emphasis on equal opportunity regardless of one's origins, the Smithsonian Institution was the gift of an Englishman born out of wedlock. James Smithson, whose tomb lies in the Crypt Room of the Smithsonian Castle, was prevented by his illegitimate birth from entering the clergy, the military, or politics. So he turned to science, and eventually became a member of the distinguished body of scientists, the Royal Society. Having no children, he willed his fortune to his nephew, with the provision that if his nephew were also childless, the funds would be used to establish an institution in the city of Washington, D.C. (which he had never visited) for the "increase and diffusion of knowledge."

Interactive touch-screen programs, two electronic wall maps, models, and two orientation theaters beckon visitors to stop first at

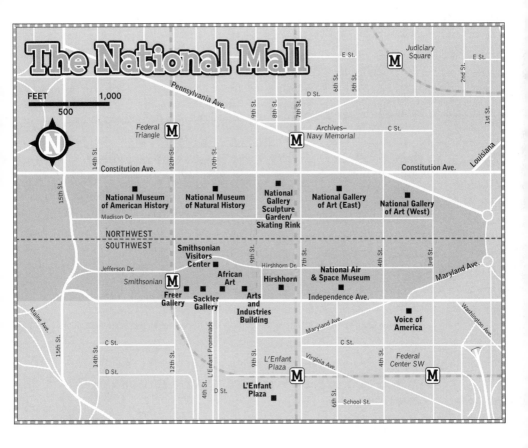

# Quick Guide to

| Attraction | Location |
| --- | --- |
| ★Smithsonian Visitor Information Center ("The Castle") | 1000 Jefferson Drive, SW |
| The Freer Gallery | Jefferson Drive at 12th Street, SW |
| The Arthur M. Sackler Gallery | 1050 Independence Avenue, SW |
| The National Museum of African Art | 950 Independence Avenue, SW |
| Smithsonian Arts and Industries Building | 900 Jefferson Drive, SW |
| Hirschhorn Museum and Sculpture Garden | Independence Avenue at 7th Street, SW |
| ★National Air and Space Museum | 7th Street and Independence Avenue, SW |
| The Voice of America | 330 Independence Avenue, SW (enter on C Street, between 3rd and 4th Streets) |
| ★National Gallery of Art | Constitution Avenue between 3rd and 7th Streets, NW |
| National Gallery of Art Sculpture Garden and Ice Skating Rink | Mall at 7th Street and Constitution Avenue, NW |
| ★National Museum of Natural History | 10th Street and Constitution Avenue, NW on the Mall |
| ★National Museum of American History | Constitution Avenue between 12th and 14th Streets, NW |

# The National Mall Attractions

| Age Range | Hours | Details on |
|---|---|---|
| All Ages | 9 A.M.–5:30 P.M. daily | Page 54 |
| All Ages | 10 A.M.–5:30 P.M. daily | Page 59 |
| All Ages | 10 A.M.–5:30 P.M. daily; Thursdays until 8 P.M. | Page 60 |
| All Ages | 10 A.M.–5:30 P.M. daily; Thursdays until 8 P.M. in summer | Page 61 |
| All Ages | 10 A.M.–5:30 P.M. daily | Page 62 |
| All Ages | 10 A.M.–5:30 P.M. daily | Page 63 |
| All Ages | 9:30 A.M.–6 P.M. daily (Memorial Day–Labor Day); 9:45 A.M.–5:30 P.M. (rest of year) | Page 65 |
| Teens | Tours: Mon.–Fri. 10:30 A.M, 1:30 P.M., and 2:30 P.M. | Page 68 |
| All Ages | Mon.–Sat. 10 A.M.–5 P.M.; Sun. 11 A.M.–6 P.M. | Page 69 |
| All Ages | Mon.–Thurs. 10 A.M.–10 P.M.; Fri.–Sat. 10 A.M.–11 P.M.; Sun. 11 A.M.–10 P.M. | Page 74 |
| All Ages | 10 A.M.–5:30 P.M. daily | Page 74 |
| All Ages | 10 A.M.–5:30 P.M. daily | Page 76 |

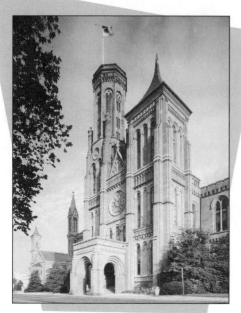

*Smithsonian Visitor Information Center (now we can see why it is called "The Castle")*

"The Castle," headquarters for the entire Smithsonian Institution. Be sure to ask for the free guide booklet and map for the Smithsonian (which is available in several languages), the brochure *10 Tips for Visiting the Smithsonian with Children,* and the Dining Guide that tells all the places to eat within the various local Smithsonian buildings. Encompassing sixteen museums, galleries, and the National Zoo, the Smithsonian Institution is also among the most outstanding research centers in the world. So extensive is its collection that only one percent of its holdings are ever on display at one time; two of its numerous facilities are located outside the Washington, D.C., area, in New York City.

The Castle has a dining room, the **Commons Restaurant,** open to the public only on weekends and holidays; brunch on Sunday is from 11 A.M.–3 P.M. and on Saturday and holidays 11 A.M.–2 P.M.; 202-357-2957. Each of the Smithsonian facilities has its own gift shop with a focus on that particular collection, including crafts from around the world, books, recordings, educational toys and games, jewelry, and Smithsonian reproductions; 202-357-2700.

Standing nine feet tall in front of "the Castle" is the imposing **statue of Joseph Henry,** inventor of the first telegraph, the electric relay, and an electric motor. The standard "unit of inductive resistance" is named in his honor, the *henry.* The sculpture shows Henry leaning on a pedestal depicting his electromagnet. His family actually lived in this building while he was secretary of the brand new Smithsonian Institution, where he worked for twenty-nine years.

> Metro: Smithsonian
> 1000 Jefferson Drive, SW
> Open daily 9 A.M.–5:30 P.M.; closed December 25
> 202-357-2020 for events information and free guided tours; for information in Spanish, 202-633-9126
> *All* Smithsonian facilities are *free;* fees are charged for some activities.
> 202-357-2700 for general information
> www.si.edu

# The Freer Gallery

**For All Ages...** The oldest of the Smithsonian's art museums, the Freer, houses an extensive collection of Asian and American art, including Chinese, Japanese, Korean, and South Asian paintings, ceramics, jades, sculptures, and miniatures, as well as Buddhist and Islamic art. You'll recognize this gallery by its Renaissance-style façade with colorful banners flying. Industrialist Charles Freer, who endowed the gallery, learned about Asian art from his friend,

**Smart Stuff**

**For Tikes...** How many peacocks can you find in this dining room? (A.)

James McNeil Whistler. All ages especially enjoy Whistler's "Peacock Room," an actual dining room that was transported in pieces from London to Detroit to Washington, D.C. Ask for the special guidebooks for children.

**Smart Stuff**

**For Tweens and Teens...** What symbol did Whistler use as his signature? How many can you find in this room? (B.)

Metro: Smithsonian

Jefferson Drive at 12th Street, SW

Daily 10 A.M.–5:30 P.M.; closed December 25

Guided tours available; phone for schedule.

Group tours must be arranged well in advance; call the Education Office at 202-357-4880, ext. 246; also ask for information about ImaginAsia.

202-357-2104 or 202-357-2700

# The Arthur M. Sackler Gallery

**For All Ages...** The closest thing to caving on The National Mall is entering the little kiosk near the Freer to descend 57 feet underground into the **Sackler Gallery** of Asian and Near Eastern Art. If you like tunnels, you can also get there through the underground exhibition passage from the Freer Gallery. In contrast to the Freer, the Sackler accommodates visiting exhibits as well as its own collection. From ancient to modern art, the Sackler houses exhibits of bronze, jade, silver, gold, lacquer, ceramics, paintings, and sculpture from the Mediterranean to Japan. A monthly calendar lists storytelling events, workshops, and other activities, and here, too, you can ask for the children's guidebook.

The gift shop has beautiful Asian handcrafted clothing, scarves, jewelry, pottery, boxes, and notepaper, as well as a large selection of books (including a special children's section), music, posters, and postcards.

Bounded by Independence Avenue and the Smithsonian Castle, the Arts and Industries Building, and the Freer Gallery, the **Enid A. Haupt Garden** actually is a rooftop garden covering the underground museums. In this formal Victorian garden, children will particularly enjoy the nine-foot-tall moon gates, the Fountain Garden's waterfall, and the animal-shaped topiaries, including buffalo. This is a good rest stop, but not a place for climbing or running; take your parasol.

Metro: Smithsonian

1050 Independence Avenue, SW

Daily 10 A.M.–5:30 P.M.; Thursdays open until 8 P.M.; closed
    December 25

Guided tours available; ask for information on ImaginAsia.

Group tours must be arranged well in advance.

202-357-4880 or 202-357-2700

# The National Museum of African Art

**For All Ages...** This is a museum kids love. Be sure to ask for the
Family Guide that children and adults can use together to explore
African art. Children can envision real people making these masks,
gongs and handmade musical instruments, pipes, statues, stools, and
other furnishings. Large color photos help explain the purposes of
many of the artifacts. This collection of ancient and contemporary
work is the only national mu-
seum that highlights sub-Sa-
haran African art and culture.

### Smart Stuff

**For Tweens and Teens...**
Find the exhibit about the
ancient African city that
flourished long before the
civilizations of Greece or
Rome. (C.)

Because the materials
used are familiar, including
raffia, beads, shells, wood,
clay, and fiber, children can
readily picture themselves
working with them. The
many representations of ani-
mals delight children of all ages. The exhibit on the ancient West
African city of Benin is notable for its beautiful metal work collection. Of particular interest in the gift shop here are handmade craft
items, CDs, videos, and tapes of African music.

Metro: Smithsonian

950 Independence Avenue, SW

Daily 10 A.M.–5:30; Thursdays until 8 P.M. in the summer;
    closed December 25

Guided tours available 1:30 P.M. Monday through Thursday
and 11 A.M. and 1 P.M. on weekends (1 hour). Arrange for
group tours at least three *months* in advance.

For schedule of family workshops, storytelling, and films, call
the Education Department at 202-357-4600, ext. 222.
Ask about the AfriKid Art programs.

202-357-2700.

# Smithsonian Arts and Industries Building

**For All Ages…** The placement of the 1940s carousel (yes, you *can*
really ride on it—for a small fee) on the Mall in front of the Arts
and Industries Building indicates that this is a kid-friendly museum.
The carousel runs from 10 A.M. to 6 P.M. daily, weather permitting.
Inside the museum are a real 1876 steam locomotive, printing
presses, an ice cream machine, a telegraph, and a 45-foot-long
model of the cruiser USS *Antietam.* Many items here celebrate the
Philadelphia Centennial Exposition of 1876, highlighting the latest
advances in American technology. The permanent collection includes such Victorian everyday objects as cookbooks and clothing,
and even copies of *Uncle Tom's Cabin.*

Mostly, visitors get an unvarnished glimpse of life in the mid-
1800s. It's a good beginning for exploration of the more complex
exhibits in some of the other Smithsonian buildings. And in the gift
shop kids can find reproductions of numerous items from toys and
games to household objects from early America.

**Discovery Theater,** located in this museum, features performances of singers, dancers, puppeteers, and mimes most of the year;
you will need to call for details.

Metro: Smithsonian
900 Jefferson Drive, SW
Daily 10 A.M.–5:30 P.M.; closed December 25
Discovery Theater information 202-357-1500
202-357-2700

Ready for a snack, or shopping, or a movie? Right across Independence Avenue is **L'Enfant Plaza** (First Street and Independence Avenue, SE; 202-485-3300), above ground, a courtyard and garden surrounded by modern office buildings, and below ground, a complex of shopping mall, restaurants, movie theaters, and parking. There's enough variety here to satisfy almost anyone's hungry tummy: yogurt, cookies, deli, pizza, hamburgers, Chinese, and an entire food court. From June through September, there are free Wednesday afternoon concerts in L'Enfant Plaza, from 11:45 A.M. to 1:45 P.M.; musical offerings include rock, jazz, and pop. So both your food *and* your entertainment are a bargain. The **U.S. Postal Service Headquarters** is at 475 L'Enfant Plaza, SW; on the ground floor, the Hall of Stamps exhibits original stamp art work and rare and unusual postal items. Open Monday through Saturday 9 A.M.–5 P.M.; closed federal holidays; 202-268-2000.

# Hirschhorn Museum and Sculpture Garden

**For All Ages…** Another grateful (and highly successful) immigrant to the U.S. gave this extraordinary collection to his adopted country. Latvian-born Joseph Hirschhorn began collecting art as a teenager, purchasing etchings in New York; then, in 1974, at the age of 75, he donated his "little gift": 2,000 pieces of sculpture and 4,000 drawings and paintings.

## Smart Stuff

**For Teens…** Find the sculpture of a world-famous fictional Spanish hero. Who was the sculptor? How would you describe his artistic style? (D.)

Going the Guggenheim one better, The Hirschhorn Museum is not only cylindrical, but stands on sculptured supports fourteen feet aboveground. American and European art from the late nineteenth century to the present fill this unique building on the Mall and an outdoor sculpture garden as well. Children who always worried that their own artistic creations didn't look "realistic" enough will be delighted to discover the abstract work of grown-up artists on all three floors. Artists in the Hirschhorn collection comprise a roster of important late nineteenth and twentieth century painters and sculptors: Calder, deKooning, Stella, Hopper, O'Keefe, Pollock, Moore, Rodin, Giacometti, Renoir, Gaugin, Picasso, and Warhol.

Best of all are the sculptures, which exemplify a huge variety of styles from the delicate dancers of Degas to the enormous wall frieze of Matisse. A good place to stretch out when the kids have had enough of standing still and paying attention, the wide open spaces of the Sculpture Garden encourage exploration. Colorful koi populate the fish pond; just be sure the kids don't climb in and join them.

It's a good idea to begin with the short orientation film in the theater on the lower level. There's also a beautiful free Family Guide (at the information desk) spotlighting works in the collection that are children's favorites and suggesting connected activities. You can use the cards enclosed to mix and match your own children's preferences, as well as to enhance your enjoyment of the works here.

## Smart Stuff

**For Tikes and Tweens...**
How many sculptures of horses can you find in the Hirschhorn?

Talk about the different styles you see; how do they make you feel? (E.)

## Helpful Hint

Teacher's Packets and Art Hunt activity guides are available as well; we strongly urge you to request these well-thought-out materials before you come. The gift shop on the lower level carries a wide variety of prints, art books, calendars, posters, note cards, jewelry, and other artistic items.

From Memorial Day through Labor Day, the **Full Circle** outdoor café (self-service) is a good cho friendly dining. From hot and cold sandwiches, delicic dogs, and personal-size pizzas to child-pleasing desserts such as jumbo chocolate chip cookies, this is an economical choice as well. Open 11 A.M.–3 P.M., weather permitting.

> Metro: L'Enfant Plaza or Smithsonian
> Independence Ave. at 7th Street, SW
> Daily 10 A.M.–5:30 P.M.; closed December 25
> Guided tours are offered; special tours for disabled visitors;
>     call to confirm times; 202-357-3235.
> Fee for audiotape tours for special exhibits
> Call regarding children's films and special programs;
>     reservations are required; 202-357-3235 (Education
>     Department).
> 202-357-2700

# ★National Air and Space Museum

**For All Ages...** Despite its overwhelming size, this museum is a hands-down favorite with kids. From its patriotic opening on July 1, 1976, in time for the Bi-centennial, it has been the most visited museum in the world, and is now celebrating its 25th birthday with a year-long celebration. Most of the aircraft housed here have actually flown, from the Wright brothers' 1903 Flyer to Lindbergh's "Spirit of St. Louis,"

**Smart Stuff**

**For Tikes...** Several exhibits show vehicles used in space. If you were to travel in a spaceship, what would you bring?

to the Apollo 11 Command Module "Columbia," through a Viking Mars Lander. For many, the most exciting space travel souvenir is something everyone *can* touch: the famous moon rock. Everywhere you turn, aircraft hover overhead. Children also love to climb into such relics as the American Airlines DC-7 and the Skylab Orbital Workshop, the backup for America's first space station.

Arrive when the museum opens, and you will need to pace yourselves; this huge museum will require at least three to four hours of your time, and some organizing. A good first stop is the Information Desk, to pick up a floor plan and a list of events. An activity board lists times for events such as storytelling, paper airplane contests, and special demonstrations. You will need to purchase tickets *immediately*

## Smart Stuff

**For Tweens...** What was the name of the first animal in space? What kind of animal was it, and what country did it come from?

(F.)

for whichever of the films in the **Langley Theater** fits your group's desires and your schedule; there are several each day, shown on an IMAX screen, five stories high and seven stories wide. These are movies all parents and teachers will approve of and all ages will enjoy. At the same time, purchase your tickets for a show at the **Albert Einstein Planetarium.** The *only* way to get tickets for these events *in advance* (up to two weeks) is by going to the box office.

Twenty-three galleries center on specific themes, including early flight, jet aviation, planetary and lunar exploration, rocketry, military aircraft, space art, computer technology in aerospace, robotics, aerial imaging, and astronomy. In the "How Things Fly" exhibit, kids can

## Parents/Teachers Take Note

Kids will enjoy this museum's Web site (www.nasm.edu/NASMAP.html), which lets them explore the museum, section by section. Since the National Air and Space Museum is so large, a visit requires advance planning. We suggest letting kids work in teams to formulate a blueprint of their tour, justifying each of the spots they have chosen.

experience numerous interactive activities such as wind and smoke tunnels and control of a full-size Cessna 150 airplane.

Just in case your kids' homing devices are on vacation, gift shops in this museum abound. Small ones are located in many of the display areas, and then there's a much larger one, if you haven't bought enough! Kids can choose from model airplane and rocketry kits to books on aeronautics and biographies of famous pilots, jewelry, and souvenirs of all kinds. A favorite with all ages is the freeze-dried "astronaut ice cream," which really does melt in your mouth.

Good reading includes: *Amelia Earhart (American Women of Achievement),* by Barbara Weisberg (tweens); *The Wright Brothers: How They Invented the Airplane,* by Russell Friedman, et al. (tweens); *The Little Prince,* by Antoine de St. Exupery (tweens and teens), also available on video; and *The Right Stuff,* by Tom Wolfe

**Smart Stuff**

For Teens... When was the first docking of U.S. and Soviet spacecraft? What is the most recent joint venture in space? How has the "cold war" affected such joint operations? Make a prediction for the future of international cooperation in space. (G.)

**Time-Saving Tip**

Taking a lunch break here is a visual treat; it's also a great time-saver if you're planning to stay a few more hours. The futuristic **Flight Line** cafeteria boasts floor-to-ceiling windows with wonderful views of the Capitol, the Mall, and the National Gallery of Art. You can select from several buffet stations and courses ranging from sandwiches, salads, hot entrees, soups, pizza, and dessert, fresh-baked bread, and pastries. Prices are reasonable and seating is ample (for 800 people—so you can bring a friend or two). Open daily 10 A.M.–5 P.M.

(teens), also a movie. *The Spirit of St. Louis,* the story of Charles Lindbergh's famous voyage, is an interesting film for tweens and teens. *Smithsonian Adventures: Hot Air Balloon* is a kit to build a five-foot-tall hot air balloon (tweens).

The **Wright Place,** a floor above the **Flight Line** cafeteria, offers table service, slightly pricier food, an extensive children's menu (grilled cheese, chicken fingers, hamburgers), and does take reservations (202-371-8777). Many plants and aviation photos decorate the restaurant, but the views are not as spectacular as downstairs. Open daily 11:30 A.M.–3 P.M.

> Metro: L'Enfant Plaza
> 7th Street and Independence Avenue, SW
> Daily 9:30 A.M.–6 P.M. (Memorial Day weekend through Labor Day); 9:45 A.M.–5:30 P.M., rest of year. Closed December 25.
> Guided tours offered; call for details.
> Fees for Planetarium, movie (202-357-1686 for IMAX film schedule), and audiotape tours.
> For school group tours, call Tour Office, 202-357-1400.
> 202-357-2700
> www.nasm.edu/
> www.educationplanet.com/search/History/Museums

# The Voice of America

**For Teens...** Famous since 1942 as a beacon of freedom and information about the United States, the Voice of America (VOA) is nearby. Since over 80 million visitors all over the world outside of North America tune in regularly, the VOA is of special interest to visitors from other countries, who might have listened to it at home. You can see a short film about VOA operations, and then take the free 45-minute tour. You can watch broadcasting in its radio and television studios and newsroom, and in 52 languages for distribution worldwide. A former broadcaster describes his own life (born in Russia in 1911) and his forty-five years as a broadcaster, writer, editor, commentator, and Chief of the Russian Service for VOA in his book *Talking to the Russian: Glimpses of History by a Voice of America Pioneer,* by Victor Franzusoff (tweens and teens).

> Metro: Federal Center
> 330 Independence Avenue, SW (enter on C Street, between 3rd and 4th Streets)
> Tours Monday through Friday at 10:30 A.M., 1:30 P.M., and 2:30 P.M.; closed holidays; reservations required.
> 202-619-3919

# ★National Gallery of Art

**For All Ages...** A beautiful blend of past and present, the National Gallery of Art has something for everyone. In two buildings, spanning four city blocks, the classical West Building and modern East Building, visitors can see art from the thirteenth century through the present, one of the finest collections anywhere in the world. Built of pink Tennessee marble, the graceful West building contains long halls of classical sculpture and courtyards adorned with seasonal plants. If you don't feel cultured in this setting, you never will!

A welcome addition is the new Micro Gallery near the Mall entrance of the West Building, where thirteen computer stations with 20-inch color monitors allow visitors to access images and information about the gallery's holdings, artists, and art-related subjects. If you are computer-comfy, you can create your own

*In the halls of the National Gallery of Art*

personal tour of the museum and print a map showing the locations of specific works of art you want to visit.

Kids will find it exciting to notice the differences between the reproductions they have seen in books and the "real thing." The best of European and American art is represented: Italian, French, British, Dutch, Flemish, German, and Spanish works. Old masters, such as Rembrandt, Raphael, Vermeer, Renoir, Monet, Jacques-Louis David, and Leonardo da Vinci, are displayed in viewer-friendly-sized rooms in the West Building. This is not a place to rush through, but if museum-fatigue sets in, take advantage of any of the small atriums spaced throughout the building, sit down, and relax.

## Helpful Hint

Because this is an especially large museum with a lot to offer, the temptation is to put on your running shoes and try to race through it all. Don't. Your best bet is to plan ahead; ask for a family guide and a floor plan, and choose what you want to see and where. Be selective; see a few things thoroughly and talk about them. Even better, request the services of a docent in advance of your trip.

In the hierarchy of gift shops, the West Building version is way up at the top. Filled with posters, prints, and postcards, stationery, calendars, a huge collection of art books, silk scarves, jewelry, and even toys and games, here's where to go for high-class souvenirs.

## Smart Stuff

For Tweens... Find the huge picture entitled "The Dead Torreador," by Edouard Manet. Kids love the goriness of this painting, but they can also be encouraged to discuss the realism of it and how it makes them feel. What do they think is the artist's opinion of bullfights?

## Smart Stuff

**For Teens...** One way to combat teens' natural tendency to plough through an exhibit ("Saw this! Saw that! Yep!") is to compare and contrast two paintings that might seem similar.

For example, look at two American works from the late nineteenth century: Winslow Homer's 1876 painting, "Breezing Up" and Mary Cassatt's 1893 painting, "The Boating Party."

What are the differences in: uses of color? appeal to the senses? feeling of movement? Ask which painting they prefer and why. (H.)

Below the West and East Buildings is a concourse connecting the two, with another gift shop, a cafeteria, and a waterfall (actually, a wall of glassed-in water from the fountain outside). The most exciting feature for kids will likely be the moving walkway linking the two buildings.

## Time-Saving Tip

The "Concourse Buffet" is among the most popular of the Mall area eateries. To museumed-out adults and kids, this is a welcome and tasty relief. With a large seating capacity (although everyone tries to sit facing the waterfall) and wide variety of choices, this cafeteria is an inviting place for all ages and degrees of appetite. Open Monday through Friday from 10 A.M. to 3 P.M., Saturday 10 A.M. to 4 P.M., and Sunday 11 A.M. to 4:30 P.M. for snacks and meals.

The special excitement of the East Wing is in the design of the building itself. The sharp angles and stark exterior hint at the dramatic, light-filled interior. Created in 1978 by architect I. M. Pei, it remains the most modern, even though not the newest, building downtown.

Although the exhibits here change frequently, their common denominator is that all represent the masters of contemporary art, including Picasso, Giacometti, Warhol, Stella, Miro, Mondrian, Rothko, Man Ray, Magritte, and Matisse. Children are amazed at the enormous works of art high above their heads as they enter. The super-size Calder mobile (children love to watch it move) and the giant Miro tapestry are colorful surprises after a visit to the more traditional West Wing. The huge elevators (necessarily so for moving large works of art) and the spiral staircase up to the Tower level hold particular appeal for younger kids. In this case, getting to the exhibits is half the fun. One dividend for young artists is that many of the objects represented in the works of art do *not* look "real"; this may be some children's first exposure to non-representational styles. Older kids will appreciate the variety of abstract styles, particularly if the artist, like Picasso (who actually began his career with representational painting), embraces a variety of approaches.

**Smart Stuff**

For Tweens and Teens... Geometry lesson: What geometric shape does the East Wing represent? (Hint: It's actually a combination of two interconnected shapes.) (I.)

**Smart Stuff**

For Tikes... Select an abstract painting and see how many objects you can "find" within it. How does the picture make you feel?

Food? On one of the upper levels in the East Wing, high enough for a grand view, is the **Terrace Café.** Upscale in both price and selection, this is not for the burgers and fries gang, but it is a delight for lunch if you are a small, classy few.

Special temporary exhibits at the National Gallery of Art are so popular that many people pick up the free "time tickets" (which admit you on a certain day and time) well in advance of their visit. But *all* visitors have access; go to the ticket counter on the main floor of the West Building early on the day of your visit to pick up tickets. Some are set aside just for this distribution.

The gift shops are filled with books of interest, of course. In addition, tweens might enjoy *Girl With A Watering Can* (Paintings from the National Gallery of Art, Washington, D.C.), by Edward Zadrzynska. The series, *Art for Children,* by Ernest Raboff, includes individual books on such artists as Picasso, Raphael, Chagall, Matisse, and Renoir (tweens).

Metro: Archives

Constitution Avenue between 3rd and 7th Streets, NW

Monday through Saturday 10 A.M.–5 P.M., Sunday 11 A.M.–6
   P.M.; closed January 1 and December 25

Guided tours: West Building Monday through Friday 11:30
   A.M. and 3:30 P.M., Saturday 10:30 A.M. and 12:30 P.M.,
   Sunday 12:30 P.M., 2:30 P.M., and 4:30 P.M.; East Building
   Monday through Friday 10:30 A.M. and 1:30 P.M., Satur-
   day through Sunday 11:30 A.M., 1:30 P.M., and 3:30 P.M..

For group tours, schedule four weeks in advance.

Foreign language tours Tuesday and Thursday; call for details.

Gallery talks Tuesday through Sunday; lectures Sunday 4 P.M.,
   concerts Sunday 7
   P.M. Call for loca-
   tions and times.

Sign language interpre-
   tation available
   with three weeks
   advance notice.

Fee for self-guiding
   tour audiotapes.

202-737-4215 or 202-737-6188. Education Department:
   202-842-6187

www.nga.gov

**Helpful Hint**
We strongly suggest that
you ask to receive by mail
the packet to help teachers/
parents plan ahead.

# National Gallery of Art
# Sculpture Garden and Ice Skating Rink

**For All Ages...** Back out into the sunlight, students enjoy wandering through the six-acre Sculpture Garden, home to a number of modern works of Claes Oldenburg, Roy Lichtenstein, Coosje van Bruggen, Tony Smith, and Magdalena Abakanowicz. Open from late October to mid-March, the circular ice rink is a wonderful spot for skating and socializing. You can even rent skates here. The newly renovated outdoor **Pavilion Café** offers fresh baked goods, salads, sandwiches, specialty pizzas, desserts, and a welcome cup of hot cocoa or coffee; there's also a children's menu. Keeping your balance on the ice is your job.

> Metro: Archives
> Mall at 7th Street and Constitution Avenue, NW
> Monday through Thursday 10 A.M.–10 P.M.; Friday through
>      Saturday 10 A.M.–11 P.M.; Sunday 11 A.M.–10 P.M.
> Phone for information about ice-skating: 202-289-3360

# ★National Museum of Natural History

**For All Ages...** You know you're not in an art gallery when you enter from the Mall and are greeted by a huge, hairy, eight-ton African bush elephant in the domed rotunda of the National Museum of Natural History. This is a favorite with children of all ages. From animals and live insects to dinosaurs (only the bones, of course), fossils, and gems, this museum has something special for everyone. Check first at the Information Desk for free, timed admission tickets and hours for the **Discovery Room** and the **Insect Zoo.** Immediately off the rotunda, start with the **Native Cultures of the Americas,** with dioramas of native peoples at everyday tasks.

For young children, the Discovery Room, with its bones, reptile skins, and even a preserved rattlesnake, offers a chance to look *and* touch. The **Dinosaur Hall,** full of skeletons of real, used-to-be-live, colossal creatures, is also a favorite with young visitors. There are two exhibits on undersea life, one on birds of the world, and a fossil collection. On the second floor, the **O. Orkin Insect Zoo** allows anyone who likes insects to get up close and personal with cockroaches, centipedes, and tarantulas. "Big Bob" is a particular favorite: a tarantula the size of a dinner plate. Speaking of meals, you can watch "Big Bob" feast weekdays at 10:30 A.M., 11:30 A.M., and 1:30 P.M. Tuesday through Friday, and weekends at 12:30 and 1:30 P.M.

For those of us who like our treasures non-mobile, the **Janet Annenberg Hooker Hall of Geology, Gems, and Minerals** has more allure. Kids especially ogle the collection of geodes that glow in the dark. In addition to the famed 45-1/2 carat Hope Diamond, this hall displays earrings worn by Marie Antoinette on her way to the guillotine, and features interactive and multimedia activities. Although these offerings are clearly state of the art, unfortunately they do not allow for creation of expensive jewelry of our own.

The museum's newest jewel is the **Discovery Center,** with its 500-seat IMAX theater, featuring movies about the environment and our cultural heritage. Hands-on activities abound here; when kids tire, they can take advantage of the food court in the new 600-seat **Atrium Café** and then drag you through the largest complex of gift shops in the entire Smithsonian.

An animated version of *The Song of Sacajawea,* read by Laura Dern, is available on video and will appeal to younger viewers. A book for tikes is *Amelia and Eleanor Go for a Ride,* by Pam M.

**Smart Stuff**

For Tweens... This museum actually has a two-part name. What is the second part? How many native cultures from the Western Hemisphere can you find displayed? (J.)

Ryan. In *A Time for Native Americans,* tweens can learn about forty-nine significant American Indians from a set of illustrated biographical cards; the packet includes a map puzzle, a time line puzzle, and a time line challenge. An activity guide to traditional North American Indian life, with creative ideas and projects, for tweens, is *More*

*Than Moccasins. Colonial Kids* is an activity book with directions for preparing authentic food, clothing, and other colonial items, as well as hundreds of activity ideas (tweens). *Dear America: Friend to Friend* is an unusual computer game, featuring six girls from different historical periods in American history (tweens). Of particular interest would be *Wounded Knee: An Indian History of the American West*, by Dee Brown, et al. (tweens and teens), based on *Bury My Heart at Wounded Knee*, by Dee Brown. *Dances with Wolves* is a movie teens will find poignant.

> Metro: Federal Triangle or Smithsonian
> 10th Street and Constitution Avenue, NW on the Mall
> Daily 10 A.M.–5:30 P.M.; closed December 25
> Free guided tours of museum highlights 10:30 A.M. and
>     1:30 P.M. daily
> Fee for iGO Interactive Audio Tour, using hand-held, touch
>     screen computer; call for details and rates.
> 202-357-2700; for Discovery Room group visits,
>     202-357-2747.

# ★National Museum of American History

**For All Ages...** Also called "the nation's attic," because of the eclectic nature of its contents, the National Museum of American History frustrates those who try to see it all in one visit. Sharing the building with Dorothy's ruby slippers from *The Wizard of Oz* are Thomas Edison's original light bulb, jazz king Dizzy Gillespie's trumpet, and the original Star-Spangled Banner. Presidential history buffs will especially appreciate a recent addition to the permanent collection: **The American Presidency.** This is one exhibit that has kept its curators particularly busy. In addition to the myriad things to see, there are some exhibits that allow children to take part: **Hands-on History,** where children participate in crafts demonstrations and other historically connected activities; and **Hands-on-Science,** which en-

courages participation in science experiments and p
portunity to play with science-related toys and game

Begin at the Informa-
tion Desk to see if you need
timed admission passes for
either of the above interactive
rooms. Also, ask for the self-
guided tour booklet "Hunt
for History" (for your appropriate age group), a floor
plan, and take a few minutes
to plot your travels through
the museum. Some of the
most popular exhibits are:
**"First Ladies: Political Role**

## Smart Stuff

**For Teens...** What scientific instrument replicated
in the National Museum
of American History was
originally introduced in
Paris in 1851 with the invitation to "witness the
earth revolve"? How does
it work? (K.)

**and Public Image,"** complete with their actual ball gowns; **"Field
to Factory,"** describing one of the largest population shifts in our
nation's history, the migration of African Americans from the rural
South to northern cities; and treasures from the land of television,
including Mr. Rogers' sweater, *Sesame Street's* Oscar the Grouch, and
Fonzie's leather jacket.

One section of this museum concentrates on military artifacts
from George Washington's tent to the experiences of GIs in World
War II. **The Hall of Trans-
portation** is a magnet for
those who adore cars, motorcycles, trains, and boats.
**"After the Revolution"** gives
us a look at the everyday lives
and activities of eighteenth-
century Americans; kids
enjoy the log house. Those

## Smart Stuff

**For Tweens...** Locate the
1902 Horn and Hardart
Automat. What was an
automat? What is its
modern-day version? (L.)

who dream of elaborate dollhouses will adore the five-story version
in this museum, furnished with turn-of-the-century (nineteenth to
twentieth!) miniatures. On the third floor is a moving exhibit of
items left by mourners at the Vietnam Veterans Memorial.

## Smart Stuff

**For Tikes andTweens...** Find a real general store and post office in the National Museum of American History. You can mail a postcard or letter here, and have it postmarked "Smithsonian Station." How old is this post office and where did it come from? (M.)

Well-stocked with books, games and toys, tapes, and historic reproductions, the gift shop has a little something for everyone. But it's the food in this museum that's a bigger draw. At the Constitution Avenue level, is the wonderful **Palm Court,** complete with potted plants, a coffee bar (open 10 A.M.–4:30 P.M. daily), and, further back, the interior of a circa 1900 confectionery shop/Victorian ice cream parlor (open 11 A.M.–4 P.M. daily). You *can* get lunch here (soup, sandwiches, and salads), and it's quite good, but the desserts are the main attraction. Sinful in size and content, these are true old-fashioned treats. A visit here will earn you lots of "brownie" points from the kids. On the lower level, the **Main Street Cafés** offer a wide selection of sandwiches, pizza, desserts, and even hot meals, and are open for breakfast, lunch, and snacks. This restaurant serves efficiently, and items are very reasonably priced. Open daily 10A.M.–5 P.M..

## Smart Stuff

**For Tikes...** If you ran your own general store, what would you like to sell?

Who says attorneys aren't creative? The U.S. Attorney for the District of Columbia tried a brief stint at poetry, and the rest is definitely history. His name was Francis Scott Key, and his poem became our national anthem, *The Star Spangled Banner.*

Some enrichment materials for experiencing this museum might include: *Ragtime,* by E. L. Doctorow (teens)—also a Broadway musical; and *Our Town,* by Thornton Wilder (tweens and teens), the classic play to read aloud and, if possible, perform. *The Big Book of American Heroes: A Young Person's Guide* (from George Washington to Maya Angelou), by Mike Janulewicz, Peter Bull, and Richard Widdows would appeal to tweens.

Metro: Federal Triangle or Smithsonian
Constitution Avenue between 12th and 14th Streets, NW
Daily 10 A.M.–5:30 P.M.; closed December 25
Guided tours are available; call 202-357-1481 for times
Fee for audiotape rentals
202-357-1481 or 202-357-2700

# Where to Stay in the National Mall Area

Since none of the Smithsonian buildings have overnight accommodations (alas!), we've tried to locate the next best things. Again, remember to ask for discounts—for any category you can think of (time of year, group, corporate, etc.). Here are a few suggestions to consider:

**Hotel Harrington**
11th and E Streets, NW
202-628-8140 or 1-800-424-8532
Metro: Metro Center

**Holiday Inn Capitol at the Smithsonian**
550 C Street, SW
202-479-4000 or 1-888-TRIP2DC
Metro: L'Enfant Plaza

**Loew's L'Enfant Plaza**
480 L'Enfant Plaza, SW
202-484-1000 or 1-800-635-5065
Metro: L'Enfant Plaza

# Answers to Smart Stuff Questions

**A.** Little ones will have fun searching for the six peacocks in this room.

**B.** Whistler's trademark was a butterfly. There are four of them in this room.

**C.** The ancient Nubian city of Kerma, 2500–1500 B.C.

**D.** The sculpture is of Don Quixote, by Giacometti, famous for his elongated "realistic" figures. Notice the difference between this sculpture and other "representational" pieces such as the huge bust of Baudelaire.

**E.** Of the numerous horse sculptures, children might like to contrast the forceful movement-oriented work of Meissonier, "A Horseman in a Storm," with the solid, static, almost primitive look of Braque's "Little Horse" and Duchamp-Villon's very abstract "Head of a Horse."

**F.** Laika was the first animal in space, a dog from the Soviet Union. Read about the U.S.–Soviet space race; in the Air and Space Museum, you might want to visit the Space Race exhibit.

**G.** The first docking of two spacecraft paired Apollo I and Soyuz I on July 15, 1975. As this book goes to press, the joint U.S.–Russian Space Station is the most recent cooperative venture. Teens will enjoy making predictions, but they need to base them on facts about the current scientific and political climates in each country.

**H.** If the kids are slow getting into this, ask how many different shades of green they can find in Homer's ocean; contrast this with the water in the Cassatt painting.

**I.** The building is actually a trapezoid, built of two interconnected triangles. You might have to go up in a helicopter to see this clearly!

**J.** The second part of the National Museum of Natural History's name is "The Museum of Man." Children will be interested in finding the geographic locations of the many different cultures.

**K.** The Foucault Pendulum, a large brass ball, swinging across the same spot knocking over one peg at a time in a large circle, is actually moving because the floor under it is rotating, along with all the rest of us, on the planet Earth.

**L.** An automat was the earliest version of convenience food: people ran around behind the walls of little windows, refilling the cubicles as customers purchased their selections. Today's vending machines are slightly more automated!

**M.** The general store/post office served Headsville, West Virginia, from 1861 to 1971, when it was moved to its present site in the National Museum of American History. Children enjoy discovering the kinds of goods that were for sale in that early time period.

# CHAPTER 4

# White House
## & Foggy Bottom

**W**ho would have thought that some of the most significant buildings in our country are built on a former swamp stabilized by landfill? The name "Foggy Bottom" comes from the misty, often foul, air that hovered above this swamp on the edge of the Potomac River. A coal depot and gasworks inhabited the area that is now home to the **White House, George Washington University, Corcoran Gallery, Kennedy Center,** headquarters for the **Organization of American States,** the **Renwick Gallery,** the mysterious **Octagon House,** and the equally mysterious **Department of State.** These days, "Foggy Bottom" is Washington vernacular for the State Department, whose edicts are sometimes a bit foggy.

## ★National Aquarium

**For All Ages...** An entire society flourishes underground in the nation's capital. No, it's not the counterculture reappearing. Our nation's oldest public aquarium, scaled just right for children, resides—of all places—in the basement of the **Department of Commerce.** Tanks full of fascinating sea creatures are set low enough into the walls to be viewed by even the smallest of "fry." One special treat is watching the sharks (Monday, Wednesday, and Saturday 2 P.M.) and piranhas (Tuesday, Thursday, and Sunday at 2 P.M.) feeding—not a sight for faint-hearted adults, but a favorite with kids. Younger children especially enjoy getting up close and personal with the marine residents of the Touch Tank. Want to pet a horseshoe crab or handle a starfish? C'mon down!

With a variety of undersea life from eels that can make an electric current (maybe they could be helpful in an energy crisis) to the strangely shaped hammerhead sharks, this aquarium has an enormous collection of denizens, but they all live on a single visitor-

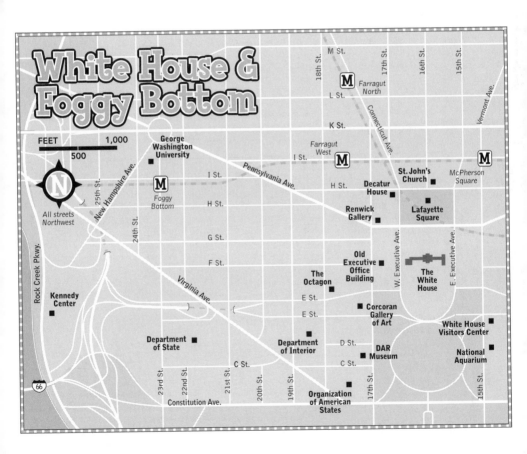

# Quick Guide to

| Attraction | Location |
| --- | --- |
| National Aquarium | 14th Street and Constitution Avenue, NW (inside the Department of Commerce building, between 14th and 15th Streets, NW) |
| White House Visitors Center | 1450 Pennsylvania Avenue, NW (inside the Department of Commerce building, between 14th and 15th Streets, NW) |
| The White House | 1600 Pennsylvania Avenue, NW |
| Lafayette Square | Lafayette Square (directly across Pennsylvania Avenue from the White House) |
| St. John's Church | 16th and H Streets, NW (across from Lafayette Square and the White House) |
| Decatur House | 748 Jackson Place, NW (on the northwest corner of Lafayette Park) |
| Renwick Gallery | 17th Street and Pennsylvania Avenue, NW |
| The Old Executive Office Building | Next to the White House on Pennsylvania Avenue (enter on 17th Street, NW) |
| The Octagon | 1799 New York Avenue, NW |
| Corcoran Gallery of Art | 17th and E Streets, NW (half-block west of the White House) |
| ★D.A.R. (Daughters of the American Revolution) Museum | 1776 D Street, NW |
| Organization of American States Building | 17th Street and Constitution Avenue, NW |
| State Department, Diplomatic Reception Rooms | 2201 C Street, NW |
| George Washington University | 2121 I Street, NW |
| ★Kennedy Center for the Performing Arts | 2700 F Street, NW (New Hampshire Avenue and Rock Creek Parkway) |

# White House/Foggy Bottom Attractions

| Age Range | Hours | Details on |
|---|---|---|
| All Ages | 9 A.M.–5 P.M. daily | Page 84 |
| Tweens and Teens | 7 A.M.–5 P.M. daily | Page 88 |
| Tweens and Teens | Tours: 10 A.M.–12 P.M. except Sundays and Mondays | Page 90 |
| All Ages | | Page 95 |
| All Ages | 9 A.M.–3 P.M. daily | Page 95 |
| Teens | Tours: Tues.–Fri. 10 A.M.–2:30 P.M. Sat./Sun. 12 P.M.–3:30 P.M. | Page 95 |
| Teens | 10 A.M.–5:30 P.M. daily | Page 96 |
| Teens | Saturday only, 9 A.M.–12 P.M. | Page 97 |
| Teens | Tues.–Fri. 10 A.M.–4 P.M. Sat./Sun. 1 P.M.–4 P.M. | Page 97 |
| Tweens and Teens | Wed.–Mon. 10 A.M.–5 P.M. Th. 10 A.M.–9 P.M.; closed Tues. | Page 98 |
| All Ages | Mon.–Fri. 8:30 A.M.–4 P.M. Sun. 1 P.M.–5 P.M. | Page 100 |
| Teens | Mon.–Fri. 9 A.M.–5:30 P.M. | Page 101 |
| Teens | Tours: Mon.–Fri. 9:30 A.M., 10:30 A.M., 2:45 P.M. | Page 103 |
| Teens | | Page 103 |
| All Ages | 10 A.M.–12 A.M. | Page 104 |

...an find something of interest. Here in the
...has some cool offspring.

...Triangle
...1 Constitution Avenue, NW (inside the De-
...of Commerce building, between 14th and 15th
...NW)
...1.–5 P.M.; closed December 25
Fee
202-482-2825

# White House Visitors Center

**For Tweens and Teens...** The large, new, White House Visitors Center offers comfortable places to sit and relax, information and displays about the White House, a video tour: *Inside These Walls* (just in case you weren't able to get up and out early enough to get tickets for a walk-through tour), and a gift shop. Most important: This is the place to get tickets for the 15-minute tours of the White House (where you will *not* actually be visiting the president himself). You can request VIP passes in advance of your visit to Washington, however; write to your congressional representative or senator 8 to 10 weeks in advance to ask for free tickets for the VIP tour. VIP tours are longer (30–45 minutes) and guided by Secret Service agents who discuss history, art, and furnishings of the White House. But they start early; these tours actually begin at 8:15, 8:30, and 8:45 A.M., so you will still have to get up and out. And lines, well there are *always* White House lines, even with the VIP tickets.

While the idea of visiting the presidential residence is exciting, the amount of time you will spend getting your tickets, waiting in lines, and then actually taking your zippy-quick tour of the mansion might just encourage you to postpone this site for a future visit. When you total up the time it actually involves, one White House tour equals visits to several other sites. But you *will* want to see the exterior, regardless. Imagine, there are some people willing to campaign for years just to become residents of the White House.

Sometimes without notice or explanation, public tours of the White House are canceled because of official functions, so call the day before you plan to visit. There are no public rest rooms or telephones there, either, so take care of all your needs at the **Ellipse Visitor Pavilion,** where the tour assembles, or at the **White House Visitors Center.** (*Residents,* of course, *do* get to use the rest rooms.)

As for breakfast, which you will most likely be pining for after the early-morning ticket line-up, you're in luck. The Ellipse Visitor Pavilion offers muffins, snacks, hot dogs, and drinks. On 15th Street, NW, across from the Ellipse, is the **Commerce Department,** which has a cafeteria open weekdays from 9 A.M.–2 P.M.; breakfast here is a bargain. After all, they *do* know something about commerce. The **BreadLine** is just a block from the White House, at 1751 Pennsylvania Avenue, NW; open weekdays 7 A.M.–6 P.M. Made-to-order sandwiches and stuffed breads (like calzones), as well as fresh salads, muffins, croissants, and other baked goods. Available "to-go." 202-822-8900.

> Metro: McPherson Square
> 1450 Pennsylvania Avenue, NW (inside the Department of Commerce building, between 14th and 15th Streets, NW)
> Daily 7:00 A.M.–5:00 P.M.
> Tours: Dated/timed tickets are required for the White House (first-come, first-served distribution). Tuesday through Saturday 7:30 A.M. Tickets are usually all distributed within less than an hour, so go *very* early (6:30 or 7 A.M.) to get in line.

On Pennsylvania Avenue in the park between 15th and E Streets, NW is a massive **equestrian monument** to a larger-than-life character. **William Tecumseh Sherman** was famous for his "scorched earth" march to the sea, capturing Georgia in 1864. He was named for the Shawnee Indian chief whom his father admired. (When his father died a few years later, and he was placed for adoption, his foster mother added the more conventional "William" as his first name.) This loquacious man who loved dancing and pretty women was as extroverted as his superior, General Grant, was taciturn. When a movement surfaced to draft him for the presidency, he answered with the now-famous response: "I will not accept if nominated, and will not serve if elected."

## The White House

**For Tweens and Teens...** The White House has been home to every president except our first. From John Adams' lonely occupation of the unfinished president's house on November 1, 1800, through the British destruction of it in 1814, through Franklin D. Roosevelt's tenure, when it became known as "the Grand Hotel," to its most recent setting for scandal, every administration has put its own stamp on the White House. Even White House children have used the residence in unorthodox ways, like the sons of President Garfield who used the East Room for their bicycle races. But it was Teddy Roosevelt who had the drab exterior repainted white, and who officially named it "The White House," emblazoning it on his presidential stationery.

In this building, members of presidential families, including one

### Smart Stuff

**For Tweens...** There are streets in Washington, D.C., named for every state. On which state's street does the president live? (A.)

*The White House State Visitors Entrance*

Which president served the shortest term?
(William Henry Harrison—31 days)
Which president served the longest term?
(Franklin Delano Roosevelt—12 years, 1 month)

president himself, were married, numerous babies, including presidential grandchildren
and one presidential child,
were born, and seven U.S.
presidents have lain in state.
Most surprising in this place

## Smart Stuff

**For Tweens...** Which president was married in the
White House? (B.)

filled with history are its size and style. Heads of most long-estab-
lished countries in other parts of the world live in much larger and
more opulent surroundings. This home for the leader of our democracy underscores his title: President, not King.

There *was* a time before Inaugural balls and festivities.
One president took the oath of office and later walked
back to his boarding house and had his dinner with the
other residents. His name was Thomas Jefferson. His new
residence, the White House, was not yet finished in 1801.

Visitors touring the
White House walk through
or past the State Dining
Room, the East Room, the
Green Room, the Red Room,
and the Blue Room, the
Vermeil Room, and the Li-
brary. Secret Service agents
are available in each room
to answer your questions.

## Smart Stuff

**For Teens...** What Confederate sympathizer, nick-
named "the Colonel,"
lived and died in the White
House after the South had
lost the Civil War? (C.)

Antiques, paintings, and other treasures collected over several administrations are on display in these areas and in the hallways. White House staff members, interns, and others are not on display, however; with one notorious exception, they do their work in another part of the building. Outside, if you see the flag flying at the White House, the president is home.

## Smart Stuff

For Teens... Carved onto the mantle of the State Dining Room is John Adams' hope for future occupants of the White House. What did he wish? Which administration do you feel has most lived up to this expectation? Which least? (D.)

The first cooking stove for the White House was purchased by President Fillmore, but nobody knew how to use it. He had to go to the U.S. Patent Office to get the information on how it worked!

For some interesting White House digging on your own, we highly recommend (for the youngest readers or listeners) Anne Denton Blair's *Arthur, the White House Mouse* and Kate Waters' *The Story of the White House.* Tikes and tweens will enjoy *Growing Up in the White House,* by Seymour Reit. Six suggestions especially for tweens are: *You Are The President* (Great Decisions series), by Nathan Aaseng; *You Are The President II: 1800–1899* (Great Decisions series), by Nathan Aaseng; Cheryl Harness's *Ghosts of the White House;* Marianne Hering's *Secret of the Missing Teacup* (White House Adventures Series); *The White House: An Historic Guide,* by The White House Historical Association with the Cooperation of the National Geographic Society; and Nancy Ann Van Wie's *Mystery at the White House: A President is Missing. Fandex Family Field Guides: Presidents* is a chronological guide to U.S. presidents and

*The Oval Office*

vice presidents (tweens). A few more suggestions: C. Brian Kelly's *Best Little Stories from the White House* (tweens and teens). *The First Ladies,* by Margaret Brown Klapthor, has a one-page photo and a one-page write-up on each first lady through Barbara Bush (tweens and teens). Teens might enjoy: *To the Best of My Ability: The American Presidents,* edited by James McPherson and David Rubel; *Theodore Roosevelt: A Life,* by Nathan Miller; *Mornings on Horseback,* by David McCullough; and *Abigail Adams: Witness to a Revolution,* by Natalie S. Bober. *An Invitation to the White House,* by former First Lady Hillary Rodham Clinton, features more than 350 photos, invitations, menus, and other memorabilia from actual White House functions (teens). A really fun read for all ages is *White House Pets,* by Margaret Truman; it's out of print, but well worth seeking through your local library.

As for movies, check out *The Candidate* (teens) and *The American President* (teens).

This area has some good choices for lunches, dinners, and snacks. **Reeves Restaurant Bakery,** at 1306 G Street, NW, is one of the oldest bakeries in the city. Here you can get an "all you can eat" breakfast buffet,

## Smart Stuff

For Tikes... Some of the funniest stories about life in the White House describe the antics of Teddy Roosevelt's six children and their pets. If you lived in the White House, what kinds of pets would you like to have there? (E.)

very reasonably priced, as well as sandwiches or hot entrees. Of course, this is a bakery, so you'll want to try at least one of the tasty homemade goodies, from pies to cakes to eclairs, to puddings. Open 7 A.M.–6 P.M. every day, but closed Sunday; 202-628-6350. **Health Zone,** at 1445 K Street, NW, is a special discovery, with its refreshing and relaxing atmosphere and its affordable pricing. All kinds of sandwiches, from vegetarian sushi to hot pastrami, are on this menu. Open 7 A.M.–4 P.M.; 202-371-2900. **Bertucci's,** at 2000 Pennsylvania Avenue, NW, requires reservations for eight or more people in a group. It's a favorite for the George Washington University students, and it's a bargain. Not only is there a large selection of pizzas, but a bottomless salad bowl accompanies them at lunch. Open Monday through Thursday 11 A.M.–10:30 P.M.; Friday through Saturday 11A.M.–11:30 P.M.; and Sunday noon to 10 P.M.; 202-296-2600. **Lindy's Bon Apetit,** at 2040 I Street, NW, serves omelettes with home fries and toast, as well as a zillion varieties of burgers, soups, and desserts, all well-priced. Open Monday through Friday 8 A.M.–8 P.M., Saturday 11 A.M.–4 P.M., closed Sunday; 202-452-0055.

> Metro: McPherson Square, Metro Center, or Federal Triangle
> 1600 Pennsylvania Avenue, NW
> Tours 10 A.M.–12 P.M. except Sundays and Mondays
> (see Visitors' Center, above, for ticket information);
> evening candlelight tours available during the Christmas
> season. No strollers permitted on White House tours.
> To hear a recording about the president's daily schedule,
> phone 202-456-2343.
> 202-456-7041

Everyone loves a nice back yard, and presidents get **The Ellipse:** a beautiful green expanse south of The White House. Its claims to fame are the Pageant of Peace (see Appendix I) and the Zero Milestone. A block of granite, the Zero Milestone is the official point used to measure the distance from D.C. to other parts of the United States.

# Lafayette Square

**For All Ages...** Lafayette Square, directly across Pennsylvania Avenue from the White House, is a major landmark with a checkered past. In recent years, it has been the site of demonstrations and protests; it was a military encampment site during the War of 1812 and the Civil War. Later, President Grant used it for a small zoo; unfortunately, some of the animals gave off unpleasant odors and had to be removed. In the center of the square, the dominant statue of **Andrew Jackson** includes four guns that were captured by Jackson at the Battle of New Orleans in 1814, an ironic touch, since the war was actually *over* before the battle began. **Lafayette,** holding forth on the southeast corner, stands near a statue of scantily clad **Columbia,** who is holding an outstretched sword. Some have suggested that she is offering, "Give me back my clothes and I'll give you your sword!"

# St. John's Church

St. John's Church is called the "Church of the Presidents," because every president since Madison has attended one or more services there, all sitting in the same reserved pew. The 1,000-pound bell in the bell tower was made from a British cannon captured in the War of 1812.

> 16th and H Streets, NW, across from Lafayette Square and
>   the White House
> Open daily 9 A.M.–3 P.M.; closed federal holidays.
> Guided tours 11:30 A.M. on the first Sunday of each month.
> 202-347-8766

# Decatur House

**For Teens...** Decatur House, on the northwest corner of Lafayette Park, was home to both a hero and a villain. It was named for Stephen Decatur, the youngest captain in the navy and the hero who defeated the Barbary pirates and captured an important British frigate during the War of 1812. But he only spent one year in the house, dying in a duel. John Gadsby, a wealthy hotelier, used the house in the 1830s and '40s to entertain the city's elite, while running a slave market in the back. Slaves were chained in the attic and the extension along H Street, and according to contemporary reports, filled the night air with their howls and cries. Fortunately, all that the house contains now is vintage décor. Period rooms in Decatur House showcase the Victorian and Federal styles of furnishings; tours last 40 minutes. A film with a significant story to tell about slavery and human rights is *Amistad* (teens).

> Metro: Farragut West or Farragut North
> 748 Jackson Place, NW
> Tours every half-hour Tuesday through Friday 10 A.M.–
>     2:30 P.M., Saturday and Sunday noon–3:30 P.M.;
> Closed January 1, Thanksgiving, and December 25.
> Admission fee; discounts for seniors over 54, and students
>     with ID; under 12, free. Also free to members of National
>     Trust for Historic Preservation.
> 202-842-0920

# Renwick Gallery

**For Teens...** The Renwick Gallery, a branch of the Smithsonian's National Museum of American Art, focuses on American crafts by major contemporary artists. Designed by James Renwick Jr., in 1859 (who also designed the Smithsonian Castle), it is a beautiful and opulent setting. Not a star attraction for kids, but an appealing spot for adults, at least on a second visit to Washington. The museum shop carries the materials for creating your own art works, handcrafted items, including hand-painted silks, and books for children and adults.

> Metro: Farragut West or Farragut North
> 17th Street and Pennsylvania Avenue, NW
> Open daily 10 A.M.–5:30 P.M.; closed December 25.

Tours by appointment; phone 202-357-2531 Monday
through Friday 9 A.M.–4 P.M.
Changing exhibitions, lectures, educational programs, craft
demonstrations, films; call for schedule.
202-357-2700.

# The Old Executive Office Building

**For Teens...** Called by some the "Victorian wedding cake," the Old
Executive Office Building was erected during President Grant's administration. When it was completed in 1888, it was the largest office building in the world. With its baroque, Second Empire
exterior, now it might be one of the most ornate. Inside, it looks
more like a palace than an office building. It houses the bulk of the
White House staff, the vice president's office, and some interns.
Tours are offered only on Saturday mornings, by advance reservation. Like the Renwick, this site can wait for your second visit.

Metro: Farragut West or Farragut North
Next to the White House on Pennsylvania Avenue, enter on
17th Street, NW
Tours Saturday only, 9 A.M.–noon, by reservation only; phone
202-395-5895 Tuesday through Friday mornings. Name,
date of birth, and social security number of each visitor
are required, and a photo ID when you arrive.
202-395-5895

# The Octagon

**For Teens...** Called by one newspaper columnist, "Washington's
second most famous haunted house," The Octagon is a good place
to visit if you like ghost stories. Built by architect William Thornton, who also designed the Capitol, for Colonel John Tayloe III,
this building has been home to a president, to a wealthy family, and
to slaves. The Treaty of Ghent (ending the War of 1812) was signed

here by President Madison in an upstairs room, and the ghost of a murdered slave girl is said to scream in the night in this house. The Tayloe family has contributed its share of ghostly legends as well. The colonel's ghost is believed to ring bells here, and the ghosts of both of his daughters are said to appear from time to time. The skeleton of a young girl, found buried in a wall by workmen, also contributes to the mystery of The Octagon.

Now owned by the American Institute of Architects Foundation, not, more appropriately, the "mystery writers association," the house displays temporary design and architectural exhibits in the former bedrooms. Downstairs is a permanent exhibit on life in the 1800s, life for the servants, that is. By the way, in keeping with its strangeness, The Octagon is *not* built in the shape of an octagon at all; it was just designed to fit on an awkwardly shaped lot. People still say there are eight angles, even though not eight sides; let us know if you find them.

> Metro: Farragut West or Farragut North
>
> 1799 New York Avenue, NW
>
> Open Tuesday through Friday, 10 A.M.–4 P.M.; Saturday and Sunday, 1–4 P.M.; closed January 1, Thanksgiving, and December 25. Admission fee; discount for senior citizens and students with ID. Guided tours Tuesday through Sunday. Story times for younger children. Call for schedule.
>
> 202-638-3221

# Corcoran Gallery of Art

**For Tweens and Teens...** "The most valuable bequest I can make you is a good name," William Wilson Corcoran wrote to his grandchildren. The father of the Corcoran Gallery of Art gave his own name to one of D.C.'s great art treasures. He was an indefatigable philanthropist to the District of Columbia, numerous nearby universities, and even individuals who lined up at his office. As a gesture of patriotism after the Civil War (he had been a Confederate sympathizer whose property was seized when he prudently left for

Europe during the War years), he put his vast art collection under the governance of a board of trustees and opened it to the public. It is one of the nation's three oldest art museums (the other two are the Boston Museum of Fine Arts and the Metropolitan Museum of Art in New York).

**Smart Stuff**

**For Tweens...** What American artist (represented in the Corcoran Gallery) was also a famous inventor? (F.)

An expansive beaux-arts building, with a huge atrium and marble staircase, the Gallery houses the Corcoran School of Art as well as an extensive collection of American art from the eighteenth century through the present. Showcasing painters such as John Singer Sargent, Alfred Bierstadt, and Winslow Homer, this museum also features such modern artists as Rothko, Nevelson, and Lichtenstein. Some rooms are devoted to specific European treasures: medieval Renaissance tapestries, Corot landscapes, nineteenth century French impressionists, Delft porcelains, and the *Salon Dore* (a completely reconstructed on-site Louis XVI-style room from a Parisian hotel).

**Smart Stuff**

**For Teens...** After viewing one of John Singer Sargent's elegant portraits, find one by modern artist Roy Lichtenstein. Both are representational, yet they are from very different styles. Which appeals to you more? Why? (G.)

The visiting exhibits: paintings, prints, and especially photographs, are often provocative and worth a special trip themselves. Works of local artists are often presented

**Smart Stuff**

**For Tweens and Teens...** Find a painting by nineteenth century landscape artist Alfred Bierstadt. What does the painting say about the American West? What elements in his painting reveal his viewpoint? (H.)

here as well. The Corcoran also offers beautiful educational materials, many educational programs, and partnering with classroom teachers for special projects or tours. Phone 202-639-1852 for information.

The museum shop here offers a selection of art books, note cards, jewelry, children's items, and other gifts, with relevant items stocked during some of the special exhibitions; open during museum hours. As for food, **the Café des Artistes** on the first floor offers light dining and snacks. Open Monday, Wednesday, Friday 11 A.M.–3 P.M., Thursday 11 A.M.–8:30 P.M. (including Tea), and Sunday 11 A.M.– 2 P.M. And the Sunday Gospel Brunch is served 11 A.M.–2 P.M., the only one of its kind we know of in the area. Reservations recommended. Phone 202-639-1786.

Metro: Farragut West or Farragut North
17th and E Streets, NW (half-block west of the White House)
Open Wednesday through Monday, 10 A.M.–5 P.M.; Thursday
    10 A.M.–9 P.M.; closed Tuesday, December 25, and January 1.
Admission: suggested adult donations; under age 12, free.
Lectures, workshops, poetry readings, international shows,
    films, a concert series, Sunday Traditions Workshops
    (for children 4–12), and specialized tours; call for schedule of events and fees, and advance arrangements.
Free tours (45 minutes) at 10:30 A.M. (except Saturday and
    Sunday) and at 7:30 P.M. Thursdays.
202-639-1700 or 202-638-3211

# ★D.A.R. (Daughters of the American Revolution) Museum

**For All Ages…** One of the best attics we know of is the third floor **New Hampshire Toy Attic** in the D.A.R. Museum. This imposing building is the property and headquarters of the Daughters of the American Revolution. Rag dolls, tea sets, tiny cast iron stoves, china dolls, and eighteenth and nineteenth century games remind children that even long ago, kids had toys. In the **Touch of Independence** section, kids can really touch a Braille flag (late eighteenth century), child-size antique furniture, and open mystery boxes, filled with eighteenth and nineteenth century items. And better than any other attic, this one isn't dusty.

For adults and older teens, the lower floors boast thirty-three period rooms, with furniture, china, glass, silver, paintings, and even costumes from earlier American historic times. The gadgets from those times will interest every age: the foot-controlled toaster, the four-sided guillotine-mousetrap, and the sausage stuffer that looks more like an exercise machine.

Naturally, the D.A.R. Museum focuses on the roles of women in American history. So our friend Sybil Ludington appears here in sculpture and painting. (Remember her? She outrode Paul Revere.)

> Metro: Farragut West or Farragut North
> 1776 D Street, NW
> Open Monday through Friday 8:30 A.M.–4 P.M., Sunday
>     1–5 P.M.
> Tours Monday through Friday 10 A.M.–2:30 P.M.,
>     Sunday 1–4:30 P.M.; advance reservations for groups;
>     202-879-3239.
> Special exhibitions: 202-879-3241
> D.A.R. Library for genealogical research, open Monday
>     through Friday 8:45 A.M.–4 P.M., Sunday 1–5 P.M.
>     Call for details: 202-879-3229. Fee.
> 202-879-3241

# Organization of American States Building

**For Teens...** Part art gallery, part rain forest, and part international offices, the Organization of American States (OAS) Building is the headquarters of the secretariat of the Organization of American States. Amidst these beautiful surroundings are regular meeting rooms where formal sessions are held in Spanish; they are open to tourists, and translation machines are also available. It's a great place for kids to hear and practice their own Spanish. When you're not listening in, you can enjoy the main floor gallery of twentieth-century art from South and Central America. Behind the building is the **Art Museum of the Americas,** with works of contemporary artists from Mexico, the Caribbean, and Latin and South America.

The richly decorated **Hall of Americas,** the **Hall of Heroes and Flags,** and the **Liberator Simon Bolivar Room** deserve a peek. Kids who are too young for a visit to a meeting room will love the main building's tropical entrance way, with palm trees and an Aztec- and Mayan-inspired fountain; the Aztec Garden nearby features a statue of Xochipilli, the Aztec god of flowers. Fortunately, sacrificial rites are no longer required.

> Metro: Farragut West or Farragut North
> 17th Street and Constitution Avenue, NW
> Open Monday through Friday 9 A.M.–5:30 P.M.;
>     closed holidays.
> Tours by appointment; for tour information,
>     phone 202-458-3927.
> Call to find out when the OAS is in session.
> 202-458-3000
> Art Museum of the Americas (201 18th Street, NW) open
>     Tuesday through Sunday 10 A.M.–5 P.M. 202-458-6016.

In this area, you might want to stop in at the **Department of the Interior** to browse in the **Indian Craft Shop,** a collection of authentic Native American Crafts, including baskets, and turquoise and silver jewelry. Open Monday through Friday from 8:30 A.M. to 4:30 P.M., it is located at 1849 C Street, NW; 202-208-4056.

> In the category of "your government at work," during the Civil War, the Department of Interior's Bureau of Indian Affairs hired a particularly literate clerk. He lost his job, however, when it was found that his desk drawers were filled with his poems, not government paperwork. His name was Walt Whitman.

There's also a **U.S. Geological Survey map store** here, and a **National Park Service office** with brochures on all U.S. national parks. Those into more consumable goods will appreciate the large cafeteria in the basement, open weekdays 7 A.M.–2:45 P.M.

# State Department, Diplomatic Reception Rooms

**For Teens...** Although the design for the outside of this building is not particularly creative, along with some of the foreign policy that emanates from it, the inside contains a surprise missed by many Washington tourists. It's a real find for adults and older teens. The diplomatic reception rooms on the eighth floor, actually used to welcome visiting dignitaries, can also welcome you. Along with a distinguished collection of eighteenth and early nineteenth century American furniture, paintings, and decorative arts are some truly historic pieces. The desk where Thomas Jefferson wrote the Declaration of Independence as well as the one at which John Adams, Benjamin Franklin, and John Jay signed the Treaty of Paris are all displayed.

A book that will appeal to future diplomats and their fellow citizens (tweens and teens) is *Talking Peace: A Vision for the Next Generation, 2nd ed.*, written by former president Jimmy Carter.

> Metro: Foggy Bottom–GWU
> 2201 C Street, NW
> Tours Monday through Friday at 9:30 A.M., 10:30 A.M., and 2:45 P.M. are 45 minutes long and for visitors over age 12; reservations four weeks in advance; 202-647-3241; bring photo ID for admittance.
> Call for details on 15-minute Public Affairs tours.
> Information and publications: 202-647-6575

# George Washington University

**For Teens...** Named for a familiar fellow, this is a renowned university that college-hopeful teens might like to explore. Its hospital, famous for treating President Reagan after his gunshot wound, was also featured on the popular television political drama *The West Wing.* And Lisner Auditorium is here; more about that in Appendix I.

> Metro: Foggy Bottom–GWU
> 2121 I Street, NW
> 202-994-1000 or 202-994-6178
> www.gwu.edu/

An eye-catching statue stands in the circle at Virginia and New Hampshire Avenues, NW, just a few blocks from the Kennedy Center. The sculpture depicts **Benito Juarez,** one of Mexico's greatest leaders. A full-blooded Zapotec Indian, and orphaned at three years of age, he went on to become a district attorney, legislator, judge, governor, and representative in Mexico's Congress. Eventually, he became president of his country, elected twice. One local wag, noting the imperious out-stretched arm pointing east, dubbed this "the go-to-your-room statue."

# ★Kennedy Center for the Performing Arts

**For All Ages...** Talk about the slow pace of government: Two hundred years ago, George Washington proposed that a national cultural center be located in Washington, D.C. In 1977, the center opened as a presidential memorial and headquarters for Washington's performing arts. The enormous and hauntingly realistic bust of John F. Kennedy stands by itself in the **Grand Foyer,** amid oceans of red carpeting and crystal and gilt décor. At the information desk, pick up a flag sheet; kids will especially enjoy craning their necks to

**Smart Stuff**

**For Tweens...** Flags have colors and words or symbols that represent something important for that state or country. Design a flag for your school or family. What colors would you include? What picture, words, or symbols would you choose?

identify the flags of states in the **Hall of States** and nations from around the world in the **Hall of Nations.** Gifts of art from many countries are displayed in halls throughout the building: sculptures, tapestries, carvings, and Boehm porcelain birds.

The six theaters here are home to a variety of performances: plays in the **Eisenhower Theater;** opera, musicals, and ballet in the **Opera House;** symphony concerts, recitals, and popular music events in the **Concert Hall;** drama, chamber music, poetry readings, and modern dance in the **Terrace Theater;** children's productions and special programs in the **Theater Lab;** and films in the **American Film Institute Theater** (soon to move to a new home in the suburbs). Although tours are given daily, the best way to enjoy the Kennedy Center is to attend a performance (see Appendix I), have a meal, or ride the elevator up to see the spectacular rooftop views of the Potomac River, Washington, and Virginia.

For theatrical and musical souvenirs, the gift shops here have the most and the best. The large shop is near the parking garage level and carries just about anything you can think of with musical and theatrical themes: note paper, mugs, jewelry, scarves, posters, CDs, and videotapes, just to name a few examples. The smaller shop, off the Plaza entrance, offers a sampling of what's to be found below.

Dining here you can be as elegant or as practical as you'd like—or as your budget permits. From the elegant and pricey **Roof Terrace Restaurant** (202-416-8555) to the **Hors d'Oeuvrerie** (202-416-8555) with table service of more modest fare (especially good for after-theater munching), to the **Encore Café** (202-416-8560), where you help yourself cafeteria-style to the same food, reap the bonus of magnificent views through a wall of floor-to-ceiling windows, and please your tummy as well as your eyes.

Metro: Foggy Bottom–GWU Free shuttle to and from Metro
    station every 15 minutes Monday through Saturday,
    9:45 A.M. to midnight, and Sunday, noon to midnight.
2700 F Street, NW (New Hampshire Avenue and Rock
    Creek Parkway)

Open 10 A.M. to midnight; Free one-hour tours Monday
through Friday 10 A.M.–5 P.M., Saturday and Sunday
10 A.M.–1 P.M., except January 1 and December 25.
Tour reservations needed for groups of 20 or more.
202-416-8341.

Ticket prices vary with events; discounts available for full-
time students, seniors, the disabled, and military grades
E–1 through E–4. Backstage tours are offered, with opportunities to explore what real theater looks like behind
the scenes (202-416-8341).

Films on the history of the Kennedy Center: two ongoing
10-minute films, one at the tour desk and one (narrated
by Caroline Kennedy Schlossberg) at the Millennium
Stage end of the Grand Foyer.

Information: 202-416-8340.

Ticket information: 202-467-4600 or 1-800-444-1324

www.kennedy-center.org (On the Web, you can find a schedule of events and theater floor plans, order tickets, or even
watch a Millennium Stage performance.)

# Where to Stay in the White House/ Foggy Bottom Area

Although many people have stayed overnight at the White House,
don't count on an invitation. Nearby, and more realistic, possibilities are:

**St. James Suites**
950 24th Street, NW
202-457-0500 or 1-800-852-8512
Metro: Foggy Bottom–GWU

**The George Washington University Inn**
824 New Hampshire Avenue, NW
202-337-6620 or 1-800-426-4455
Metro: Foggy Bottom–GWU

**The River Inn**
924 25th Street, NW
202-337-7600 or 1-800-424-2741
Metro: Foggy Bottom–GWU

**Swissotel Washington–The Watergate**
2650 Virginia Avenue, NW
202-965-2300 or 1-800-424-2736
Metro: Foggy Bottom–GWU

**Doubletree Guest Suites New Hampshire Avenue**
801 New Hampshire Avenue, NW
202-785-2000 or 1-800-222-TREE
Metro: Foggy Bottom–GWU

**Allen Lee Hotel**
2224 F Street, NW
202-331-1224 or 1-800-462-0186
Metro: Foggy Bottom–GWU

**State Plaza Hotel**
2117 E Street, NW
202-861-8200 or 1-800-424-2859
Metro: Foggy Bottom–GWU

# Answers to Smart Stuff Questions

**A.** The president lives in the White House, at 1600 Pennsylvania Avenue.

**B.** Forty-eight-year-old Grover Cleveland married Frances Folsom Cleveland, 27 years his junior (age 21), June 2, 1885, shortly after her college graduation.

**C.** An elderly and unrepentant Confederate, named Frederick Dent, had a bedroom close to the North Portico, where he lived out the rest of his life. The ex-slave-owner's coffin rested in the Yankee White House before his burial. How did he merit such treatment? His daughter Julia had married the general of the victorious Union forces, President Ulysses S. Grant.

**D.** The quote reads: "I Pray Heaven to Bestow the Best of Blessings on THIS HOUSE and on All that shall hereafter Inhabit it. May none but Honest and Wise Men ever rule under this Roof."

**E.** Funny examples were Alice Roosevelt's blue macaw, named Eli Yale, and her green snake, called Emily Spinach. Quentin Roosevelt's pony, Algonquin, was once smuggled upstairs to his master's room in the White House elevator.

**F.** Samuel F. B. Morse, inventor of the telegraph (and guess what code?).

**G.** Sargent's soft, muted colors emphasize the three-dimensional realism of his subjects; Lichtenstein's bold colors and strong lines evoke two-dimensional, comic-book-style art.

**H.** Bierstadt romanticized the American West with grand vistas, dramatic use of light and shadow, and a perspective that seems to invite the viewer into his magnificent scenery. Students might want to connect Bierstadt's work with the history of westward expansion.

CHAPTER

5

Tidal Basin

**F**rom the long slash of black granite in memory of our Vietnam War dead, to the eerie-looking architecture evoking the concentration camps during the Holocaust, the memorials around the Tidal Basin area are worth a thoughtful, unhurried visit. They include the oldest monument, the landmark obelisk of the **Washington Monument,** and one of the newest, the **F.D.R. Memorial.** Each tells a distinct story and each has a unique appeal.

## Vietnam Veterans Memorial

**For Tweens and Teens...** For youngsters to whom the Vietnam War compares in historical remoteness to the War of 1812, a visit to the Vietnam Veterans Memorial will be eye-opening. Children, spouses, siblings and friends crowd around the carved names of loved ones killed in this conflict, and leave letters, flowers, mementos, and tears. Some of these items are displayed in the National Museum of American History; most are in a government warehouse in Glen Dale, Maryland, which is itself becoming another memorial. Maya Lin, who, as a young Yale senior, designed the monument, described it as

Food! Don't come to this area, which spans Constitution Gardens, the Lincoln Memorial, the Tidal Basin, and the Jefferson Memorial, without eating first or packing a picnic. Though there are restrooms, there are no restaurants here. Since there is a lot of walking, wear your most comfortable walking shoes. And bring your water bottle!

a "rift in the earth—a long, polished black stone wall, emerging from and receding into the earth"—perhaps like our human existence. At each end of the wall, visitors can look up names (alphabetically) and locations of inscriptions, which are listed on the wall by dates; park

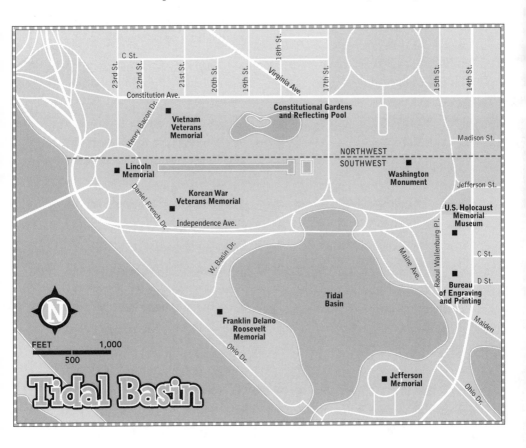

# Quick Guide to

| Attraction | Location |
| --- | --- |
| Vietnam Veterans Memorial | West end of the Mall (near the Lincoln Memorial, between the Reflecting Pool and Constitution Avenue) |
| Constitution Gardens and Reflecting Pool | 17th and 23rd Streets, NW (near the Lincoln Memorial) |
| ★Lincoln Memorial | West end of the Mall, at 23rd Street, NW (between Constitution and Independence Avenues, NW) |
| Korean War Veterans Memorial | Near the Lincoln Memorial (between the Reflecting Pool and Independence Avenue, NW) |
| ★Franklin Delano Roosevelt Memorial | West Potomac Park (between Korean War Veterans Memorial and Jefferson Memorial, and between Tidal Basin and Potomac River) |
| ★Jefferson Memorial | South end of 15th Street, SW, southeast side of the Tidal Basin |
| ★Bureau of Engraving and Printing | 14th and C Streets, SW |
| U.S. Holocaust Memorial Museum | 100 Raoul Wallenberg Place, SW |
| Washington Monument | 15th Street near Constitution Avenue, NW (at west end of Mall) |

# Tidal Basin Attractions

| Age Range | Hours | Details on |
| --- | --- | --- |
| Tweens and Teens | 24 hours, daily | Page 110 |
| All Ages | 24 hours, daily | Page 115 |
| All Ages | 24 hours, daily | Page 117 |
| Tweens and Teens | 24 hours, daily | Page 119 |
| All Ages | 24 hours, daily | Page 120 |
| All Ages | 24 hours, daily | Page 123 |
| Tweens and Teens | Mon.–Fri. 9 A.M.–1:40 P.M. | Page 124 |
| Tweens and Teens | 10 A.M.–5:30 P.M. daily, and Thursdays until 8 P.M. | Page 126 |
| All Ages | 8 A.M.–12 P.M. daily (April–August); 9 A.M.–5 P.M. (Sept.–March) | Page 130 |

*A view of the Washington Monument from the Vietnam Veterans Memorial*

rangers can answer questions. This memorial will pack an unexpected emotional punch with youngsters still untouched by war or death.

In recent years, two sculptures have been added to this site. One, by Frederick Hart, "Three Servicemen," reminds us how young these soldiers were. The other, by Glenna Goodacre, the Vietnam Women's Memorial, pays tribute to the women who also served.

## Smart Stuff

**For Tweens...** Imagine you have a sibling or friend fighting in a war far away. Write him a letter. What kinds of things do you think he would want to know?

Of the numerous books written on the Vietnam War and on this memorial, here are some to take a look at: *The Wall*, by Eve Bunting (tikes); *Always to Remember: The Story of the Vietnam Veterans Memorial*, by Brent Ashabranner (tweens); *A Wall of Names: The Story of the Vietnam Vet-*

## Smart Stuff

**For Teens...** Imagine that you are a soldier serving in Vietnam. You are about to participate in a major battle. Write a letter home to your parents, a sibling, or a best friend. What would you want them to remember about you?

*erans Memorial,* by Judy Donnelly (teens); and *Shrapnel in the Heart: Letters and Remembrance from the Vietnam Veterans Memorial,* by Laura Palmer (teens). Some movies of this era are harsh and quite graphic; they are still moving testimonies to this traumatic period in our country's history. Here are a few: *The American Experience: Vietnam, a Television History* (tweens and teens); *Guardians of Stone,* with James Earl Jones, who plays a guard at Arlington National Cemetery (tweens and teens); *Dear America: Letters Home from Vietnam* (tweens and teens); *Vietnam: The War at Home* (teens); *In Country* (from the book by Bobbie Ann Mason)

**Smart Stuff**

For Tweens... Many people come with paper and pencil, and make "rubbings" of names they find on the wall. You might want to make a rubbing of something you'd like to preserve from a statue or monument.

about post-traumatic stress disorder (teens); and *1969,* about the reaction to the war, at home in the U.S. (teens). There are three more, which we recommend only for older teens: *Born on the Fourth of July,* based on the true story of Ron Kovic; *The Killing Fields;* and *Platoon.*

> Metro: Foggy Bottom–GWU
> West end of the Mall, near the Lincoln Memorial, between
>      the Reflecting Pool and Constitution Avenue
> Daily 24 hours; National Park Service rangers on duty 8 A.M.
>      to midnight.
> 202-619-7222 (Public Affairs), 202-426-6841, or 202-634-
>      1568 (Information Kiosk)

# Constitution Gardens and Reflecting Pool

**For All Ages...** A scenic, fifty-two acre park with gardens, a six-acre lake, squirrels, birds, and occasional ducks, and a more permanent

## Parents/Teachers Take Note

If only these stones could talk. When youngsters learn the history of these fifty-six brave men, they will appreciate the significance of their pledging [their] "lives, [their] fortunes, and [their] sacred honor" to the revolutionary cause. All financially comfortable and well-educated, they were not rabble rousers, but thoughtful citizens who knew they would have to make personal sacrifices on the new nation's behalf. According to folklore, nine fought and died in the Revolutionary War; five were captured by the British as traitors; two lost sons serving in the Revolutionary Army; two had sons who were captured by the British; twelve had their homes destroyed; the wife of one was jailed and died in captivity; several had to go into hiding, along with their families; some died in poverty after their property was seized or burned. Freedom always has a price.

information center, is home to a one-acre island memorializing the fifty-six signers of the Declaration of Independence. Cross a wooden bridge and you'll see a semicircle of large granite bench-like blocks, each carved with the name, signature, town, and occupation of one of the Declaration's signers. This is a lovely spot for picnicking, biking, or just lolling in the grass.

The Reflecting Pool, modeled on such star attractions as the pools at Versailles and the Taj Mahal, is a pretty good attraction in itself. In the summer it's often filled with ducks, and, frozen in the winter, with ice skaters.

Metro: Foggy Bottom–GWU
17th and 23rd Streets, NW, near the Lincoln Memorial
Daily 24 hours
202-426-6841

# ★Lincoln Memorial

**For All Ages...** An appropriate memorial to a larger-than-life historical figure is the nineteen-foot-high marble seated statue of the brooding President Abraham Lincoln. Its home, the elegant rectangular monument, has become, since its dedication, a symbol of civil rights, justice, and the positive power of our democracy. Ironically, at that ceremony (in 1922) Dr. Robert Moton, then president of Tuskegee Institute (noted African American college) and the renowned Booker T. Washington, were compelled to sit in the segregated section for non-white spectators. In recent years, from African American soprano Marian Anderson's performance on the steps in 1939 (after she was barred from Constitution Hall), to Martin Luther King Jr.'s famous "I Have a Dream" speech here in 1963, the site itself has become a place of history.

With its 36 columns representing the existing states in the Union at the time of Lincoln's death, the memorial is decorated with carved inscriptions from his speeches, allegorical murals, and names of the 48 states (at the time of the monument's dedication) on a frieze above the colonnade. The sculpture of Lincoln itself is like a magnet for visitors. Sculptor Daniel Chester French contributed a powerful figure to the ages. Father of a deaf child, it is believed by many that French gave each of Lincoln's hands the

*Abraham Lincoln, one of Washington, D.C.'s most visited statues*

American Sign Language position for one of his initials (his left hand forms the "A" and his right, the sign for "L").

In the basement of the memorial is the Legacy of Lincoln Museum, originally proposed by a group of students from Scottsdale, Arizona. Exhibits contain excerpts from some of Lincoln's famous speeches and a photographic history of many of the notable events that have occurred here; a video tells the building's history. An information booth and bookstore are also on the premises. At night, the view from the Lincoln Memorial steps is particularly moving; to the east is the sparkling dome of the U.S. Capitol and to the west, across the river in Virginia, you can see the eternal flame at the grave of another slain president, John F. Kennedy.

## Smart Stuff

**For Tweens...** After researching Civil War Washington, D.C., youngsters might like to compile albums of their original "old" letters from Washington to friends or family living far away. Kids especially love trying to make the paper look aged.

## Smart Stuff

**For Tweens and Teens...** Abraham Lincoln has become an icon, so it's hard to ferret out the fictional from the real. If you can, find out what personality traits he exhibited. Which of these do you think were *helpful* in his capacity as president and commander in chief of the Union forces? Which might have been detrimental?

Any visit to the Lincoln Memorial should provoke discussion about his life and times. Books on the subject abound, of course, but here are a few suggestions: *Abraham Lincoln (Famous Americans),* by Lola M. Schaefer (tweens); *Abe Lincoln's Hat,* by Martha Brenner (tweens); *Abe Lincoln: Log Cabin to White House* (Landmark Books), by Sterling North (tweens); *A Memorial for Mr. Lincoln,* by Brent Ashabranner (tweens); *House of Spies: Danger in Civil War Washington,* by Margaret Whitman Blair (tweens); *Lincoln: A Photobiography,* by Russell Freedman (tweens); *Abe Lincoln Grows Up,* by Carl Sandburg (tweens); *Lincoln As I Knew Him: Gossip, Tributes and Revelations from His Best Friends and Worst Enemies,* by Harold Holzer (teens); *Lincoln,* by Gore Vidal (teens); and any of Carl Sandburg's classic volumes on Lincoln (older teens). There are also movies; two classics are: *Young Mr. Lincoln* (tweens and teens), starring Henry Fonda; and *Abe Lincoln in Illinois* (tweens and teens), with Raymond Massey.

> Metro: Foggy Bottom–GWU or Smithsonian
> West end of the Mall, at 23rd Street, NW (between Constitution and Independence Avenues, NW)
> Open 24 hours; rangers on duty 8 A.M. to midnight, except December 25
> Interpretive tours: arrange in advance; phone 202-426-6842 (Mall Ranger Station; Education Specialist)
> 202-426-6895.

# Korean War Veterans Memorial

**For Tweens and Teens...** Don't forget, west of the Reflecting Pool, the memorial to the "Forgotten War." The Korean War Veterans Memorial, dedicated in 1995 (over forty years after the War's end), consists of nineteen larger-than-life stainless steel sculptures of soldiers on patrol, a circular Pool of Remembrance, and a 164-foot-long black granite wall etched with the faces of real support troops, taken from actual photos of U.S. soldiers, sailors, airmen, and marines. Sixty percent of the $18 million needed for this moving memorial was donated by Korean War veterans; no government funds were used.

> Metro: Foggy Bottom–GWU
> Near the Lincoln Memorial, between the Reflecting Pool and Independence Avenue, NW
> Daily 24 hours; rangers on duty 8 A.M. to midnight.
> 202-619-7222

# ★Franklin Delano Roosevelt Memorial

**For All Ages...** For an entire generation, Franklin Delano Roosevelt symbolized the presidency: For millions, he was the only president they had ever known. His memorial, set on 7½ acres beside the picturesque Tidal Basin, is also unique among the presidential monuments. It is a memorial not only to the man, but also to the unsettled times he transcended to lead a nation. The structure pulls us into the story: four outdoor "rooms," one for each of Roosevelt's terms, complete with evocative sculptures, quotes from his memorable speeches, and artistically designed waterfalls over rough-cut granite blocks. At the end is a bronze sculpture of F.D.R. himself, seated in a well-camouflaged wheelchair (find the tiny wheels at the edges of the chair). A new sculpture of F.D.R. has been added, after six years of efforts on the part of disability rights advocates. This one shows the president seated in the wheelchair he designed and built from a kitchen chair and bicycle wheels. The contrast of this very human-size statue

## Smart Stuff

**For Tikes and Tweens...**
Do you personally know anyone who uses a wheelchair? Try this experiment: Sit on a tricycle and try to open your door and go into your house or apartment without standing up. How would your life be different if you were confined to a wheelchair?

*President Franklin D. Roosevelt, with his dog, Fala, at the F.D.R. Memorial*

with the larger-than-life scale of the memorial portrays the vulnerability of Roosevelt's body as opposed to the invincibility of his spirit, a legacy for us all. An elegant standing likeness of Eleanor Roosevelt is featured as well—the only monument to a first lady. Adults should anticipate an emotional experience. Children need some advance preparation to understand such a huge and significant slice of American history. In addition, a discussion about the status and history of citizens with disabilities would be a logical digression. In a dramatic way, Roosevelt has come to symbolize the triumph of an individual *and* a nation over enormous challenges.

**Smart Stuff**

**For Tweens...** Interview a neighbor, friend, or family member about World War II. How was life during that period different from your life today? (A.)

In any library or bookstore, you will find many books on F.D.R. Here are a few suggestions: *Franklin D. Roosevelt,* by Wyatt Blassingame (tweens—this one is out of print, but you might find it in your library); *Eleanor Roosevelt: A Life of Discovery,* by Russell Freedman (tweens); *Franklin Delano Roosevelt,* by Russell Freedman (tweens); *No Ordinary Time: Franklin and Eleanor Roosevelt,* by Doris Kearns Goodwin (teens); and *Eleanor: The Years Alone,* by Joseph P. Lash (teens). We can recommend several films: *Sunrise at Campobello* (tweens and teens), with Ralph Bellamy, Greer Garson, and Hume Cronyn; and *The Grapes of Wrath,* starring a young Henry Fonda, taken from John Steinbeck's classic book (teens). For music, try Woody Guthrie's plaintive ballads and the political folksongs of The Weavers.

**Smart Stuff**

**For Teens...** Interview a relative, family friend, or neighbor about experiences during the Great Depression in the United States. What kinds of social changes occurred as a result of the Depression? (B.)

Metro: Smithsonian (Independence Avenue exit), plus about a
mile walk
West Potomac Park, between Korean War Veterans Memorial
and Jefferson Memorial, and between Tidal Basin and Potomac River
Daily 24 hours; rangers on duty 8 A.M. to midnight.
202-426-6841

# Tidal Basin

A nice change from its early incarnation as a "whites only" public
beach, the Tidal Basin is now a beautiful pool, reflecting the under-
stated splendor of the Jefferson Memorial. Every spring, 3,700 ornamental cherry trees form a decorative pink necklace around the
Basin. And surrounding them are tourists by the thousands. A gift
from Japan to the United States in 1912, the trees fell on hard times
during World War II when several "patriots" took buzz saws to some
of them. Again in April 1999, some smaller culprits wreaked havoc;
a family of beavers was eventually captured and spirited away by the
National Park Service. The major culprits these days are people who
block your view when you're trying to take a photo.

Metro: Smithsonian (Independence
Avenue exit) and
walk west two
blocks and south
on 15th Street
Fifteenth Street and
Ohio Drive in East
Potomac Park
202-619-7222

*The Jefferson
Memorial in cherry
blossom season*

# ★Jefferson Memorial

**For All Ages...** The simple dignity of his memorial belies the complexity of this astonishing man, Thomas Jefferson. An amateur architect (who would have loved the domed rotunda of his memorial), naturalist, inventor, anthropologist, astronomer, musician, and one of his country's leading statesmen, he, along with Benjamin Franklin, exemplified America's version of the "Renaissance man." The man to whom agrarian life was the ideal, looks out across a landscape of water and greenery; to his back is the Potomac River, and beyond, the shoreline of his beloved Virginia.

**Smart Stuff**

**For Tikes...** What is the only monument in Washington, D.C., without corners? (C.)

The neoclassical form, with its Ionic columns, was a favorite with Jefferson. He used it in designing the Virginia State Capitol, the University of Virginia, and his own home, Monticello. The 19-foot bronze statue of Jefferson is surrounded by quotations from his writings, carved into the walls. Inscribed on the frieze over the entrance from the Tidal Basin, depicting Jefferson with other members of the committee selected to draft the Declaration of Independence, is his philosophy: "I have sworn upon the altar of God eternal hostility against every form of tyranny over the mind of man." From Mr. Jefferson's steps, you can look past the Washington Monument to the White House, a beautiful view. At night, the illuminated memorial is a spectacle in itself.

Below the Jefferson Memorial are displays commemorating Jefferson's role as the United States began. The gift shop here has reproductions of colonial quill pens and other items from Jefferson's era, as well as postcards and Washington souvenirs, and there is also a small bookstore. From spring through fall, a kiosk at the nearby Tourmobile Stop sells snacks.

Books about Jefferson are numerous. A few suggestions are: *Meet Thomas Jefferson,* by Marvin Barrett (tweens); *Jefferson's Children: The Story of One American Family,* by Shannon Lanier and Jane Feldman (tweens); *Thomas Jefferson: Man on a Mountain,* by

Natalie S. Bober (tweens and teens); *American Sphinx: The Charac-ter of Thomas Jefferson,* by Joseph J. Ellis (teens); *Jefferson* (Abridged), by Saul K. Padover and Samuel K. Padover (teens); and *Jefferson and Monticello: The Biography of a Builder,* by Jack McLaughlin (teens).

> Metro: Smithsonian (Independence Avenue exit) and walk
>      west two blocks and south on 15th Street
> South end of 15th Street, SW, southeast side of the Tidal
>      Basin
> Daily 24 hours; rangers on duty 8 A.M. to midnight
> Interpretive tours by request 8 A.M. to midnight; closed De-
>      cember 25
> 202-426-6841; bookstore: 202-426-2177

## Smart Stuff

**For Tikes...** On the shore opposite the Jefferson Memorial is a **stone lantern** from the people of Japan, commemorating friendship between our two coun-tries. It is lit at the beginning of the Cherry Blossom Festival. You might like to design a statue that will commemorate friendship between the U.S. and an-

**Hains Point,** at the very tip of East Potomac Park, marks the convergence of the Washington Channel and the Potomac River. A dramatic bronze sculpture, **"The Awakening,"** grabs visitors' atten-tion. It features two huge outstretched arms arising out of the ground. No other parts of the body have yet emerged, as far as we know.

# ★Bureau of Engraving and Printing

**For Tweens and Teens...** You can't take it with you, but it's still pretty exciting to see. The Bureau of Engraving and Printing produces the

## Smart Stuff

**For All Ages...** Do you have "old money" or "new money" in your pocket? Pull out a $1, $5, $10, or, if you're lucky, $20 bill, and look on the front next to the president's portrait. See if you can find where this bill was printed. Hint: If you have new money, with the jumbo-size portrait, it won't tell the city. But all bills, old and new, tell the date the Department of the Treasury was established. Can you find it? (D.)

greatest amount of paper money, security documents, and stamps on the globe. You can take a tour of this facility that prints over $11.4 billion annually in currency. Even though it's a far cry from their allowance, kids enjoy watching the sheets of money roll off the presses and be cut, sorted, and stacked as familiar bills. In the gift shop, visitors can buy shredded money that didn't pass inspection—in bags, pens, and paperweights, or postcards of bills with their pictures in the middle, but, alas, nothing they can use to pay for souvenirs. As for lunch or snack-time, try the **cafeteria** at the **U.S. Department of Agriculture** (14th Street and Independence Avenue, SW; 202-488-7279 or 202-720-5505 for the visitor center). Ten food stations offer variety inexpensively.

> Why does your homework shred in the washer, but your lunch money just gets wrinkled?
>
> Quality, quality. U.S. "paper" money is made of 75 percent cotton and 25 percent linen. The average life of a dollar bill is still only eighteen months; this probably includes several accidental washings!

*[handwritten notes in margin:]*
7 - 9 bfast
6:30     9 - 11 cont
11 - 2 lunch
2 - 3:30
snacks

An interesting book for more information about money in the U.S. is *Money, Money, Money,* by Nancy Winslow Parker (tweens and teens).

Metro: Smithsonian

14th and C Streets, SW

Tours Monday–Friday, 9 A.M.–1:40 P.M., 40 minutes; pick up
    timed tickets at kiosk on 15th Street SW (be in line at
    8 A.M.); extended summer hours

For VIP tour tickets, contact your senator or congressperson
    three months in advance of your trip. VIP tickets re-
    quired for 45-minute tours.

202-874-3188 or 202-874-3019

www.moneyfactory.com

# U.S. Holocaust Memorial Museum

**For Tweens and Teens...** Who would have ever guessed that a museum that promises to depress you thoroughly and take a minimum
of three hours of your time would be one of the most popular sites in
Washington, D.C.? At least two million people annually go through
this grim monument to one of the darkest periods in human history.
In a clever and unnerving combination of styles and materials, the
architecture itself evokes the setting of the concentration camps in
which six million Jews and
millions of others, including
Gypsies, Soviet POWs, dissi-
dents, homosexuals, Jehovah's
Witnesses, Poles, and the disabled, were murdered in the
Holocaust.

## Smart Stuff

**For Teens...** As you read
the history of the rise of
the Nazi party, what signs
were there that this was
not just another fringe
political group? Do you
think it could happen
here? Why or why not?

With a fifth-floor library
at the top, where high school
students and others can do research, the museum's permanent exhibits fill the next three
floors in descending order.
Visitors literally descend gradually into the harrowing exhibits on the
chaos of this era. The identity card you are issued on entry gives the
history of an actual Holocaust victim; consult your booklet as you

progress through the displays to find out what that person was actually undergoing during each time period. Through oral histories, multimedia presentations, photographs, artifacts, and an actual Polish freight car like those used to transport Jews from the Warsaw ghetto to Treblinka, visitors participate in an overwhelming experience.

Children under age eleven would find this fare inappropriately overpowering. The exhibit "Daniel's Story: Remember the Children" is designed for them, preferably eight and older. Located on the first floor, and available *without* tickets, this exhibition chronicles the story of a fictional but historically accurate German family from their comfortable home to a concentration camp. Though it is clear that Daniel survives, his story, told through a child's eyes, packs a significant emotional punch. Children are encouraged to express their feelings in writing or pictures at the end of the exhibit, and to post them in a special museum mailbox. The Children's Wall memorializes the 1.5 million children murdered in the Holocaust. Consisting of 3,300 tiles painted by American schoolchildren, it is strikingly beautiful and arresting.

> ## Smart Stuff
> For Tweens and Teens... Suppose you were a friend of Daniel's. What might you have tried to do for him or his family? What risks—if any—would you have been willing to take for them?

> ## Helpful Hint
> Because of the powerful impact of this museum, it's a good idea to do some reading and discussing *before* visiting the U.S. Holocaust Memorial Museum. The books listed are only a sample of the rich variety of materials available.

The **Museum Shop** contains books on the Holocaust, audio and videotapes, personal histories, and a wide selection of related books for young readers.

Below are some appropriate choices to look at here or before you come. An unusual offering in this genre is *The Children We Remember*, by Chana Byers Abells, a very sensitive treatment for the youngest readers, who will need an adult to help them interpret this difficult subject (tikes). *The Diary of A Young Girl*, by Anne Frank, is a classic, especially for tweens and teens. *Smoke and Ashes: The Story of the Holocaust*, by Barbara Rogasky, is a thoughtful reader-friendly account (tweens and teens). *Maus I* and *Maus II*, by Art Spiegelman, especially appeal to young teens because of the allegorical cartoon format. Another diary, preserved and found after the war, is *Scroll of Agony: The Warsaw Diary of Chaim A. Kaplan*, an eyewitness account (teens). *Night*, by Elie Wiesel, (teens), is just one of his moving Holocaust-inspired works; *Edith's Story*, by Edith Velmans (teens), based on diaries, reminiscences, and letters, is the true story of a young girl during World War II; *Different Voices: Women and the Holocaust*, edited and introduced by Carol Rittner and John K. Roth, is exceptional reading for older teens. All ages should take a look at . . .*I Never Saw Another Butterfly: Children's Drawings and Poems from Terezin Concentration Camp 1942–1944*. *The Auschwitz Chronicle*, by Danuta Czech (older teens) comes highly recommended. Per Anger, who served with this famous Swedish diplomat, wrote *With Raoul Wallenberg in Budapest: Memories of the War Years in Hungary*, interesting reading for older teens. A chronological collection of stories by different writers, *Out of the Whirlwind: A Reader of Holocaust Literature*, edited by Albert H. Friedlander, guides the mature reader through this time period. No modern list would be complete without *Schindler's List: A Novel*, by Thomas

## Helpful Hint

To avoid waiting in a long line for same-day, time-specific passes, check out advance passes, even though there is a small service charge. Also, if you know someone who has a special museum membership, get in touch right away; you might be able to get advance passes through him or her.

Keneally, the book from which the film was made (older teens). We also recommend several films, appropriate for teens: *Schindler's List, Life Is Beautiful, Jakob the Liar,* and *Europa, Europa.*

If you have an appetite, there is a **small cafeteria-style café** in an annex next to the museum. The menu (not kosher) is limited to sandwiches, fruit, drinks, and desserts. Open daily 9 A.M.–4:30 P.M.

Metro: Smithsonian

100 Raoul Wallenberg Place, SW

Daily 10 A.M.–5:30 P.M.; Thursday until 8 P.M., April 1 through early September; closed Yom Kippur and December 25. Last admission 2 hours before closing.

Free entrance passes 10 A.M. on 14th Street side of building. Limit 4 passes per person. Get in line early, as only a limited number of tickets are given out each day. Allow at least 3 hours for your actual visit, and *wear comfortable shoes.*

Advance passes: service charge for advance passes, phone 1-800-400-9373. For group reservations, phone 202-488-0455.

Information on frequently asked questions is available at the Information Desk, or by writing to: U.S. Holocaust Museum, Communications Dept., 100 Raoul Wallenberg Place, SW, Washington, DC 20024-2150.

202-488-0400

Authorized and erected at the turn of the twentieth century, the **statue of John Paul Jones** (at Independence Avenue and 17th Street, NW) memorializes a man with a checkered past but an indomitable will at the right historical moment. After some run-ins with fellow colonial merchant mariners, Jones fled to Fredericksburg, Virginia, where he appended the "Jones" to his original last name ("Paul"). His successful exploits as commander of several ships in the Revolution led up to his famous encounter with a British vessel, where, out-manned and out-gunned, he outwitted the English captain and boarded his ship as Jones' own ship was sinking. When the enemy captain had earlier asked for Jones' surrender, Jones had replied: "I have not yet begun to fight!" His remains rest appropriately in the chapel of the U.S. Naval Academy in Annapolis.

## Washington Monument

**For All Ages...** At 555 feet, 5 inches, the world's tallest freestanding masonry structure is visible from nearly everywhere in the city. No cement is used to hold the granite blocks together, but don't worry, the Washington Monument is supposed to be able to withstand even a 145-mile-per-hour tornado gale. The fact that it sways one-eighth of an inch in high winds shouldn't make you seasick; trust us, no one can feel it.

Ride the elevator to the five hundred-foot level and look out at the amazing views of all of the District of Columbia. When you're ready to descend, there's another interesting choice: You can again use the elevator, or walk down with an interpreter-led tour (see below—it is a *very* long walk); the guide will point out memorial stones set into the walls from many different sources.

This two-tone memorial is a monument to getting things done in a democracy. It was first discussed as a possibility in 1783; then, after many false starts, the monument's fund-raising actually began in 1833. At last, on July 4, 1848, the cornerstone was laid. Each existing state was ex-

*The Washington Monument*

pected to contribute. Short of funds, Alabama started a new trend, sending a stone instead. Then, over a hundred individuals, towns, states, and nations, including the Pope and the Cherokee Nation, sent stones to be included in the monument. Construction had stopped by the time of the Civil War, as the project had run out of money. Cattle continued to roam and Union troops to train on the monument grounds. In 1876, President Grant approved federal funding to complete the memorial. It was dedicated at last in 1885, and opened to the public in 1888. The marble used to complete it was from a different quarry than the original, and is thus a slightly different shade. At that time, only men could use the elevator; it was considered too dangerous for women, so *they* had to climb up the 897 steps to see the view. It must have been hard to be so delicate! One of the mysterious auxiliary benefits of the whole project was the construction of an enormous sculpture of Washington dressed in a Greek toga. It can now be seen guarding the escalators in the National Museum of American History.

Kids might enjoy reading *George Washington (Famous Americans)*, by Lola M. Schaefer (tikes and tweens); *The Adventures of George Washington*, by Mickie Davidson (tweens); *George Washington's Socks*, by Elvira Woodruff (tweens); and *George Washington*, by Cheryl Harness (tweens). For teens, two books of special interest are: *Washington: The Indispensable Man*, by James Thomas Flexner; and *Citizen Washington* (historical fiction), by William Martin.

## Smart Stuff

**For Teens...** Before he left office, President Washington warned against becoming involved in the affairs of other nations. In which wars, if any, do you think he would have approved U.S. involvement? Why?

Metro: Smithsonian

15th Street near Constitution Avenue, NW (at west end of Mall)

*reservations*
*w³.nps.go*

*1 -800 -*
*967 -*
*2283*

Daily 8 A.M. to midnight, April through August and
9 A.M.–5 P.M., September through March; closed July 4 and
    December 25.
Timed admission tickets: Get in line *before* 7:30 A.M. Also
    through Ticketmaster in advance: 800-505-5040 (small
    fee).
Tours *down* the steps of the Monument: 10 A.M. and 2 P.M.,
    limited to the first 25 who show up; the National Park
    Service suggests calling ahead.
202-426-6841

# Where to Stay in the Tidal Basin Area

As far as selecting places to stay in this area, we recommend consulting the list at the end of the previous chapter, White House/Foggy Bottom. The same choices are also the closest ones for touring this part of the city.

# Answers to Smart Stuff Questions

**A.** Some examples include rationing, Victory Gardens, war news from newsreels shown in movie theaters, and women in jobs that were traditionally men's.

**B.** Teens might want to discuss some of these topics: migration from family farms and the farm belt, hoboes, shanty towns, the "Bonus Army" (a demonstration to urge Congressional action to deliver unemployed servicemen a bonus promised to veterans in 1924), soup kitchens, apple vendors, the election of F.D.R., the influx of thousands of professionals and clerical workers to the Washington, D.C., area to man the newly formed agencies, bread lines, the National Youth Administration (arranging part-time jobs for thousands of high school and college students, so they could continue their education), women as their families' main wage earners, the culture of frugality (just ask a Depression-era survivor!).

**C.** The Jefferson Memorial

**D.** "Old" money notes the city of its printing in the seal to the left of the president's portrait. All bills show the green emblem of the Department of the Treasury to the right side of the president, with the date 1789 at the bottom.

CHAPTER

6

G'TOWN

# Georgetown
## & Embassy Row

Fashion is fickle. The section of Washington known as Georgetown has gone from commercial hub to ramshackle homes and trash-filled alleys to elegant, renovated town houses for the city's movers and shakers. Named for two Georges who had first owned the land (neither King George nor George Washington), George Town was founded by an immigrant Scottish community. Previously a thriving port, it was granted its charter by the Maryland Assembly in 1751. From its official incorporation in 1789 until 1871, George Town had a government separate from her prestigious neighbor, the District of Columbia. At that point, Congress abolished George Town's status as a separate municipality and dubbed the region "Georgetown."

A young senator named John F. Kennedy and his growing family lived here until they moved to a much larger home on Pennsylvania Avenue. Today, Georgetown is still a stylish and pricey area of town houses, trendy shops, restaurants, a university, and historic buildings. However, in some ways it clings to its historic roots: It has no Metro stop and little parking for cars.

**Embassy Row** is also a class act. The stately mansions lining Massachusetts Avenue make an interesting neighborhood. The British Embassy, with its statue of a victorious Winston Churchill, sits next door to the modern, glass-supported Embassy of Brazil. The opulent Embassy of Iran made a wonderful spot for State Department functions when that country and the U.S. severed diplomatic relations. If you're lucky enough to visit in the spring, splurge for a ticket to the Embassy Row House Tour; you can see where other people get to rub important elbows.

# ★Chesapeake and Ohio Canal National Historical Park

**For All Ages...** Begun in 1828 as the harbinger of a more rapid era of transportation, the C & O Canal has become a site where its visitors can slow down and enjoy their leisure time. In competition

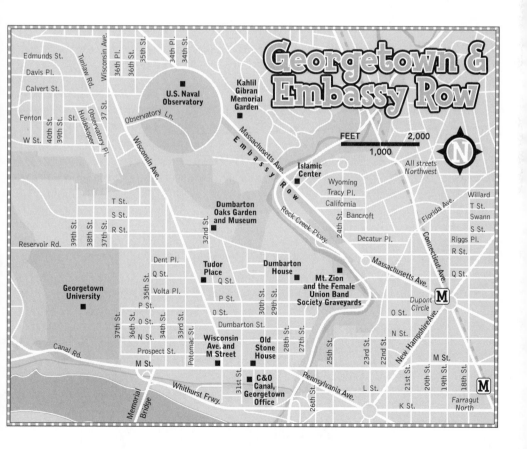

# Quick Guide to

| Attraction | Location |
| --- | --- |
| ★Chesapeake and Ohio Canal National Historical | Between 30th and Thomas Jefferson Streets, Georgetown Park and 11710 MacArthur Boulevard |
| ★Old Stone House | 3051 M Street, NW |
| Georgetown University | 37th and O Streets, NW |
| Tudor Place | 1644 31st Street, NW |
| Dumbarton Oaks Garden and Museum | 1703 32nd Street, NW (between R and S Streets) |
| ★Wisconsin Avenue and M Street, NW | |
| Embassy Row | Dupont Circle; walk north on Massachusetts Avenue, NW |
| Islamic Center | 2551 Massachusetts Avenue, NW |
| U.S. Naval Observatory | 3450 Massachusetts Avenue NW, on Observatory Circle |

# Georgetown/Embassy Row Attractions

| Age Range | Hours | Details on |
|---|---|---|
| All Ages | Georgetown: 9 A.M.–4:30 P.M. daily. Great Falls: 9 A.M.–4:30 P.M. daily (Tavern). Park hours vary. | Page 137 |
| All Ages | 8:30 A.M.–4:30 P.M. daily (Memorial Day–Labor Day); 8:30 A.M.–4:30 P.M. Wed.–Sun. (rest of year) | Page 141 |
| Teens | | Page 142 |
| Teens | Tours: Tues.–Fri. 10 A.M., 11:30 A.M., 1 P.M., 2:30 P.M., and Saturday 10 A.M.–3 P.M. on the hour | Page 143 |
| Tweens and Teens | Tues.–Sun. 2 P.M.–5 P.M. Gardens 2 P.M.–6 P.M. daily (April–Oct.) 2 P.M.–5 P.M. rest of year | Page 144 |
| Tweens and Teens | | Page 146 |
| Tweens and Teens | Walk or ride by any time | Page 148 |
| Tweens and Teens | 10 A.M.–5 P.M. daily; closed Fridays to non-Muslims 1 P.M.–2:30 P.M. | Page 152 |
| Tweens and Teens | 7:30 P.M. Mondays (Nov.–March); 8:30 P.M. Mondays (April–Oct.) | Page 153 |

with the more successful railroads, the canal lost out as a major commercial artery for the city. Today's barges carry people instead of coal, with costumed guides singing and narrating the history of the canal. Kids brought up with remote-controlled vehicles will especially enjoy the power behind this replica of a nineteenth-century canal barge; it is pulled by mules. Youngsters and adults will wonder at the technology of canal lift locks that regulate the water levels along the way.

Originally designed to connect Washington, D.C., to Pittsburgh, Pennsylvania, the canal stretches a mere 184 miles, from Georgetown into Cumberland in western Maryland; it was never completed to Pittsburgh. Hikers, bikers, and canoeists travel the canal and its towpath, delighting in the views. Natural rock sculptures, abundant foliage, and picturesque waterfalls provide spectacular vistas throughout its length. A number of famous visitors have enjoyed the canal and the trails alongside it. One who made a difference was the late Justice William O. Douglas, a committed outdoorsman. When he heard, in 1954, that plans had been approved to *pave* over the canal and turn it into a freeway, he embarked on a protest hike. With thirty-six other hardy souls, he walked the distance from Cumberland, Maryland, to the canal's end in Georgetown. During the eight days of walking, the protesters were greeted enthusiastically in every town they passed. By the time they arrived in the District, they had sparked a conservation movement that found its support in the *Washington Post* and in the National Park Service. Both reversed their positions from favoring the freeway to supporting the canal's preservation as a national historic landmark. Finally, Congress officially granted protected status in 1971. The towpath was dedicated in honor of Justice Douglas in 1974.

Because this area is 15 miles northwest of Washington itself, a car would make your visit more convenient and easier to schedule. Check with Metro Bus; phone 202-636-3425.

Refreshments are available at the **Great Falls Tavern and Museum,** but packing a lunch to bring along is a better way to be sure of satisfying your hunger.

> Metro: Foggy Bottom–GWU (very long walk); call Metro
> Bus for better transportation information: 202-637-7000
> Between 30th and Thomas Jefferson Streets, Georgetown
> The Canal follows the Maryland shore of the Potomac River
> from Georgetown to Cumberland, Maryland.
> Georgetown Office of the C&O Canal: 1057 Thomas Jefferson Street, NW; daily 9 A.M.–4:30 P.M.; book shop open
> 10 A.M.–4 P.M. weekends; 202-653-5190

**Great Falls Tavern and Museum:**

> 11710 MacArthur Boulevard; daily 9 A.M.–4:30 P.M., closed
> January 1 and December 25; films and programs; phone:
> 301-299-3613, 301-299-2026, 301-767-3714
> Park hours vary, generally sunrise to sunset; call for details.
> Fee for barge rides.
> Hour-long day trips and two-hour evening trips can be scheduled (in advance) for groups at special rates.
> 202-653-5190
> www.parkexplorer.org

# ★Old Stone House

**For All Ages...** Built in 1765, this is Washington's oldest building. Five rooms hold sturdy furnishings from the eighteenth century. Costumed guides lead visitors through the house, and demonstrate skills of early American life, including weaving, candle-dipping, quilting, spinning, and colonial-style cooking. There's also a lovely cottage garden for picnicking, if you have come prepared, or just strolling, if you haven't.

Ready for breakfast? Or a sandwich? Try longtime favorite **Booeymonger,** nearby at 3265 Prospect Street, NW (open Monday through Friday 7:30 A.M. to midnight, Saturday and Sunday 8 A.M. to midnight). Their creations are as clever as their names: Tuna

Turner, Scheherazade, or Peter Pan, just to name a few. This is actually a bargain Georgetown–style. Phone: 202-333-4810. For Vietnamese fare, **Miss Saigon** (3057 M Street, NW; Monday through Friday, 11:30 A.M.–11 P.M., Saturday and Sunday, noon to 11 P.M.) provides interesting and delectable specialties, including a number of vegetarian selections. Phone: 202-333-5545. Craving pizza or spaghetti? **Geppetto,** at 2917 M Street, NW (Monday through Thursday noon to 11 P.M., Friday and Saturday, noon to 12:30 A.M., Sunday, noon to 10:30 P.M.), though tiny, has a wonderful menu. Get take-out, and walk down by the C & O Canal to picnic. Phone: 202-333-2602.

> Metro: Foggy Bottom–GWU (very long walk); check with Metro Bus, as the 30-series buses all go from downtown into Georgetown; 202-637-7000
>
> 3051 M Street, NW
>
> Daily 8:30 A.M.–4:30 P.M., Memorial Day through Labor Day; 8:30 A.M.–4:30 P.M. Wednesday through Sunday rest of the year; closed holidays
>
> Guided tours Tuesday through Sunday 9 A.M.–5 P.M.
>
> 202-426-6851

# Georgetown University

**For Teens...** The oldest and largest Jesuit university in the United States, Georgetown University was founded by John Carroll, a cousin of one of Maryland's signers of the Declaration of Independence, in 1789. Unusually tolerant for its time, it was open from the start to students of "every religious profession." From its beginning to the present day, Georgetown has been connected with luminaries; Carroll was friendly with George Washington, Benjamin Franklin, and the Mar-

## Smart Stuff

**For Teens...** Father Patrick Healy has a building named after him on the Georgetown campus. See if you can find out why he was famous. (A.)

quis de Lafayette, and of course, Georgetown is the alma mater of a recent president, Bill Clinton. A special note: After the Civil War, the University changed its school colors to blue and gray, honoring students on both sides, who had died in the conflict. Georgetown University's reputation for scholarship, as well as its beautiful architecture, make it a worthwhile stop, especially for college-bound teens.

> Metro: Foggy Bottom–GWU (very long walk); call Metro
>    Bus: 202-637-7000
> 37th and O Streets, NW
> Leavey Center, 3800 Reservoir Road, NW, houses the bookstore and food courts.
> 202-687-0100
> www.georgetown.edu/

# Tudor Place

**For Teens...** When he wasn't designing the Capitol, Dr. William Thornton turned his talents to this beautiful neoclassical mansion. A home for Georgetown's mayor, Thomas Peter, Tudor Place was completed in 1816. Peter knew a good thing when he saw one; his wife, Martha Custis Peter, was the granddaughter of Martha Washington, and much of the furniture was inherited or purchased from Mount Vernon. There's even a touching letter from George to Martha, written in June 1775, just before he marched off to take command of the fledgling Revolutionary Army. Such other luminaries as the Marquis de Lafayette, Robert E. Lee, Henry Clay, John Calhoun, and Daniel Webster either slept, sat, or partied here.

Peter's descendants, Confederate sympathizers, were forced to rent rooms to Union soldiers to keep the house from procurement as a Union hospital. Fortunately, you can tour today without being asked about *your* political sympathies.

A lovely five-acre, Federal-style garden contains ancient boxwoods, a lily pond, fruit trees, secluded seating alcoves, and a bowling green. But don't bring your bowling ball.

Metro: Dupont Circle (long walk); check with Metro Bus:
    202-637-7000
1644 31st Street, NW in Georgetown
Guided tours only (45 minutes): Tuesday through Friday 10
    A.M., 11:30 A.M., 1 P.M., and 2:30 P.M., and Saturday on
    the hour, 10 A.M.–3 P.M.; closed major holidays.
Reservations suggested; tours on special topics can be arranged.
Fee.
202-965-0400
www.tudorplace.org

# Dumbarton Oaks Garden and Museum

**For Teens...** Of historic interest, spanning many centuries, Dumbarton Oaks houses a unique art collection. Pre-Columbian art and artifacts are displayed here in a beautiful series of circular glass pavilions. Included are Olmec jade figures, textiles, jewelry, and funerary pottery. In the renowned Byzantine collection, visitors can see illuminated manuscripts, jewelry, mosaics, icons, and other works of art.

## Smart Stuff

**For Teens...** What is the United Nations, and why was it formed? Of the agencies it has spawned, which ones do you feel have made significant contributions? (B.)

The twentieth century has also been well-represented. The Dumbarton Oaks Conversations held in the music room in 1944, with representatives from around the world, eventually led to the founding of the United Nations. Harvard University received the property in 1940 from Mr. and Mrs. Robert Woods Bliss, and currently maintains it as a research facility for pre-Columbian, Byzantine, and landscape architecture studies.

The ten acres of formal gardens offer terraced settings for roses, wisteria-covered arbors, an orangery, and gorgeous fall foliage. It is considered one of the finest gardens in the U.S. Nearby is **Dumbarton Oaks Park,** twenty-seven acres of woodland, especially beautiful in the spring and early summer. It is accessible only on foot, and reachable via Lovers' Lane (honest!), off R Street between Avon Place and 31st Street, NW. Open daily 8 A.M. to dusk. Phone: 202-282-1063.

> Older teens and adults are more apt (than younger kids) to enjoy this beautiful mansion and its gardens.

Metro Bus: 202-637-7000

1703 32nd Street, NW (between R and S Streets)

Open Tuesday through Sunday 2–5 P.M.; closed holidays. Donation.

Gardens open daily 2–6 P.M., April through October; 2–5 P.M. rest of year; closed federal holidays and in bad weather; fee April through October.

202-339-6400 or 202-339-6409 (Docent Office, for tours); recording: 202-339-6401

www.doaks.org

Completed in 1805, **Dumbarton House** perfectly exemplifies Federal-style architecture, with its entire layout exactly symmetrical. The National Society of Colonial Dames of America has had its headquarters here since 1928, and has restored and furnished it with exquisite period antiques. On display are children's items from museums throughout the U.S., as well as historic documents signed by George Washington, Thomas Jefferson, and Dolley and James Madison.

Metro: Dupont Circle (long walk); Metro Bus: 202-637-7000

2715 Q Street, NW in Georgetown

Guided tours only. Reservations needed for groups of 10 or more.

Open Tuesday through Saturday 10 A.M.–12:15 P.M., September through July; closed August 1 through Labor Day, federal holidays, and December 23 through January 2.

Donation; free for students with ID.

202-337-2288 (recording)

Nearby, off 27th and Q Streets, NW, is the almost forgotten burial place of 6,000 to 10,000 early Washingtonians, mostly African American, the **Mount Zion** and **Female Union Band Society Graveyards.** Comprising a total of three acres, just a short distance from Rock Creek Parkway, these burial grounds hold special historic value. There are plans to restore a burial vault here, which is supposed to have been a hiding place for slaves heading northward on the Underground Railroad.

## Smart Stuff

**For Tweens...** Imagine you were a slave in Civil War times, trying to make the perilous journey from your home plantation near Richmond, Virginia, to the "free North," somewhere in Pennsylvania, across the Mason-Dixon Line. What kinds of signs and symbols would you use to signal the people after you to show them where it would be safe to stop along the way? (C.)

# ★Wisconsin Avenue and M Street, NW

If all this history has made you hungry, you can be thankful that you have more than colonial food at your disposal. American cuisine in an eclectic setting is a hallmark of **Clyde's** (3236 M Street, NW, open every day; for hours and reservations, phone 202-333-9180). Known for burgers, chili, crab cakes, and big traditional breakfasts, Clyde's also serves eggs Benedict with a grilled portobello mushroom in place of the ham; Sunday brunch, too. If you're brave enough to drive, Clyde's will treat you to two hours of parking at the underground Georgetown Park Mall's garage, a genuine bargain. For Mediterranean sandwiches and desserts, try **Bistro Met,** at 3288 M Street, NW (daily, 11:30–2 A.M.), just down the street from Georgetown Park. Phone: 202-333-2333. Indian food at its tastiest is offered at **Aditi** (3299 M Street, NW; Monday through Saturday, 11:30 A.M.–2:30 P.M. and 5:30–10 P.M.; Sunday 12–2:30

P.M., lunch only; open 'til 10:30 P.M. Friday and Saturday nights.) Vegetarians can find lots of choices here. Locals recommend the assorted appetizers. Phone: 202-625-6825. Reservations encouraged for groups. Hankerin' for some ribs? Head for **Old Glory** (3139 M Street, NW; Monday through Thursday, 11:30–2 A.M.; Friday through Saturday, 11:30–3 A.M.; Sunday, 11–2 A.M.; late night menu after 11:30 every evening), where the spareribs, barbecued chicken, pit-grilled burgers, and grilled veggies are just waiting for you. This is a southern roadhouse-style stop, complete with live music Tuesday, Thursday, and Saturday. Phone: 202-337-3406. Reservations are needed for more than six. Y'all come! Georgetown is actually full of restaurants of all sizes and price ranges, but mostly tiny and expensive. It's a good place to explore.

**For Tweens and Teens...** Fortified for shopping? There's plenty of it here. From fashionable and pricey boutiques to street-corner vendors, there's plenty to discover. Aficionados of hand-crafted items, used books, antiques, art books and prints, funky or fine jewelry, and secondhand or preppy duds can all find something. So bring your wallet!

Starting several blocks above the mecca of Wisconsin and M Streets, NW, and strolling south on Wisconsin Avenue, kids will enjoy **Commander Salamander** (1420 Wisconsin), specializing in offbeat teen fashions (they'll spray a color streak in your hair or do a make-up application, too); **Appalachian Spring** (1415 Wisconsin), with its one-of-a-kind, handmade, American crafts pieces; **Betsey Johnson** (1319 Wisconsin), where you'll find playful, bright-colored teen clothes; **Olsson's Books and Records** (1239 Wisconsin), an independent chain with a wide selection; **Hats in the Belfry** (1237 Wisconsin), where there's a style for everyone to try on; and **Movie Madness** (1222 Wisconsin), with posters and postcards for film fans. Just below M Street, still on Wisconsin, are **Georgetown Tees** (1075 Wisconsin), for souvenir tee shirts, and **Peace Frogs** (1071 Wisconsin) to take home lots of frogs—on clothing and accessories, of course.

At this point, you have reached **The Shops at Georgetown Park** (3222 M Street), where, inside an ornate Victorian setting there are four stories of shops and restaurants, including **FAO Schwarz, Liberty of London, Ferragamo, Tommy Hilfiger, Sharper Image,** and **Polo/Ralph Lauren.** While this is certainly not a discount shopping center, it's a great place to grab a bite, admire the surroundings, and at least window shop. It's also an attractive place to sit and relax, and a haven on a rainy day.

Now for M Street. Young people will want to check out **Urban Outfitters** (3111 M Street), for contemporary clothing and home furnishings; **Steve Madden** (3109 M), with the clunkiest and chunkiest women's shoe styles; **Downtown Locker Room** (3101 M), for sports garb; **Deja Blue** (3005 M), for second-hand jeans; **Barnes & Noble** (3040 M), the largest books and music store in the area; **Eddie Bauer** (also at 3040 M), with its cozy jackets and sturdy sportswear; **American Hand Plus** (2906 M), for American and international handmade treasures; and **Animal Sensations** (2914 M), an art gallery with emphasis on the light-hearted. On 29th Street, just below M, is **Spectrum Gallery** (1132 29th Street, NW), where thirty local professional artists show their paintings, prints, pottery, photography, and sculpture; prices are reasonable.

> Metro: Foggy Bottom (long walk); Metro Bus: 202-637-7000 for the 30-series bus schedules.
>
> Parking is tough, but at the Shops at Georgetown Park (Mall), parking is validated in the underground lot if you spend $10 or more in a store here; no problem.

# Embassy Row

**For Tweens and Teens...** Helping Washingtonians to be citizens of the world are the more than 130 nationalities with embassies in Washington, D.C. Massachusetts Avenue, popularly known as "Embassy Row," is the home for many. While most are not open to the public, the variety and beauty of their exteriors are certainly worth a look. You can take a long, leisurely walk along this appealing route, or—*this* is a nice time to have the use of a car.

## Smart Stuff

**For Tweens and Teens...** Washington, D.C., as the capital, is the only city in the country to house foreign embassies. But consulates are found in other U.S. cities. Find out the difference between these terms. Are there any consulates in your city? If so, which ones? (D.)

Flags and coats-of-arms outside the embassy doors are not only decorative but also interesting; kids might enjoy trying to figure out the countries represented before they sneak a peak at the signs by the doors. Three embassies allow public tours. The **Indonesian Embassy** (2020 Massachusetts Avenue, NW, phone: 202-775-5200; reservations required for weekdays) was formerly the home of the Walsh family, whose daughter, Evelyn, was the last private owner of the Hope Diamond (now in the National Museum of Natural History). The **Indian Embassy** (2107 Massachusetts Avenue, NW, phone: 202-939-7000) offers tours 9:30 A.M.–6 P.M. on weekdays. The **Finnish Embassy** (3301 Massachusetts Avenue, NW, phone: 202-298-5800) invites visitors for tours by appointment only, 10 A.M.–4 P.M. daily; call regarding their regular art shows, which are open to the public.

Also along Massachusetts Avenue, NW, you will find the **Embassy of Great Britain** (3100 Massachusetts Avenue, NW); the **Embassy of Brazil** (next door); the **South African Embassy** (3051 Massachusetts Avenue, NW); the **Embassy of Turkey** (2525 Massachusetts Avenue, NW); the **Japanese Embassy** (2520 Massachusetts Avenue, NW); the **Embassy of Ireland** (2234 Massachusetts Avenue, NW); the **Greek Embassy** (2221 Massachusetts Avenue, NW); the **Embassy of Togo** (1708 Massachusetts Avenue, NW); the **Embassy of Chile** (1732 Massachusetts Avenue, NW); the **Australian Embassy** (1601 Massachusetts Avenue, NW; for educational information, phone: 1-800-833-1787); and the **Embassy of the Philippines** (1607 Massachusetts Avenue, NW). Other embassies are spread throughout the city, wherever their governments could afford the real estate or felt strategic necessity. The **Canadian Embassy** is a large, modern complex, very near the Capitol building. The **Embassy of France** is an elegant mansion nestled into a spacious residential setting along pricey Reservoir Road in the northwest section of the city. The **Embassy of Israel** and the **Embassy of Jordan** make strange neighbors, sitting together on International Drive, NW, in nearly the same kind of proximity their countries occupy in the Middle East.

*Wife Of. . . : An Irreverent Account of Life in Powertown,* by Sondra Gotlieb (teens), while out of print, is so much fun that it's well worth a trip to your library. The author's husband, the former Ambassador from Canada, also wrote his version, *I'll Be With You in a Minute, Mr. Ambassador: The Education of a Canadian Diplomat in Washington,* by Allan Gotlieb (teens). Other works worth taking a look at, also for teens, are *In Confidence: Moscow's Ambassador to America's Six Cold War Presidents (1962–1986),* by former Soviet ambassador to Washington, Anatoly Dobrynin; *Then, They Were Twelve: The Women of Washington's Embassy Row,* by Marilyn Sephocle; and *Black Georgetown Remembered: A History of Its Black Community from the Founding of 'the town of George' in 1751 to the Present Day,* by Kathleen M. Lesko, Valerie Bobb, Carroll R. Gibbs, and Samuel Harvey. Movies are an enjoyable way to explore our "official" connections with other countries. Start with *The Mouse That Roared* (tweens and teens) for a fun-filled time. *Wag the Dog* (teens) and *The Gods Must Be Crazy* (tweens and teens) are fascinating; life almost imitates art. *The Girl Who Spelled Freedom* (tweens and teens) tells the story of a young Cambodian refugee who becomes a national spelling champion. Teens might enjoy a game offered by Close Up Publishing: *U.S. Response: The Making of U.S. Foreign Policy;* it involves role-playing of six real-life foreign policy situations.

Metro: Dupont Circle; walk north on Massachusetts Avenue, NW; D.C.'s Yellow Pages directory lists addresses of all embassies and consulates. Check with Metro Bus for route/fare: 202-637-7000.
www.YellowPages.com

The irrepressible force that was **Sir Winston Churchill** is beautifully captured in the **statue** gracing the front lawn of the **British Embassy.** In a metaphor for his intimate connection with the United States, one foot rests on English soil, and the other, on American soil (as he enjoyed telling Congress, "If my father had been an American, and my mother, British, instead of the other way 'round, I might have got here on my own!"). The force of his indomitable will was largely responsible for girding England to the lonely task of defender of the free world, while Hitler's armies overran Europe. As the British prime minister during history's most widespread conflict, he worked with President Roosevelt to bring Britain the help it needed to survive its onslaught, temporarily, alone. With his characteristic disdain for personal safety, he appeared everywhere, and everywhere he went, he flashed his famous "V" for "victory" sign. His *A History of the English-Speaking Peoples* won him the Nobel Prize for Literature, but clearly, the prize he was proudest of was the one that came with the defeat of the Axis powers in 1945. In 1963, the U.S. made Churchill an honorary citizen.

A tranquil setting on Massachusetts Avenue, between 30th and 34th Streets, NW, is home to the **Kahlil Gibran Memorial Garden** in Normanstone Park. Honoring the famous Lebanese-American poet and philosopher, author of *The Prophet,* the simple footbridge, benches, and fountain provide a wonderful contrast to the trappings of empire in the imposing British Embassy, just across the street. The sensitive bronze head, resting on a curved, poolside wall, reminds visitors of Gibran's philosophy. Inscribed on the limestone benches are quotations from his writings. Open daily all year.

## Smart Stuff

**For Tikes...** On the grounds of the British Embassy is a statue of Winston Churchill, the famous British prime minister during World War II. One hand is raised in the sign of the letter "V." What do you think that signifies? Make up a hand sign of your own and teach it to your friends. What would it signify?

# Islamic Center

**For Tweens and Teens...** The jewel of the Islamic Center, and its most conspicuous building, is the sparkling white and delicately spired mosque, adorned by twenty-four stained glass windows. Visitors will appreciate the intricate and colorful art on the pillars, walls, ceilings, and lush carpets underfoot. The only part of the Islamic Center open to the public, this is the largest and most ornate mosque in the United States. Angled on its lot, the mosque was designed to face Mecca.

> While this is a very exotic-looking building, the mosque is more exciting for youngsters viewed from the outside than on a tour.

## Smart Stuff

**For Tweens...** Islam is one of several faiths that avoid representations of the human form in religious art. You will notice calligraphy (beautiful and elaborate writing) and repetitive geometric designs that form never-ending patterns. In addition, what familiar shapes and forms from nature can you find in the decorative motifs? (E.)

Surprisingly, the Islamic Center wasn't founded until the middle of the twentieth century. After World War II, the Ambassadors of Egypt, Iran, Turkey, and Afghanistan worked together to establish this religious site. Announced by the Mu'azzin from a 160-foot-high minaret, prayers are held five times a day.

Next to the mosque is a small bookstore with souvenirs, books, and some traditional items of clothing. One particularly helpful book for those wishing to learn more about Islam is *Islam: A Very Short Introduction,* by Malise Ruthven (teens and adults).

Metro: Dupont Circle

2551 Massachusetts Avenue, NW

Daily 10 A.M.–5 P.M.; closed Fridays to non-Muslims from
1–2:30 P.M.

Prayers five times daily.

NOTE: Strict dress code enforced; no shorts or short dresses;
women must wear long sleeves and cover their heads
(scarves are made available on site). Everyone must re-
move shoes before entering.

Call a week ahead if you are interested in the one-hour
guided tour. Also call ahead if you are bringing a group,
tour or not.

202-332-8343

# U.S. Naval Observatory

**For Tweens and Teens...** Here's an opportunity to visit the Navy's
oldest scientific office (established in 1830) and look through an
enormous telescope to see sights even older. On a clear night, the
twenty-six-inch refractor telescope permits views of the moon, the
stars, and even the planets, as far away as 25,000 light-years. The
tour includes a thirty-minute
video, a look at the night sky
through an observatory telescope, and a view of the
atomic clock that keeps official U.S. time. Some visitors
have told us about glow-in-
the-dark tee shirts they purchased here.

## Helpful Hint

The tour at the Observa-
tory is recommended for
*older* tweens and teens,
and lasts about an hour
and a half.

Call Metro Bus: 202-637-7000 for transportation information
3450 Massachusetts Avenue, NW, on Observatory Circle
Mondays, November through March at 7:30 P.M.; April
through October at 8:30 P.M.; closed major holidays.
Call before 5:30 P.M. to be sure the sky is clear enough.

*Not* well-designed for disabled visitors.

1½ hour tours; be in line at least one hour in advance. Only the first ninety people are admitted, but up to thirty spaces might be already reserved.

For group reservations, call 202-762-1438

202-762-1467

Embassy Row is not famous for its local restaurants. But if you do get hungry while exploring this area, there are a few spots near the Observatory. **Rocklands** (2418 Wisconsin Avenue, NW; phone: 202-333-2558) is known for its barbecued fresh meat and a noted selection of hot sauces; open 11:30 A.M.–10 P.M. Monday through Saturday; Sunday 11 A.M.–9 P.M. **Austin Grill** (2404 Wisconsin Avenue, NW; phone: 202-337-8080) is open Monday through Thursday 11:30 A.M.–11 P.M.; Friday–Saturday 11:30 A.M. to midnight; Sunday 11:30 A.M.–10:30 P.M., and offers Tex-Mex selections at reasonable prices. Head back down Massachusetts Avenue toward Dupont Circle for other choices (see chapter 7).

# Where to Stay in Georgetown

Yes, there *are* places to stay in Georgetown. Bus service is more convenient than the subway for this area, as you've already discovered. Take a good look at your map in planning where to stay.

### Georgetown Suites
1111 30th Street, NW
202-298-7800
1000 29th Street, NW
202-298-1600 or 1-800-348-7203
Metro: Foggy Bottom (15-minute walk)

### The Georgetown Inn
1310 Wisconsin Avenue, NW
202-333-8900 or 1-800-368-5822

### Holiday Inn Georgetown
2101 Wisconsin Avenue, NW
1-800-HOLIDAY

# Where to Stay Near Embassy Row

If for some reason you really want to rub significant elbows on Embassy Row, there *are* places to stay in this area. Just remember, one pays for status.

### Hilton Washington Embassy Row
2015 Massachusetts Avenue, NW
202-265-1600 or 1-800-445-8667
Metro: Dupont Circle

### Westin Fairfax
2100 Massachusetts Avenue, NW
202-293-2100 or 1-800-937-8461
Metro: Dupont Circle

# Answers to Smart Stuff Questions

**A.** In the era after the Civil War, known as the "Golden Age of Black Washington," African Americans were given voting rights, and many held responsible jobs. Some were even elected to Congress. During this time, Father Patrick Healy became president of Georgetown University, the first black American to head a major university.

**B.** The United Nations is an organization of member nations, formed to stimulate conflict resolution through negotiation rather than armed conflict. Its member agencies include: the International Labor Office (ILO), the World Health Organization (WHO), the Food and Agricultural Organization (FAO), and the U.N. Educational, Scientific, and Cultural Organization (UNESCO), among others.

**C.** The Underground Railroad had a rich set of coded signals from designs on hanging quilts to the venerable spirituals sung in the fields. The ingenuity of a people officially prevented from learning English as a written language is astounding.

**D.** *Embassy* denotes the Ambassador's residence and any other buildings connected with that country's diplomatic mission, while the term *chancery* only covers the diplomatic offices. *Consulates* handle more day-to-day affairs (like visa and passport issues). *Attachés* are diplomats who attend to cultural, scientific, or commercial matters.

**E.** Tree branches, leaves, flowers, birds, deer, and many other animals.

CHAPTER 7

# Dupont Circle
## & Adams Morgan

Originally in a section of Washington called "The Slashes," Dupont Circle is still best in the daytime. In the 1870s, when Connecticut Avenue was finally paved, this area became an attraction for the wealthy and powerful, whose mansions are modern-day clubs, association headquarters, embassies, offices, and galleries. The circle was renamed in 1882, in honor of Union Admiral Samuel Francis du Pont, a hero of the ironclad ships in the Civil War. In 1884, Congress erected an equestrian statue here that the du Pont family found unsatisfactory; the du Ponts instead hired Daniel Chester French (sculptor of the Lincoln statue at the Lincoln Memorial) and Henry Bacon (designer of that memorial) to create the present grand neoclassical centerpiece for the small park at the center of the traffic circle.

Dupont Circle today attracts a much different group. You'll find chess-players, brown-bag-lunchers, tattered-jeans-clad students, sunbathers, musicians, young lovers (straight and gay), and political demonstrators. This is truly an intersection of major streets and lifestyles.

# Anderson House: The Society of the Cincinnati Museum

**For Tweens and Teens...** Another piece of high-class history is the Society of the Cincinnati, headquartered in Anderson House. Founded in 1783 for descendants of American and French officers who fought in the Revolutionary War, members have met every three years since 1784. The Society took its name from Cincinnatus, a Roman patriot; he agreed to serve as head of state during an emergency and then happily returned to his farm when his tenure ended. The example of this citizen-statesman appealed to the

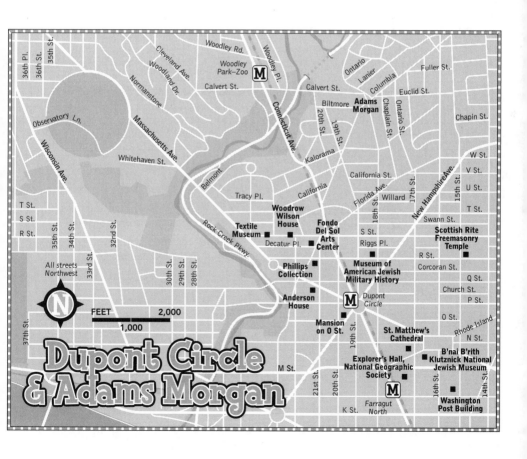

# Quick Guide to Dupont Circle

| Attraction | Location |
| --- | --- |
| Anderson House: The Society of the Cincinnati Museum | 2118 Massachusetts Avenue, NW |
| The Phillips Collection | 1600 21st Street, NW (at Q Street) |
| Textile Museum | 2320 S Street, NW |
| ★Woodrow Wilson House Museum | 2340 S Street, NW |
| Fondo Del Sol Visual Arts Center | 2112 R Street, NW (at Florida Avenue) |
| National Museum of American Jewish Military History | 1811 R Street, NW |
| St. Matthew's Cathedral | 1725 Rhode Island Avenue, NW |
| B'nai B'rith Klutznick National Jewish Museum | 1640 Rhode Island Avenue, NW (in the B'nai B'rith Building) |
| ★Explorers Hall, National Geographic Society | 17th and M Streets, NW |
| Scottish Rite Freemasonry Temple | 1733 16th Street, NW |
| Mansion on O Street | 2020 O Street, NW |
| The Washington Post Building | 15th and L Streets, NW |
| Adams Morgan | Area surrounding intersection of 18th Street, NW, and Columbia Road, NW |

# Adams Morgan Attractions

| Age Range | Hours | Details on |
| --- | --- | --- |
| Tweens and Teens | Tues.–Sat. 1 P.M.–4 P.M. | Page 159 |
| Teens | Tues.–Sat. 10 A.M.–5 P.M.; Thurs. until 8:30 P.M.; Sun. 12 P.M.–7 P.M. | Page 163 |
| All Ages | Mon.–Sat. 10 A.M.–5 P.M.; Sun. 1 P.M.–5 P.M. | Page 165 |
| Tweens and Teens | Tues.–Sun. 10 A.M.–4 P.M. | Page 167 |
| Tweens and Teens | Tues.–Sat. 12:30 P.M.–5:30 P.M. | Page 169 |
| All Ages | Mon.–Fri. 9 A.M.–5 P.M.; Sun. 1 P.M.–5 P.M. | Page 169 |
| All Ages | Sun.–Fri. 6:30 A.M.–6:30 P.M. Sat. 7:30 A.M.–6:30 P.M. | Page 171 |
| Tweens and Teens | Sun.–Fri. 10 A.M.–5 P.M. | Page 172 |
| All Ages | Mon.–Sat. and holidays 9 A.M.–5 P.M.; Sun. 10 A.M.–5 P.M. | Page 174 |
| Teens | Mon.–Fri. 8 A.M.–3:30 P.M. | Page 176 |
| Teens | | Page 176 |
| Teens | Tours by reservation only: Mon. 10 A.M.–3 P.M. (except at noon) | Page 177 |
| Teens | | Page 178 |

founders, one of whom was the great-grandfather of Larz Anderson, owner of Anderson House. In fact, a mural here depicts the Marquis de Lafayette receiving membership in the Society from George Washington, with Anderson's great-grandfather as a witness.

## Smart Stuff

**For Tweens and Teens...** As your mother always told you, be kind to your friends. When the fledgling United States took on the powerful Great Britain, it needed all the help it could get. Can you find which three (yes, *three*) countries recognized the U.S. as a new country and also declared war on England? Why do you think these countries would undertake such a course of action? (A.)

As befits the home of a former ambassador (to Japan) and his heiress wife, the museum overflows with opulence. In addition to whole rooms decorated with antique furnishings, some ceilings and walls are covered in 23-karat gold leaf. Kids will like the miniature Revolutionary War figurines engaged in "battle." American Revolution displays and George Washington memorabilia will be of particular interest to students of the Revolutionary War.

## Smart Stuff

**For Teens...** History books tell us that perhaps only one-third of the colonial populace supported independence at the time of the Revolution, with one-third of the citizens working for the *British* cause. Assume you were a middle class colonial merchant, with a family to support. Which side would you have chosen and why?

One noted book about the major players in the American Revolution is *Patriots: The Men Who Started the American Revolu-*

*tion,* by A. J. Langguth (teens). *Can't You Make Them Behave, King George?, Will You Sign Here, John Hancock?,* and *Shh! We're Writing the Constitution,* all by Jean Fritz, will be educational and fun to read for tweens. A movie for the entire family to share is *1776,* a musical that truly brings the Founding Fathers and this historical period alive.

> Metro: Dupont Circle
> 2118 Massachusetts Avenue, NW
> Tuesday through Saturday, 1–4 P.M.; closed major holidays.
> Library open by appointment only, Monday through Friday,
>    9 A.M.–5 P.M.
> 202-785-2040

# The Phillips Collection

**For Teens...** For modern art in an antique setting, try a visit to the Phillips Gallery, America's first museum of contemporary art. Established in 1921 by Duncan Phillips, heir to a steel fortune, the collection is housed in the family's brownstone mansion, giving an accessible and comfortable feeling to the exhibition. This wonderful collection outgrew its home, so a starkly modern addition was added to the building. Still, not everything can be displayed at once, so works are rotated regularly. A list of artists represented reads like a "who's who" of modern art: Picasso, Renoir, Bonnard, Van Gogh, Monet, Miro, Klee, Mondrian, Rothko, Kandinsky, O'Keeffe, and Hopper are all included.

> With appropriate preparation before visiting the Phillips, all ages will enjoy this beautiful museum. Call to request the Family Fun Pack geared to the time of your visit. Also speak with the Tour Coordinator to schedule a group tour.

A child-friendly educational resource for the permanent collection is called the "Art of the City—Family Fun Pack." It is available free, on site or in advance, and offers background information and activities for kids and adults. "Conversations with Art," a special worksheet for high school students, involves young people in learning to appreciate and critique a work of art. A workbook for adults and children to enjoy together, "A Parent-Child Guide: A Child's Adventure into the Artists' World of Color," is also available for a small contribution.

Renoir's "Luncheon of the Boating Party," the most popular work in the Phillips, has a double appeal. Not only does it exemplify the beautiful palette and style of the Impressionists, but it actually contains portraits of people the artist knew as well. Just like members of the "boating party," anyone who needs to rest a bit can find comfortable seating in any of the Phillips' rooms.

While small, the gift shop is chock-full of wonderful books, cards, games, jewelry, scarves, tapes, and surprises that represent work by the artists in the collection. **The Café** (Tuesday through Saturday, 10 A.M.–4:15 P.M.; Sunday 2–6:15 P.M.) is tiny, but offers delectable goodies; this might be a good place to select a cookie or pastry to take along as you continue your walk in the Dupont Circle area. There is a separate entrance directly into the gift shop and from there into the Café, so it is not necessary to pay admission to the museum to stop in to shop or snack.

> Metro: Dupont Circle
> 1600 21st Street, NW, at Q Street
> Tuesday through Saturday 10 A.M.–5 P.M., Thursday until 8:30 P.M.; Sunday noon–7 P.M. Closed January 1, July 4, Thanksgiving, and December 25.
> 45-minute guided tours available Wednesday through Saturday 2 P.M.
> Call in advance to schedule group tours; Director of Education Programs: 202-387-2151, ext. 214, or Tour Coordinator, ext. 247.
> Concerts Sunday 5 P.M., September through May.
> Family programs: Call for information.

Artful evenings on Thursdays: live music, gallery talks, and
    films
Admission fee; discounts for seniors and students with ID.
    Additional fees for special exhibits.
202-387-2151
www.phillipscollection.org/

Getting hungry? Luckily, you're in an area of D.C. that is absolutely loaded with restaurants. A new one, part of a Colorado
chain recently opened in Washington, is **Chipotle Mexican Grill.**
It's at 2600 Connecticut Avenue, NW; phone: 202-299-9111. For a
good all-around variety of selections, try **Wrap Works,** at 1601 Connecticut Avenue, NW (Sunday through Thursday 11 A.M.–11 P.M.,
Friday through Saturday 11 A.M. to midnight), phone: 202-265-
4200. In addition to all kinds of "wraps," including barbecued meats
and vegetarian selections, an assortment of "plates" is offered; The
Texas Plate, for example, includes barbecued chicken or steak, with
garlic mashed potatoes, beans, relish, and salad; a California plate offers fire-roasted vegetables over garlic mashed potatoes. And don't
miss out on the famous fresh fruit smoothies. **Raku,** at 1900 Q
Street, NW (Sunday through Thursday 11:30 A.M.–10 P.M., Friday
through Saturday 11:30 A.M.–11 P.M.) is a good (small) spot for delectable international treats, including tapas, noodles, "Peking duck"
in rice paper pancakes, salads, and sushi; phone: 202-265-7258. The
glass walls open for sidewalk café-style dining, and you can stop by
and pick up a menu, since Raku also delivers; delivery phone: 202-
232-8646. Devotees of pad thai? Satay? Try **Thaiphoon,** at 2011 S
Street, NW (weekdays 11:30 A.M.–10:30 P.M., Saturday and Sunday
11:30 A.M.–11 P.M.); phone 202-667-3505.

# Textile Museum

**For All Ages...** Even if you didn't grow up in a log cabin with a loom,
you will be amazed at the accomplishments of weavers from all over the
world when you visit the Textile Museum. Such countries as India,

## At the Textile Museum

China, Indonesia, Guatemala, Mexico, and Peru are represented by a lovely variety of offerings. Those who are familiar with Native American cultures will recognize and appreciate the original Navajo rugs.

Craft demonstrations, as well as workshops, special please- touch exhibits, and an interactive Activity Gallery allow visitors literally to get the feel of these creations. Kids can learn to use a loom, practice decorating textiles by coloring or stamping patterns on them, spin wool on a hand-held spindle, trace the sources for natural dyes, practice various stitching techniques on a Plexiglas board, and use the computer station for a variety of changing learning activities. Seminars, lectures, videos, and photographs provide insight into the history and lifestyles of the cultures behind the work.

An interesting note, especially for kids who are perfectionists: It is a tradition in many cultures for textile artists to weave an intentional flaw into their work, to remind themselves that only God is perfect.

For beautifully handcrafted scarves, rugs, blankets and other weavings, visit the gift shop.

Metro: Dupont Circle
2320 S Street, NW
Monday through Saturday 10 A.M.–5 P.M., Sunday 1–5 P.M.;
    closed federal holidays and December 24.

*Celebration of Textiles Day*

Donations.
Docent-led tours
Monday
through
Wednesday,
Friday, and Saturday 10 A.M.–4 P.M.,
Thursday 1-4 P.M.
Highlight tours Wednesday, Saturday, Sunday 1:30 P.M., September through May
Other tours by appointment; call the education department
(ext. 35) at least two weeks in advance to schedule a tour
for your appropriate age group.
202-667-0441
www.textilemuseum.org

# ★Woodrow Wilson House Museum

**For Tweens and Teens...** The only presidential museum in Washington, this was the last home of Woodrow Wilson, until his death in 1924. Wilson and his second wife, Edith, remained in the District after his presidency because he wanted to pursue research in the Library of Congress. Unfortunately, he was already ill when they moved in, and the house is a tribute to Mrs. Wilson's attention to

### Smart Stuff

**For Tweens...** If you were an archaeologist looking at the objects in this house, what could you tell about people's lives in the early 1920s in the U.S.?

and concern for his needs. Mrs. Wilson lived the rest of her life (she lived long enough to attend John F. Kennedy's inauguration) in a home she preserved from the date of her husband's death. Visitors will see it as it was during Wilson's life here, including his Victrola with a wooden needle, his old movie projector, an ornate wooden icebox, and even groceries in the lower level kitchen pantry. Some interesting period clothing (including shoes) is displayed in both Wilsons' closets.

The 45-minute tour is preceded by a half-hour film, narrated by Walter Cronkite, describing the life of our twenty-eighth president. Youngsters who have studied the early part of the twentieth century, the League of Nations, or the United Nations will find the Woodrow Wilson House Museum particularly interesting. Idealism isn't just for the young.

## Smart Stuff

**For Teens...** Edith Bolling Galt Wilson, President Woodrow Wilson's second wife, was roundly criticized for controlling access of even the highest level officials to her husband during his recovery from a stroke. In her memoirs, she emphasized that this was the course his doctors had strongly advocated. If the U.S. were faced with a similar presidential health crisis, what safeguards would you recommend?

You might want to search out the 1944 biographical movie *Wilson*, which delivers a thought-provoking portrait of this intriguing figure. There are many Woodrow Wilson books available: *Woodrow Wilson (United States Presidents)*, by Anne Schraff (tweens); *Woodrow Wilson (Presidential Biography Series)*, by Sallie G. Randolph (tweens and teens); *Woodrow Wilson (Penguin Lives)*, by Louis Auchincloss (teens); and *Woodrow Wilson: World Statesman*, by Kendrick A. Clements (older teens) are a few worth exploring.

Also worth a look is the tiny gift shop, stocked with books, souvenirs, and memorabilia on President Wilson and his years in public life.

Metro: Dupont Circle
2340 S Street, NW
45-minute guided tours Tuesday through Sunday 10 A.M.–
    4 P.M.; closed major holidays
Special tours for school groups; call to schedule
Admission fee; discounts for seniors and students with ID
202-387-4062

# Fondo Del Sol Visual Arts Center

**For Tweens and Teens...** An alternative, artist-operated museum, Fondo Del Sol promotes Hispanic culture through the arts. Contemporary and folk art are featured along with pre-Columbian and religious artifacts. Fondo Del Sol is a participant in the nineteen-member gallery association that holds a collective open house on the first Friday of each month (except August through September).

Metro: Dupont Circle
2112 R Street, NW, at Florida Avenue
Tuesday through Saturday, 12:30–5:30 P.M.
Admission fee; student rate
202-483-2777

# National Museum of American Jewish Military History

**For All Ages...** All kinds of war artifacts are on exhibit here, from the Revolutionary War to the present, documenting Jewish Americans' contributions to U.S. military service. You can see bugles, stirrups, binoculars, hand-painted illustrated maps of troop movements, flags, posters, photographs, and weapons. Young feminists will be especially happy to find an exhibit about Jewish women who served in the U.S. military (they weren't all behind the lines making chicken soup).

Several books we found of interest are for teens: *Where They Lie: A Story of the Jewish Soldiers of the North and South. . .,* by Mel

Young; and *Hearing a Different Drummer: A Holocaust Survivor's Search for Identity,* by Benjamin Hirsch.

> Metro: Dupont Circle
> 1811 R Street, NW
> Monday through Friday 9 A.M.–5 P.M., Sunday 1–5 P.M.,
>     closed Jewish and federal holidays
> Guided and self-guided tours; school groups should call in
>     advance.
> Donations
> 202-265-6280

**For Tweens and Teens... Dupont Circle shopping** has a split personality. South of the circle are the pricey, high-end retailers like **Liz Claiborne, Brooks Brothers, Rizik's,** and **Burberry's;** window shopping here is fun. North of the circle are the more eclectic shops, bookstores, and galleries. **Backstage,** at 2101 P Street, NW, has everything for the stage-struck: theatrical makeup, sheet music, and scripts. **Beadazzled,** 1522 Connecticut Avenue, NW, displays a dazzling array of beads that you can use creatively— make earrings, a necklace, a belt, or a bracelet out of your carefully selected choices. **Cherishables,** 1608 20th Street, NW, offers American folk arts and crafts, in addition to furniture. **Ginza,** 1721 Connecticut Avenue, NW, whisks you away to the folk art of Japan.

**Kramerbooks and Afterwards,** 1517 Connecticut Avenue, NW, is a favorite haunt for locals. Though narrow and crowded, don't miss it unless you're in a big group. Way before the Borders and Barnes and Noble folks dreamed up serving cappuccino and magazines, Washingtonians were already nestling into the cozy niches of Kramerbooks to read and sip. Open 24 hours on weekends. **Newsroom,** 2011 S Street, NW, relocated in the last year or so. If you're looking for a periodical in almost any foreign language, allow yourself time to browse here. Look for your hometown's newspaper, too.

If you're sleuthing out a mystery book, head for **Mystery Books** at 1715 Connecticut Avenue, NW. Real-live book detectives will hunt for any out-of-print edition for you at **Second Story Books,** 2000 P Street, NW; you can search through the huge quantity of used books yourself if you don't mind a little dust. The standards are here, too: **Olsson's Books and Records** is at 1307 19th Street, NW, and **Supercrown,** at New Hampshire Avenue and P Streets, NW.

This area is full of small art galleries, particularly along R Street, west of Connecticut Avenue. While the collections are interesting, including Chinese and Southeast Asian art and antiques and American and English furnishings, they're generally not of interest or affordability to youngsters.

# St. Matthew's Cathedral

With vaulted ceiling frescoes and chapels filled with candles, the interior of St. Matthew's Cathedral is a delight to the eye. Completed in 1895, after only two years of construction, it is decorated with Italian-style mosaics and pillars topped with gilded Corinthian capitals. Beneath the ninety-foot dome, the central altar, a gift from the Archbishop of Agra, is in traditional Mogul style, also seen in the Taj Mahal.

Historically, St. Matthew's has been the site of memorable events. Funeral Mass for President John F. Kennedy was said here on November 25, 1963, and Pope John Paul II celebrated Mass here when he visited Washington in 1979. Traditionally, a "Red Mass" is celebrated in October, coinciding with the historical opening of the judicial year as far back as the Middle Ages. (Red vestments symbolize the scarlet robes worn by royal judges attending such a mass centuries ago.) Members of Congress, Supreme Court justices, heads of government agencies, the White House Cabinet, the diplomatic corps, members of the legal profession, and, occasionally, the president, are in attendance to pray for guidance in their official duties. A good thing to agree on.

> Metro: Farragut North or Dupont Circle
> 1725 Rhode Island Avenue, NW
> Sunday through Friday 6:30 A.M.–6:30 P.M.,
> Saturday 7:30 A.M.–6:30 P.M.
> Guided tours Sunday 2:30 P.M. or by appointment
> 202-347-3215

# B'nai B'rith Klutznick National Jewish Museum

**For Tweens and Teens...** Documenting twenty centuries of Jewish history, the B'nai B'rith Klutznick National Jewish Museum gives an insightful picture of a significant American ethnic group. Changing exhibits of contemporary sculpture and painting on Judaic themes are featured in this specialized museum and exhibit hall. Ceremonial and folk art objects, both ancient and modern, as well as an impressive collection of ritual and religious items, such as Torahs, menorahs, prayer shawls, kiddush cups, candlesticks, Passover seder plates, and religious books form an impressive display. A Sports Hall of Fame celebrates American Jewish athletes, such as Sandy Koufax, "Red" Auerbach, and Hank Greenberg.

A reminder of the importance of religious tolerance is the letter on display from George Washington to the Touro Synagogue in Rhode Island after his visit there: "The Government of the United States. . .gives to bigotry no sanction and to persecution no assistance. . . ." The museum also houses a library rich in Jewish Americana, available for researchers to enjoy. A little-noted treat is the small, outdoor sculpture garden.

A large selection of books, contemporary Jewish

## Smart Stuff

**For Tweens and Teens...** Incorporated in the Bill of Rights as the First Amendment is the stipulation that "Congress shall make no law respecting an establishment of religion, or prohibiting the free exercise thereof. . . ." Why do you think this particular freedom appears so early in our nation's history? If these provisions were *not* in our Bill of Rights, how do you think our American society would be different? What are some current issues concerning religious freedom in our country?

crafts, children's gifts, jewelry, and ceremonial items are available in the Museum Shop.

*The Chosen,* by Chaim Potok (tweens and teens) tells a gripping fictional story about two young boys that reveals some of the differences among observant Jews; this is also available on video. Harry Kemelman wrote a whole series of funny novels, beginning with *Saturday the Rabbi Went Hungry,* enjoyable for tweens and teens. *To Life!* By Harold S. Kushner (teens), provides insight into Judaism. One instructive movie about anti-Semitism is *Gentleman's Agreement,* with Gregory Peck (tweens and teens). *Hester Street* is an enlightening movie, also for teens, about what it was like for Jewish immigrants to the United States early in the twentieth century. *Avalon,* for teens, extends the timeline to post World War II Jewish life.

Metro: Farragut North
1640 Rhode Island Avenue, NW, in the B'nai B'rith Building
Open Sunday through Friday 10 A.M.–5 P.M.; closed major
    Jewish holidays and some federal holidays
Guided tours by appointment only
Donations
202-857-6583; gift shop: 202-857-6608
http://bnaibrith.org/museum

By now, you've noticed that all over the Dupont Circle area there are restaurants, cafes, and carryouts, so food is plentiful. Here's a double-decker treat: **Café Luna,** on the first floor, serves pizza and pasta; upstairs at **Skewers,** you'll find Middle Eastern fare; all at 1633 P Street, NW (Sunday through Thursday 11:30 A.M.–11 P.M., Friday through Saturday 11:30 A.M.–12:30 A.M.); phone: 202-387-7400. Grilled eggplant with yogurt, grilled vegetable sandwich, fillet mignon on pita, shish kabob, kufta (looks like a long hot dog, but it's made of chick peas and spices, like felafel), and a wide variety of vegetables and salads are found at Skewers. **Bua,** at 1635 P Street, NW (daily 10:30 A.M.–10:30 P.M.) offers Thai food and a good selection of vegetarian entrees; phone: 202-265-0828. For pizza and pastas, visit **Bertucci's,** 1218 Connecticut Avenue, NW (Monday through Thursday 11 A.M.–10 A.M., Friday and Saturday 11 A.M.– 11 P.M., Sunday 11 A.M.–9 P.M.); phone: 202-463-7733.

Dedicated in 1909, this seated statue of one of our country's most beloved poets presides over one of D.C.'s busiest intersections (Connecticut Avenue and M Street, NW). The mythological figures **Henry Wadsworth Longfellow** has bequeathed to us touch something special in our national psyche. Perhaps it is fitting that the creator of "Paul Revere's Ride," "The Song of Hiawatha," "Evangeline," and "The Wreck of the Hesperus" should sit where he does, in traffic. Maybe he's reminding us to slow down and live.

# ★Explorers Hall, National Geographic Society

**For All Ages...** A real-life National Geographic "special," this is an exhibit for kids of all ages. Whatever you like in nature, it's here: astronomy, biology, geography, weather, space science, and exploration of the planet, all on the first floor of the Society's headquarters. The can't-miss-it centerpiece is the world's largest globe, hand-painted, Earth Station One; it's an eleven-foot, 1,100-pound sphere, explored with electronic buttons that answer questions.

In the permanent display, "Geographica: A New Look at the World," kids can learn about the peoples and customs of the world, touch a tornado, and operate interactive computer displays to learn about the earth and space. Youngsters of a certain age will be attracted to the seven-pound Goliath frog, preserved in all its glory; others might prefer

## Smart Stuff

**For Tweens and Teens...** As Earth's population grows, we look increasingly to our oceans for relief. In what ways can we use our oceans productively for humankind?

## Smart Stuff

**For Teens...** In prior centuries, exploration meant discovering new territories or learning about uninhabited areas of the earth. In the latter part of the twentieth century, exploration focused on outer space. What do you think are our obligations to the environments we explore?

*National Geographic* magazine's colorful and extraordinary displays of photographs.

The most relevant and enjoyable reading materials for a visit to this special place would be any issues of the *National Geographic* magazine, with its familiar yellow cover, or, for younger children, *National Geographic World*. Subscriptions to either of these magazines make special gifts, for individuals or schools; past issues are available at the gift shop, as well as at used bookstores and second-hand shops. An enjoyable game for tikes (on up) is *Take Off!*—a world geography game with a huge laminated map. Two more games are *Where In the World?*, which consists of five games on five levels of play, about world geography (capitals, languages, religions, etc.) for tweens and teens; and *National Geographic History Voyage*, which brings players to unknown destinations where they can learn all about new places—a game of geography and mystery (tweens and teens). The gift shop at Explorer's Hall offers beautiful books, maps, magazines, and videos.

> Metro: Farragut North or Farragut West
> 17th and M Streets, NW
> Monday through Saturday and holidays 9 A.M.–5 P.M., Sunday 10 A.M.–5 P.M.; closed December 25
> Free films, usually Tuesdays, noon, October through April
> Lecture and film information, 202-857-7700
> 202-857-7588
> www.nationalgeographic.com

# Scottish Rite Freemasonry Temple

**For Teens...** An elaborate building guarded by two sphinxes, the Scottish Rite Freemasonry Temple stands out from its surroundings. Completed in 1915, it is the headquarters for the Masons of the District of Columbia. Fourteen presidents, from George Washington to Gerald Ford have been Masons. Dedicated to "spreading the light of knowledge and fraternity," these days the Masons focus on support for children with learning disorders. A lengthy tour, not great for most children, does give you the opportunity to see the 1,000-pipe organ, the Hall of Masonic Heroes, and the J. Edgar Hoover Law Enforcement Room. But if your tween or teen is a member of DeMolay or Job's Daughters, this site would be of special interest.

> Metro: Dupont Circle
> 1733 16th Street, NW
> Monday through Friday, 8 A.M.–3:30 P.M.; call for tour
>     information
> 202-232-3579

# Mansion on O Street

**For Teens...** A well-kept Washington secret, this small Victorian inn is owned and run by an eccentric dowager, H. H. Leonard; it offers twelve different bed-and-breakfast rooms, publicized only by word-of-mouth, and often visited by celebrities. You don't have to stay overnight to visit this unusual mansion. Tours are offered, and it's a place for a shopping adventure. Everything—and we do mean *everything*—is for sale, from small pieces of jewelry and knickknacks to sculptures and huge paintings. Bring a truck (parking, however, is a real challenge here).

> Metro: Dupont Circle
> 2020 O Street, NW
> 202-496-2000

# ★The *Washington Post* Building

**For Teens...** When it broke the Watergate scandal nearly thirty years ago, the *Washington Post's* reputation became world-famous, second only, perhaps, to the *New York Times*. The diligent reporting and journalistic skills of the *Post's* Bob Woodward and Carl Bernstein eventually resulted in the only resignation of a president, Richard Nixon, in our country's history.

Youngsters who are interested in news and how a major newspaper is produced will find its headquarters a fascinating place. However, visitors are not likely to see the big presses rolling; since the *Post* is a morning newspaper, most of it is printed during the night. But to see how many people it takes and how much activity it requires to bring the daily news into publication is indeed a surprise. You will never look at a newspaper in quite the same way again!

Several books of interest to current events buffs will be: *All the President's Men,* by Carl Bernstein and Bob Woodward (teens), which is also a movie (teens), with Robert Redford, Dustin Hoffman, and Jason Robards; *The Chain Gang: One Newspaper versus the Gannett Empire,* by Richard McCord (teens); *Our Man in*

## Smart Stuff

**For Tweens and Teens...** Thomas Jefferson once said that given the choice between a democracy with no newspapers and newspapers with no democracy, he'd choose the latter. Why do you think he would make such a choice? Do you agree?

Framed on a wall, and highly visible when you tour the building, is a cutout of a classified ad promotion that reads, "I got my job through the *Washington Post*." It is signed by President Gerald Ford, who took office after Nixon resigned.

*Washington,* by Roy Hoopes (teens)—a detective novel, whose major figures are two famous journalists; A *Time of Change: A Reporter's Tale of Our Time,* by Harrison E. Salisbury (teens); and *Simon Says: The Best of Roger Simon* (teens)—what fun journalism can be!

> Metro: McPherson Square or Farragut North
> 15th and L Streets, NW
> Call for tour arrangements a few months before your trip.
> Guided tours Monday 10 A.M.–3 P.M. on the hour (except
>     noon); reservations required—call several *months* in
>     advance; children must be over 11 or in fifth grade.
> 202-334-7969
> www.washingtonpost.com

# Adams Morgan

**For Teens...** Colorful and exciting, this tiny international neighborhood combines ethnic variety and bohemian style. Chock-full of restaurants, cafes, clubs, and shops, Adams Morgan is a mecca for young people and those who appreciate creative offerings. The two main streets to explore are 18th Street, NW, running north and south, and Columbia Road, NW, running diagonally northeast and southwest. Originally a major trail for Native Americans, this area was named Lanier Heights, until integration (D.C. was the first major U.S. city to integrate its schools voluntarily) fostered the combining of students from two schools. The primarily white Adams School merged with the largely African American Morgan School, and the residents decided to change the name of their neighborhood to Adams Morgan.

In addition to the original American-born mix, residents now hail from Southeast Asia, South America, Central America, the Caribbean, and Central Africa, among other places. As a result, the restaurants and stores, packed with handmade items and ethnic clothing from all these faraway lands, are an adventure to investigate. **Paula's Imports,** at 2405 18th Street, NW, houses an unusual assortment of jewelry, shoes, bedspreads, and other gifts from Africa, India, and Pakistan. African-inspired textiles set the stage for designer ethnic garments at **Khismet Wearable Art** (1800 Belmont Road, NW).

Unusual treasures you can find in Adams Morgan include architectural details, such as stained and leaded glass windows, chandeliers, fireplace mantels, and hardware, which you'll discover at the **Brass Knob** (2311 18th Street, NW). Hand-painted furnishings, pillows, and wrought iron fill **Skynear & Co.** (2122 18th Street, NW).

This is clearly not an area for younger kids; adults (and *only* adults) will love its clubs and cafés at night—come by taxi, as parking is nearly impossible and walking is less than safe. However, it's a very intriguing and educational neighborhood for teens to visit in the daytime.

Locals love secondhand anything, so you can browse endlessly. For old books, try **Idle Time Books** at 2410 18th Street, NW. Like most such places, it's a dusty hunt for treasure here, and politics is the topic of choice. Prefer music? **DCCD,** at 2432 18th Street, NW, has mostly modern music, LPs, and new and used CDs, which you can listen to before you buy, and also—gasp!—video games. **Flying Saucer Discs,** at 2318 18th Street, NW, features obscure titles and every genre you can think of.

In a city blasé about international cuisine, visitors still flock to Adams Morgan for the genuine article in ethnic fare. For inexpensive and exotic Ethiopian specialties, visit **Meskerem** (Sunday through Thursday noon to midnight, Friday and Saturday noon to 1 A.M.), at 2434 18th Street, NW, phone: 202-462-4100. If you've never had Ethiopian food before, be sure to wash your hands before you get started—they're your silverware, along with a spongy form of flat bread, called injera. Lots of stews are offered and described; "alicha" indicates the milder-spiced versions, while "watt" refers to the spicier dishes. And they *are* high-wattage, with plenty of green chiles.

**Mixtec** (daily 11 A.M.–10 P.M.), 1792 Columbia Rd., NW, phone: 202-332-1011, is primarily for carnivores, so sharpen your canines. Mexican favorites include camarones vallarta (shrimp in green tomatillo sauce) and anrollados mexicanos (large flour tortillas encasing various fillings). If you're brave enough for rooftop dining with youngsters, **Star of Siam** (Monday through Thursday 5–10 P.M., Friday 5–11 P.M., Saturday noon–11 P.M., Sunday noon–10 P.M.) 2446 18th Street, NW, phone: 202-986-4133, offers a wonderful view and food to match. Prices are reasonable, and traditional Thai food includes spicy curries, pad thai with shrimp, and ba mee Siam (a *very* spicy noodle-beef-pork-chicken-egg-and-vegetable dish). And how about Persian food? **The Caravan Grill** (Monday through Thursday 11:30 A.M.–10:30 P.M., Friday and Saturday 11:30 A.M.–11:30 P.M., Sunday noon–10:30 P.M.), at 1825 18th Street, NW, phone: 202-518-0444, is the place to find. A hidden entrance and a fenced-in courtyard, Middle Eastern music, and a delicious buffet in addition to the regular menu make this a star attraction for locals. Vegetarian-friendly dishes, with rice and beans, or marinated meats and poultry cooked to order, kebabs, yogurt soup, and warm flatbread are some of the interesting treats that await you in this secluded setting. Keep looking; it's a find.

> Metro: Dupont Circle (exit at Q Street and head up Connecticut Avenue, NW to Columbia Road, NW or Metro to Woodley Park/Zoo and walk over the Duke Ellington Bridge (Calvert Street, NW) and go right for a block to intersection of Columbia Road and 18th Street
> Or—take a cab.

# Where to Stay in the Dupont Circle/Adams Morgan Area

In the Dupont Circle/Adams Morgan area, the majority of the hotels are closer to Dupont Circle; Adams Morgan has small bed and breakfasts. The exception is the Washington Hilton, which has some notoriety of its own (it was outside this hotel that President Reagan was shot).

### Carlyle Suites Hotel
1731 New Hampshire Avenue, NW
202-234-3200 or 1-800-964-5377
Metro: Dupont Circle.

### Doyle Washington Hotel
1500 New Hampshire Avenue, NW
202-483-6000 or 1-800-423-6953
Metro: Dupont Circle.

### Embassy Square, a Summerfield Suites Hotel
2000 N Street, NW
202-659-9000 or 1-800-833-4353
Metro: Dupont Circle.

### Washington Hilton and Towers
1919 Connecticut Avenue, NW
202-483-3000 or 1-800-445-8667
Metro: Dupont Circle (long walk)

# Answers to Smart Stuff Questions

**A.** The three countries were: France, Holland, and Spain.

CHAPTER

8

Chinatown
& Gallery Place

The colorful **Chinatown Friendship Archway** (at 7th and H Streets, NW) beckons visitors to the five-block area of D.C.'s Chinatown, a fitting symbol for this section of the city. An area filled with art and history, the **Chinatown/Gallery Place** neighborhood has spots that are unique Washington sights. They include the **FBI Building** and the **National Law Enforcement Officers Memorial;** cultural treats like the **National Museum of Women in the Arts,** the **National Museum of American Art,** and the **National Portrait Gallery;** brain food for history buffs, like the **National Archives** and **Ford's Theater;** and ethnic delights for the tummy in Chinatown. Although some of these spots might not be awash with tourists, this area touches a variety of interests and is well worth a visit. You don't have to be an FBI agent to uncover good things to do here.

# National Museum of Women in the Arts

**For Tweens and Teens...** Amazing as it may seem, there actually *were* women artists before the twentieth century, and here's the place to see their work. In addition to such relatively recent notables

# Quick Guide to

| Attraction | Location |
| --- | --- |
| National Museum of Women in the Arts | 1250 New York Avenue (at 13th Street, NW) |
| Willard Inter-Continental Hotel | 1401 Pennsylvania Avenue, NW |
| The Shops at National Place | F Street (between 13th and 14th Streets, NW) |
| Ronald Reagan Building and International Trade Center | 1300 Pennsylvania Avenue, NW |
| ★Pavilion at the Old Post Office | 1100 Pennsylvania Avenue, NW |
| ★National Archives | Constitution Avenue at 8th Street, NW |
| U.S. Navy Memorial and Naval Heritage Center | 701 Pennsylvania Avenue, NW |
| ★FBI (Federal Bureau of Investigation) Building | 935 Pennsylvania Avenue, NW (enter on E Street) |
| ★Ford's Theater National Historic Site and Petersen House | 511 10th Street, NW |
| Smithsonian American Art Museum and National Portrait Gallery | 8th and F Streets, NW |
| The Chinatown Friendship Archway | Bordered by 6th, 7th, H, and I Streets, NW |
| National Law Enforcement Officers Memorial | Between E and F Streets and 4th and 5th Streets, NW |

# Chinatown/Gallery Place Attractions

| Age Range | Hours | Details on |
| --- | --- | --- |
| Tweens and Teens | Mon.–Sat. 10 A.M.–5 P.M. Sun. 12 P.M.–5 P.M. | Page 185 |
| | | Page 191 |
| All Ages | Mon.–Sat. 10 A.M.–7 P.M. Sun. 12 P.M.–5 P.M. | Page 192 |
| All Ages | Visitors Center: Mon.–Sat. 9 A.M.–6 P.M., Sun. 12 P.M.–5 P.M. | Page 193 |
| All Ages | Tower: 8 A.M.–10:45 P.M. (summer) 10 A.M.–5:45 P.M. (winter) | Page 194 |
| Tweens and Teens | 10 A.M.–5:30 P.M. (fall–winter) 10 A.M.–9 P.M. (spring–summer) | Page 195 |
| Tweens and Teens | 24 hours, daily. Center: Mon.– Sat. 9:30 A.M.–5 P.M. (March–Oct.) Tues.–Sat. 9:30 A.M.–5 P.M. (rest of year) | Page 198 |
| Tweens and Teens | Tours: Mon.–Fri. 8:45 A.M.– 4:15 p.m. | Page 201 |
| Tweens and Teens | 9 A.M.–5 P.M. daily | Page 202 |
| All Ages | 10 A.M.–5:30 P.M. daily | Page 205 |
| | | Page 208 |
| All Ages | 24 hours, daily. Visitors Center: Mon.–Fri. 9 A.M.–5 P.M.; Sat. 10 A.M.–5 P.M.; Sun. 12 P.M.–5 P.M. | Page 208 |

*(continues)*

# Quick Guide to

| Attraction | Location |
|---|---|
| National Building Museum | 401 F Street, NW |
| Lillian and Albert Small Museum (Jewish Historical Society) | 701 3rd Street, NW (at G Street) |
| Mary McLeod Bethune Council House National Historic Site | 1318 Vermont Avenue, NW |
| African American Civil War Memorial | 1000 U Street, NW |
| Howard University | 2400 6th Street, NW |
| Lincoln Theater | 1215 U Street, NW |

as Georgia O'Keeffe, Mary Cassatt, Elaine de Kooning, Lila Cabot Perry, Frida Kahlo, and Helen Frankenthaler, visitors can explore work by artists of much earlier times: Lavinia Fontana, Rachel Ruysch, and Elizabeth Vigee-Lebrun (painter in the court of Marie Antoinette). Sculptor Camille Claudel, the unhappy mistress and student of Auguste Rodin, is also represented here. In addition to the permanent collection on the third floor, the museum hosts a series of changing exhibits, from photographs to books.

# Chinatown/Gallery Place Attractions

| Age Range | Hours | Details on |
|---|---|---|
| Tweens and Teens | Mon.–Sat. 10 A.M.–5 P.M.; Sun. 12 P.M.–5 P.M. (June–Aug.); Mon.–Sat. 10 A.M.–4 P.M.; Sun. 12 P.M.–4 P.M. (rest of year) | Page 210 |
| Teens | Mon.–Fri. 10 A.M.–4 P.M. | Page 212 |
| Tweens and Teens | Sun.–Thurs. 10 A.M.–4 P.M. | Page 212 |
| All Ages | Mon.–Fri. 10 A.M.–5 P.M. Sat./Sun. 2 P.M.–5 P.M. | Page 213 |
| Teens | | Page 214 |
| Teens | | Page 215 |

Ironically, the interior of this Renaissance Revival building, with its pink marble, ornate chandeliers, and grand, sweeping staircase tailor-made for the most elegant of weddings, was originally a Masonic lodge. It's a nice reminder that women not only belong in the halls of Congress; they belong in the halls of museums, too.

In this museum, the only one dedicated to women in the arts (including performing arts, writing, and visual arts), youngsters can have an enriched experience. "Artventure," available at the information desk, is a self-guided tour booklet; it suggests ways to appreciate the art on display, especially for six- to twelve-year-olds. A much wider range of ages will enjoy the "Case for Comparison" box, available at the front desk. Ending with a self-portrait, the characteristics children are encouraged to explore are: how they would describe themselves, what they think they look like, and how they feel about themselves, all directed toward observations of works in the permanent collection. The Education Resource Center, which has developed these projects, also offers others: special family tours and events; educational programs for children, teens, adults, and teachers; and role model workshops for teens. In addition, concerts, theatrical, and dance performances, films, workshops, book signings, and trips are some of the many offerings of this national resource.

## Smart Stuff

**For Teens...** Explore the work of two American women artists, one from the twentieth century and one from an earlier period. What differences can you find in subject matter and style? How do you think the eras in which they lived influenced their work?

The gift shop here is a wonderful place to find something special, and is open every day during museum hours. From postcards to Christmas ornaments and seasonal items of all types to books, costume and fine jewelry, handmade pottery and women-crafted works, stuffed animals and toys, you can spend a long time selecting and collecting. There are books on many of the artists whose work is on exhibit here, for a variety of reading levels.

On the mezzanine level you can partake of edible artistic creations for lunch only (Monday through Friday, 11:30 A.M.-2:30 P.M.; reservations, 202-628-1068). Choose from Greek salad, sandwiches (both hot and cold, with artsy names), full-course hot meals, and desserts, and fortify yourself to move on to your next site.

Additional options include the **Capital City Brewing Company,** at 11th and H Streets, NW (the entrance is in the back of the building), where jukebox music and a family-friendly menu offer welcome in a noisy, spacious atmosphere (11 A.M.–11 P.M. Sunday through Tuesday, and open 'til midnight Thursday through Saturday). Choose from full-course meals like grilled salmon to grilled bratwurst sandwiches, chicken salad, or club sandwiches. Tours of the brewery are sometimes available, too. Phone: 202-628-2222. On the same block, tasty Thai food is another find, at **Haad Thai** (1100 New York Avenue, NW; Monday through Friday 11:30 A.M.–2:30 P.M. and 5–10:30 P.M.; Saturday and Sunday noon–11 P.M.). Here you'll get skewers of vegetables and chicken or meats, crispy appetizers, and all the familiar choices Thai-eaters delight in, in a colorful setting; phone: 202-682-1111.

Metro: Metro Center

1250 New York Avenue at 13th Street, NW

Monday through Saturday 10 A.M.–5 P.M., Sunday noon to
    5 P.M.; closed January 1, Thanksgiving, and December 25.

For information on special exhibits and programs, phone: 202-
    783-7370. Ask to have a copy of "Artventure," a self-guiding
    tour booklet for kids, sent to you in advance of your trip.

Donations

202-783-5000 or 1-800-222-7270

www.nmwa.org

# Willard Inter-Continental Hotel

In a city known more for politics than elegance, here's a place that combines the two. Recognized from the beginning as a spot to see and be seen, the lobby of the Willard was the site where lobbying began. Sam Ward, the brother of Julia Ward Howe, an influential fellow in his own right, was frequently seen in the Willard's lobby with wealthy clients during the mid-1800s. Known as "King of the Lobby," he could be called Washington's first lobbyist.

The Civil War period was a significant time for the Willard Hotel as well as for the country. Sam's sister Julia penned "The Battle Hymn of the Republic" here. The Peace Convention, made up of remnants of the 36th Congress, met here in February 1861, in a vain attempt to avert the Civil War. During the War, both northerners and southerners stayed here, but used separate floors and entrances; however, the American flag always flew over the building.

Staying in what is now the Presidential Suite the night before his inauguration, President Abraham Lincoln was asked by owner Henry Willard if there were anything he needed. Lincoln had forgotten his bedroom slippers, so Willard quickly borrowed a pair from his wife's grandfather, who had the biggest feet in town. In the morning, the slippers were returned with a note of thanks, and they are still a Willard family treasure.

The ornate décor, with its heavy crystal chandeliers, Italian marble, and intricate mosaics, is a twentieth century restoration of early 1900s elegance. Just a peek into the lobby is a step into a bygone age. And you don't have to lobby for anything!

Metro: Metro Center
1401 Pennsylvania Avenue, NW
202-628-9100 or 1-800-327-0200
www.livinghistoryonline.com/Willard.htm

# The Shops at National Place

**For All Ages…** If you're ready for some modern shopping, guess what—there's a mall right here in the midst of it all. Housed in the **National Press Building** and adjoining the **J. W. Marriott Hotel,** the Shops at National Place offer four levels comprising seventy-five shops and various eateries. **Capitol Image** provides those Washington souvenirs you've been searching for; **Alamo Flags** sells flags, flags, flags *and* other souvenirs; **Electronique** has all the latest electronic gadgets; **Best of Times,** just in case you need a watch or clock; **Lids** has hats with college and sports logos; toys can be found at **Curious Kids;** and clothing stores abound.

You have your choice of cuisine at the Food Hall for reasonable prices. Ethnic dishes from China, Japan, and Italy, among others, are tempting. All the old stand-by fast foods are available as well, including pizza, subs, sandwiches, fudge, and ice cream.

**Money-Saving Tip**

Call in advance to get information on special discount meal arrangements for groups. Phone: 202-783-9090

Metro: Metro Center
F Street between 13th and 14th Streets, NW
Open Monday through Saturday 10 A.M.–7 P.M., Sunday
noon to 5 P.M.
202-662-1250

# Ronald Reagan Building and International Trade Center

**For All Ages...** Named for a popular president who wanted to reduce the size of government, this building is second in size only to the Pentagon. Using an acre's worth of glass in its 125-foot-high atrium, this enormous structure showcases sculptures and a variety of artifacts, including a huge hunk of the Berlin Wall, and long hallways of government offices and impressive works of art.

The Reagan Building also houses the **Washington, D.C., Visitor Information Center,** an important first stop on your trip. The 3,200-square-foot center is across the street from the Metro, through the Wilson Plaza entrance to the building. Here's *the* place to go for the latest information on where to stay, eat, or shop, cultural opportunities, and services for tourists, including plenty of souvenirs for sale. All the maps, visitor guides, and interactive information kiosks you could dream of are here, as well as stacks and stacks of brochures. Tired of pushing buttons and collecting papers? Try this: TALK with one of the real and knowledgeable information specialists on hand to help you discover Washington for yourself (you might want to have a notebook handy). In addition to a fine restaurant and cafés, there's a food court in the basement level, with twenty individual vendors serving foods from around the world.

*Trade Is Everybody's Business,* from Close Up Publishing, focuses on the sometimes confusing world of international trade, in a teen-friendly manner.

> Metro: Federal Triangle
> 1300 Pennsylvania Avenue, NW
> Visitors Center open Monday through Saturday 9 A.M.–6
>     P.M., Sunday noon to 5 P.M.
> Visitors Center: 202-DCVISIT

# ★Pavilion at the Old Post Office

**For All Ages...** It's worth stopping by the Pavilion at the Old Post Office for two sights. One is the terrific architecture of this beautifully preserved Washington landmark; the other is the dramatic view from the clock tower's big glass windows. A true time-saver, the lines here are much shorter than at the Washington Monument, and the size of the windows is a whole lot bigger. Come one, come all. Another treat, on your way up, is a tour of the **Congress Bells,** which were a gift from England in honor of the U.S. bicentennial. The **Washington Ringing Society** holds practice rings on Thursday evenings between 6:30 and 9:30 P.M. (during which time the tower is closed). If you're lucky enough to be in town at the opening of Congress or a national holiday, you will hear a phenomenal one-and-a-half-hour "full peal."

There's a reason this is called the Pavilion *at the Old Post Office,* and we bet you can guess it. Built in 1899 as the country's postal headquarters, and repeatedly scheduled for demolition in the late twentieth century, this Romanesque jewel was rescued by concerned citizens who formed a campaign called "Don't Tear It Down." Well, they didn't, and you should see it. The stunning interior space of the building, ten stories high with a glass ceiling (here it's okay!) houses a food court and an assortment of shops, in addition to TICKETplace, Washington's only discount outlet for day-of-show theater tickets. (Details in Appendix I.)

And the Pavilion hosts entertainment almost every day—take your chances as to what you'll find. High school and college groups often provide concerts, as do other musicians. Or you might find clowns, jugglers, dancers, or other creative performers, generally at lunchtime but sometimes around 5 P.M. as well.

Except for its attraction to tour busloads of visitors, the Pavilion is a convenient and inexpensive place to grab a delicious lunch or quick snack. Ranging from spicy chicken wings to ice cream, there's a huge variety to choose from, including sandwiches and some ethnic foods, Indian and Asian among them. (Summer hours: Monday through Saturday 10 A.M.–9 P.M., Sunday noon to 8 P.M.; winter hours: Monday through Saturday 10 A.M.–8 P.M., Sunday noon to 7 P.M.)

Metro: Federal Triangle
1100 Pennsylvania Avenue, NW
Tower tour hours: summer 8 A.M.–10:45 P.M.; winter
    10 A.M.–5:45 P.M.
National Park Service guides take tours up every 5–7 minutes;
    meet a guide in the lower lobby near the 12th Street en-
    trance or catch the glass elevator at the patio area in the
    Food Court; elevator holds ten at a time.
Closed major holidays
202-289-4224 or 202-606-8691 for clock tower information

# ★National Archives

**For Tweens and Teens...** Talk about a firm foundation, this neoclassical building surrounded by seventy-two Corinthian columns, and topped with a sculpted pediment, rests on 8,500 pilings; it was built on an old creek bed that ran through the city—and certainly this is *not* the place to have water in the basement! At the building's Constitution Avenue entrance are two massive bronze doors, weighing six-and-a-half tons apiece. In its rotunda, you can see the three major documents on which the U.S. government was founded: the Declaration of Independence, the Constitution, and the Bill of Rights. Speaking of a democratic heritage, one of only four remaining copies of the Magna Carta

*The Declaration of Independence at the National Archives*

of 1297 (purchased and donated by one of democracy's most colorful participants, H. Ross Perot), shows how it all began. Just how important these are is reflected in their living quarters; by day their helium-filled bronze-and-glass cases are protected by armed guards, and by night they do a disappearing act—they sink slowly into an underground vault, reinforced against theft, fire, and even nuclear attack.

Not just a museum, the Archives is a working center for genealogical research. You can even investigate your own heritage here; author Alex Haley found his "roots" in the Archives and enriched us all. Ask a staff member how to get details on researching your family's past.

## Smart Stuff

**For Tweens and Teens...** Instead of just going about the business of waging a revolution, the Continental Congress decided to have a written Declaration of Independence. Why do you think they felt the need for such a document?

Custodian of our democracy's valuables, the Archives building contains the collection of only two to five percent of our government's documents; billions of pieces of paper have to be sorted through each year, to select what is to be preserved. The collection includes maps, charts, passport applications, naturalization papers, ship manifests, photographs, immigrant passenger lists, reels of movie film, and some particularly interesting audiotape cassettes (one with an eighteen-and-a-half-minute gap) from the Watergate era. Also included are some surprises, which you will see if you take the tour: President Kennedy's doodles during the Cuban Missile Crisis, a photo of Elvis Presley with President Richard Nixon, and a display of unlabeled presidential baby photos.

**Smart Stuff**

For Teens... The United States is one of the very few countries in the world to have a *written* constitution. Why do you think our founding fathers considered this necessary? What's your opinion?

Want to go to the movies? A small theater in the building shows free films several days a week (call for details); these may include documentaries, archival material, TV kinescopes, and even feature films. You can tour the gift shop without reservations, and take home replicas of historic documents, campaign buttons, and books about genealogy. Phone: 202-501-5235.

Books that might be of interest are: *Johnny Tremain,* by Esther Forbes (tweens/teens), which is also a movie; *All the President's Men,* by Bob Woodward and Carl Bernstein (teens/adults)—and this one, of course, is a movie as

**Smart Stuff**

For Tweens and Teens... Which famous Revolutionary War figure had a son who was a Tory? (A.)

well. *The U.S. Constitution and Fascinating Facts About It,* by Terry L. Jordan, is fun for tweens and teens; *The American Reader: Words That Moved a Nation,* by Diane Ravitch, Ed. is for teens. *U.S. History Through the Eyes of Everyday People* (teens); *Words of Ages: Witnessing U.S. History Through Literature* (teens); *The First Amendment: America's Blueprint for Tolerance* (teens); and *The Bill of Rights: A User's Guide, 3rd Ed.* (teens) are all by Close Up Publishing. At least browse for awhile through *The Powers that Be,* by David

Halberstam (teens). The film *Yankee Doodle Dandy* (tweens and teens) will please everyone, with James Cagney in his Oscar-winning performance; *The Hunt for Red October* (tweens/teens) is an exciting adventure about the cold war; and *Manhattan Project* (teens) explores the moral dilemma of using nuclear weapons. Close Up Publishing offers a series of videos: *Ordinary Americans: The Collection,* including *Vietnam, Civil Rights Movement,* and *The Red Scare.* Two additional Close Up videos for teens are: *Profiles of Freedom: A Living Bill of Rights;* and *Democracy and Rights: One Citizen's Challenge.*

Just in case anyone's hungry (breakfast? lunch? snack?), across the street (diagonally) is the *Dutch Mill Deli,* 639 Indiana Avenue, NW (Monday through Friday 7 A.M.–3 P.M.); phone: 202-347-3665. A big salad bar and a hot buffet bar offer an array of choices; there are plenty of deli sandwich choices, thick fries, soups, and desserts; even pancakes and waffles are available for breakfast.

Metro: Archives-Navy Memorial
Constitution Avenue at 8th Street, NW
Fall/winter 10 A.M.–5:30 P.M.; Spring/summer 10 A.M.–9 P.M.;
    closed December 25. Beginning July 2001, closed for two
    years for renovations; call to check.
Children under 16 must be with an adult.
Behind-the-scenes tours weekdays 10:15 A.M. and 1:15 P.M.,
    1½ hours
Call 9 A.M.–4 P.M. to reserve tour space four weeks in advance;
    202-501-5205
Researchers, make an appointment with an archivist: 202-501-5400
Visitors must pass through x-ray security to enter.
202-501-5000 or 202-501-5402 for research information

# U.S. Navy Memorial and Naval Heritage Center

**For Tweens and Teens...** Even if you get seasick in the bathtub, you will appreciate the beautiful cascading fountains and naval flags that adorn the U.S. Navy Memorial (across Pennsylvania Avenue from the National Archives). Sculptor Stanley Bleifeld's statue, *The Lone Sailor* (note: photo op here), and an engraving of the Navy Hymn complete the atmosphere conducive to patriotism, meditation, rest, and picnicking. Representing all who have served in the U.S. Navy, the sailor watches over fountains and waterfalls (which contain water from the seven seas) and the world's largest stone map of the earth. Summertime weekly concerts by the U.S. Navy band and drill exercises by the U.S. Navy Ceremonial Guard entertain evening visitors; spring lunchtime concerts by various high school and college choral and instrumental groups might especially appeal to kids who are themselves members of musical groups.

Nearly hidden on the northeast corner of the Memorial plaza is the **Naval Heritage Center,** which, like the hold of a ship, is mostly "below deck" (underground). With or without saltwater in your veins, you'll find something of interest. *The Homecoming,* another of Bleifeld's evocative sculptures, greets you at the entrance. Through

## Smart Stuff

**For Tweens and Teens...**
Six U.S. presidents served in the navy; two of them held the post of assistant secretary of the navy. Can you name all of them? (Hint: the two navy assistant secretaries had the same last name.) (B.)

interactive videos, you can learn about naval history, ships, and aircraft. In the Navy Memorial Log, check out people you know who have served in the navy, and if they are not registered, ask for an enrollment form. Two hundred years of naval history are etched into thirteen glass panels on the Wave Wall. On display are paintings and portraits from the Navy Art Collection to the Presidents' Room (with portraits of presidents who served in the navy). The 70 mm surroundsound movie *At Sea* is shown several times a day; and a live tribute, *American Anthem,* is also offered at selected times.

The Ship's Store offers nautical merchandise not found at most other D.C. sites. As for books and movies to take a look at before or after your visit, check out: *A Boy's Will,* by Erik Christian

Haugaard and Troy Howell (tweens); *John Paul Jones: Hero of the Seas,* by Keith Brandt (tweens and teens); and *John Paul Jones: A Sailor's Biography* (Bluejacket Books), by Samuel Eliot Morison (teens). We suggest watching *Mutiny on the Bounty* (tweens and teens) and *Mr. Roberts* (teens).

> Metro: Archives-Navy Memorial
> 701 Pennsylvania Avenue, NW
> Daily 24 hours; Naval Heritage Center open Monday
> through Saturday 9:30 A.M.–5 P.M. March through
> October; Tuesday through Saturday 9:30 A.M.–5 P.M.,
> rest of year. Closed January 1, Thanksgiving, and
> December 25.
> Concert schedule, phone 202-433-4011 or 202-737-2300,
> ext. 711
> *At Sea* times vary; call for details. Fee, except for military
> with ID.
> For *American Anthem* reservations, phone 1-800-777-2238;
> fee discounted with student ID.
> 202-737-2300, ext. 733 or 1-800-821-8892

With the lone exception of Thomas Jefferson, no other American citizen has so exemplified the extraordinary potential of man as **Benjamin Franklin** (whose **statue** stands at Pennsylvania Avenue and 10th Street, NW). A skillful statesman, scientist, journalist, and inventor, Franklin lent his ingenuity to so much that touched his eighteenth century countrymen. His founding of the first lending library and the first volunteer fire department, as well as his invention of the lightning rod, have enriched life in subsequent centuries. In years when contemporaries were either retired or deceased, he labored here and abroad as one of America's founding fathers. It is interesting that this statue, portraying him dressed in his finest, as minister to France, is merely entitled, "Printer." This memorial was the gift of Stilson Hutchins, somewhat of a newspaperman himself. He founded the *Washington Post.* The statue's location, upon its unveiling in 1889, placed it directly in front of the old *Post* building.

# ★FBI (Federal Bureau of Investigation) Building

**For Tweens and Teens...** Some people think it was a crime to spend $126 million to build the concrete bunker known as the J. Edgar Hoover FBI Building. But kids (over seven) *love* to visit here. Loads of guns, of course, objects of all kinds that hide secrets (weapons or microfilm), and posters of the Ten Most Wanted Criminals (hope you don't recognize anyone! But two bad guys *were* caught because visitors had seen their pictures here) are among the high points of the hour-long tour.

Kids can also watch laboratory technicians examine bloodstains or fingerprints and see the forfeiture unit where jewelry, furs, artwork, silverware, and firearms are recovered from drug or tax evasion cases. You can hear stories of famous criminals, watch a safety film made by Bill Cosby, and watch the U.S. Crime Clock as it records the violent crimes taking place in this country. The exciting finale is the shooting of a paper "bad guy" by a real FBI agent with a submachine gun. (Write to the FBI to request one of these free paper targets. Kids need to know they are *not* to try such an exercise at home, however.)

## Smart Stuff

**For Tweens...** If we have police in our home cities and state troopers in our states, what kinds of crimes are tackled by the FBI? (C.)

## Parents/Teachers Take Note

**For Teens...** Many law-abiding Americans have FBI files, where personal information about them is stored. What do you think of this practice? One classroom exercise might be to divide the group into *pro* and *con* groups and have them research, write, and/or present oral arguments on this subject. Perhaps an audience of social studies or U.S. history students from another grade could judge the results.

## Smart Stuff

**For Tweens and Teens...** Which of the following can FBI laboratories do?

1. Detect forged handwriting.
2. Reconstruct the model and make of a car from just a paint chip.
3. Discern whether a single hair came from an animal or human, man or woman, and determine the individual's race as well. (D.)

We came across a spy game that might be fun to try: *Spy Alley.* It's an award-winning strategy game of suspense and intrigue, for tweens and teens. Margaret Truman's mystery books about various Washington sites and scenes would be fun for teens to read.

Just in case anybody is hungry right at this very moment, lucky you. Right across Pennsylvania Avenue are both **McDonald's** and **Wendy's.** Need we say more?

> Metro: Metro Center or Federal Triangle
> 935 Pennsylvania Avenue, NW (enter on E Street)
> Tours only; Monday through Friday 8:45 A.M.–4:15 P.M., one hour long; closed holidays. At busy times, lines form by 7:30 A.M. Between April and August, arrange for tickets ahead of time; call the tour office. Better yet, contact your senator or representative three to four months in advance for time-specific VIP tickets.
> 202-324-3447

# ★Ford's Theater National Historic Site and Petersen House

**For Tweens and Teens...** The site of one of our country's best-known tragedies, Ford's Theater has undergone numerous disasters. Originally a church, it burned to the ground in 1862, shortly after

*The Presidential Box at Ford's Theater*

it was turned into a theater; some claimed that the site was cursed by having a theater built on it. Its owner, John Ford, rebuilt it as a larger theater, opening in August 1863.

Prior to the fateful night, Lincoln had seen a number of plays here, one of which starred the famous actor, John Wilkes Booth.

Lincoln's assassination took place on April 14, 1865. After that, everyone opposed re-opening the building as a theater, and in 1866, it was purchased by the government and used as an army medical museum. Among other oddities on exhibit was Lincoln's assassin John Wilkes Booth's spinal column, with its bullet hole. On July 9, 1893, several floors of the deteriorated building caved in, killing twenty-two government workers and wounding over a hundred. It wasn't until the 1960s that the building was restored by the National Park Service as a working theater. The photographs by Matthew Brady, taken just after Lincoln's assassination, were used to ensure authenticity. Presidents since that time have always attended the theater here, but no one sits in the Presidential Box.

**For Tweens...** Be sure to ask for the Junior Ranger booklet, with its scavenger hunt for specific Lincoln memorabilia such as the pistol used in the assassination and clothing he wore. It also contains activities and games. When a child completes the booklet, he is awarded a Junior Ranger badge.

## Smart Stuff

**For Tweens...** If you had been in charge of President Lincoln's Secret Service detail, what provisions would you have made for his safety?

In the basement of the building is the **Ford's Theater Museum.** Depicting the assassination, exhibits here include the gun used by John Wilkes Booth to kill Abraham Lincoln.

## Smart Stuff

**For Teens...** If Abraham Lincoln had survived the assassination attempt, what do you think might have been different afterward? (E).

In the general wealth of materials about Abraham Lincoln, there are books specifically about the assassination. Several we can suggest are: *Back to the Day Lincoln Was Shot!,* by Beatrice Gormley (tweens); *The Day Lincoln Was Shot,* by Jim Bishop (teens); and *Mary Suratt: An American Tragedy,* by Elizabeth Steger Trendal (teens). Of course, there are classic Civil War movies to enjoy: *Friendly Persuasion* (tweens and teens); *Shenandoah* (teens); and *Gone with the Wind* (teens).

And across the street, there's good food at the **Star Saloon,** 518 10th Street, NW (Monday through Friday 11:30 A.M.–10 P.M., Saturday 5 P.M.–10 P.M.); phone: 202-347-6333. Hot and cold traditional American choices include hamburgers, barbecued pork, noodles with sauces, and fancy homemade desserts. You might need a reservation, so check first.

Metro: Metro Center
511 10th Street, NW
Daily 9 A.M.–5 P.M.; closed December 25
Theatrical performances Tuesday through Sunday 7:30 P.M.,
    Thursday at 1 P.M., and Saturday and Sunday 2:30 P.M.
    Further information in Appendix I.
202-347-4833
www.nps.gov/foth/index2.htm

# Smithsonian American Art Museum and National Portrait Gallery

**For All Ages...** Before this elegant Greek Revival building was completed in 1867, it was the home of the Patent Office, and had as its top floor the largest room in America—the setting for a raucous party celebrating Lincoln's second inauguration. Part of the Smithsonian Institution, the building is

**Helpful Hint**

Both museums are slated for face-lifts for several years, beginning January 2000, so if they are on your itinerary, call to find out their reopening dates.

divided into two art museums; it houses the world's largest collection of American art (and no wild parties that we know of) on one side, and a selection of portraiture from the staid to the outrageous on the other.

A big hit with kids is the fiberglass and epoxy cowboy on bucking bronco guarding the front of the **Smithsonian American Art Museum.** You can tell them that this is definitely a place for "cowboys and Indians," since inside are portraits of American Indians that would make Jean Jacques Rousseau proud. There is a wide variety of work to see, from the familiar paintings of Winslow Homer to the sparkling piece by James Hampton titled *Throne of the Third Heaven*, giving kids a

**Smart Stuff**

**For Tweens and Teens...**
From the depictions of Native Americans you see, what do you think the artists thought of this ethnic group? How can you tell? Do you think their attitudes were common at the time?

new appreciation for aluminum foil. The 37,500 works of art should have something to appeal to every age.

## Smart Stuff

For Tikes... How about making a collage? After looking at James Hampton's *Throne of the Third Heaven*, made from aluminum foil, younger kids might begin to think about what other materials could be used for art. An enjoyable home or school art project could be assembling a collage from objects collected during their Washington, D.C., trip (string, wrappers, paper cups, safety pins, ticket stubs, etc.).

The **Saturday Art Stop** is a once-a-month program stressing creative art experiences, designed for six- to twelve-year-olds. This is a worthwhile program to look into when the museum reopens.

Metro: Gallery Place-Chinatown
Smithsonian American Art Museum: 8th and G Streets, NW
Daily 10 A.M.–5:30 P.M.; closed December 25. Beginning
    January 2000, closed for three years for renovations; call
    to check.
Group tours; call for details.
202-357-2700
www.americanart.si.edu

**The National Portrait Gallery** (scheduled to reopen in 2004) is the place to see paintings of famous Americans, some as you've never seen them before. Faces to gawk at run from some formal renderings of the founding fathers to all kinds of representations of famous citizens. The likenesses of Babe Ruth, Ernest Hemingway, Davy Crockett, and Helen Keller are all under the same roof. Some interesting highlights are: the diminutive painting of Andrew Jackson sporting one of the first pairs of bifocals; the portrait of Benjamin Franklin that became the model for the $100 bill; and the famed life-size portrait of George Washington by Gilbert Stuart (which will be on tour while the Gallery is being renovated). Also of note are works by the subjects, themselves: the self-portraits of Samuel F. B. Morse (whose likeness truly belongs in this Old Patent Office building), and Billy Dee Williams, whose exuberance is reflected in his art. Perhaps the most incongruous piece portrays the head of the showman P. T. Barnum on the body of a beetle. No comment.

The Calendar of Events is free and published six times a year; you can ask to be on the mailing list and receive notice of events for families (registration is required). Call 202-357-2729.

Around the corner on 7th Street is Chinatown, where you'll find plenty of small ethnic restaurants with noodle dishes, curries, and Szechuan and Cantonese fare. **New Big Wong Restaurant** (610 H Street, NW; open Monday through Sunday, 11 A.M.–11 P.M.; 202-628-0491) is very family-friendly, and offers free delivery if your order is over $10.

There are countless books and films about famous Americans, including *The Story of My Life,* by Helen Keller (tweens and teens); *Edison: Inventing the Century,* by Neil Baldwin (teens); and the movies *Edison: The Man* (tweens and teens); and *The Story of Alexander Graham Bell* (tweens and teens).

## Smart Stuff

**For Tikes...** After seeing a man's head on an insect's body, can you think of strange combinations that would be interesting or funny? Did you ever see a picture of a mermaid or a minotaur?

Metro: Gallery Place-Chinatown
National Portrait Gallery: 8th and F Streets, NW
Daily 10 A.M.–5:30 P.M.; closed December 25; closed January 2000 for several years of renovations; call for reopening schedule.
Guided tours; call for details
202-357-2700
www.Americanart.si.edu

You can take your cloak, but not your dagger, to the brand new **International Spy Museum Complex** (800 F Street, NW), slated to open in the spring of 2002.

Celebrating the art and craft of spying, this museum will house a fascinating collection of artifacts and information about espionage and some activities that help visitors become imaginary participants in this mysterious enterprise. The complex will include a museum, a full-service restaurant, a café, and a gift shop, where shoppers can indulge their fantasies of living the life of Agent 007. The password is "FUN." Phone: 202-393-7798.

# The Chinatown Friendship Archway

Designating the formal entrance to the District's Chinatown, bordered by 6th, 7th, H, and I Streets, NW, is the Chinatown Friendship Archway. You won't want to miss seeing it. Hundreds of dragons in the Ming and Kuing dynasty styles decorate the lavish structure, one of the world's largest single-span archways. The parade for the Chinese New Year, in January, passes under this arch. The mayors of both the District of Columbia and Beijing, China, were present at its dedication in 1986. In this neighborhood, also, are now a huge Convention Center (soon to be joined by a second one) as well as the MCI Center (more about these in Appendix I). This is a colorful area for delicious food and interesting souvenirs; explore it during the day. One restaurant you might like to try is very plain but has excellent Chinese food: **Full Kee,** at 509 H Street, NW (Sunday through Thursday 11 A.M.–1 A.M., Friday and Saturday 11 A.M.–3 A.M.); 202-371-2233.

# National Law Enforcement Officers Memorial

**For All Ages...** A very different kind of memorial to fallen heroes commemorates those who have died on our nation's streets, in cities and small towns, protecting us here at home. In a beautifully landscaped setting, the National Law Enforcement Officers Memorial enshrines the names of officers killed in the line of duty from 1794 until the present. If you're planning a visit in May, you might want to attend the annual candlelight vigil (during National Police Week), when new names of fallen officers are added to the memorial wall. Names have been inscribed in a random order, but directories are available nearby. To date, the names of more than 14,500 officers are inscribed on blue-gray marble walls along two tree-lined "pathways of remembrance." A bronze statue of an adult lion protecting its cubs guards each entrance, symbolic of the protection, courage, and strength of law enforcement officers. An inscription on the east wall cites the memorial's motto: "In valor there is hope."

Less than two blocks away is the Visitors Center and Museum, with an interactive video system that highlights biographical information and photographs about each officer, along with the location of their names on the memorial wall. Additional photographs and historic exhibits line the walls. The museum educators here have done an exceptional job preparing materials for all ages of kids; individual activity books are available for each grade from kindergarten through eighth, and it's a great idea to call and ask for these in advance.

It's always interesting to read about law enforcement officers; try: *My Dog Is Lost,* by Ezra Jack Keats (tikes); *Policeman Small,* by Lois Lenski (tikes); *Angie's First Case,* by Donald J. Sobol (tikes and tweens); and *A Day In the Life of a Police Cadet,* by John H. Martin (tweens). Movies include: *The Great Mouse Detective* (tikes and tweens); and *The Big Sleep* (tweens and teens).

## Helpful Hint

Located in the Visitors Center, the gift shop offers all sorts of commemorative objects with the Memorial's name and logo. T-shirts, of course, as well as hats, flags, patches, posters, books, and even videos are available to purchase and take home as mementos. Part of the money from these purchases helps maintain an endowment for this memorial.

Metro: Judiciary Square
Between E and F Streets and 4th and 5th Streets, NW
Visitors Center and Museum: 605 E Street, NW
Daily 24 hours; Visitor Center Monday through Friday
    9 A.M.–5 P.M., Saturday 10 A.M.–5 P.M., Sunday noon to
    5 P.M.; closed January 1, Thanksgiving, and December 25
Guided tours by appointment.
202-737-3400
www.nleonmf.com/TheMemorial/memdefault.html

# National Building Museum

**For Tweens and Teens...** Originally called "Meigs' Red Barn," this building was for clerks processing military pensions in the 1880s, and even today is often referred to as the Pension Building. Its designer, Army General Montgomery C. Meigs, wanted to provide government workers there with the latest in skylighting, ventilation, and safety. The result is an Italian Renaissance-style edifice that is unique on the outside and breathtaking within.

> Anyone especially interested in architecture and the District's neighborhoods, monuments, and landmark buildings, as well as urban planning, will enjoy this introduction to the city.

Taking up a whole city block, the exterior is dark red brick with a touching terra cotta frieze encircling the building. The work of sculptor Casper Buberl, the frieze depicts the homeward procession of veterans, a humanistic view of war. It is not coincidence that the interior with its vaulted ceiling and eight massive Corinthian columns (brick, but painted to look like marble, a cost-cutting device) has been the site of inaugural balls since Grover Cleveland's in 1885. The unfinished building at that time only lacked a roof, so a tarpaulin was stretched across the top; a result was that canaries released to add to the festivities flew to the top, froze in the frigid air, and fell unceremoniously onto the dance floor below.

Two permanent upstairs exhibits tell about the building itself and about Washington, D.C., its neighborhoods, and its landmark buildings. There are hands-on, large-scale models, as well as interactive games, that provide an appealing introduction to the city. Temporary exhibits, a major Smithsonian crafts fair, and other special programs also make use of the Great Hall's imposing space. Family programs, demonstrations, music, films, and a variety of hands-on experiences introduce children to architecture and construction.

**The Museum Shop** on the ground floor features books on architecture as well as toys, crafts, and graphics. As for snacks and lunch, you can find these at the **Courtyard Café** on weekdays from 9 A.M.– 5 P.M.; choose from bakery items, salads, sandwiches, and drinks.

David Macaulay's wonderful series of books is internationally renowned. Take a look at any one of them: *City, Pyramid, Castle, Cathedral, Unbuilding* (this one deals with the underground systems which support a modern city), and *Mill*. All ages will find these fascinating. Teens would like *Frank Lloyd Wright: A Biography*, by Meryle Secrest.

Metro: Judiciary Square

401 F Street, NW

Open Monday through Saturday, 10 A.M.–5 P.M., Sunday noon
to 5 P.M., June through August; Monday through Saturday
and holidays 10 A.M.–4 P.M., Sunday noon to 4 P.M., rest of
the year. Closed January 1, Thanksgiving, and December 25.

Activity booklets available for purchase.

Guided tours (one hour) Thursday through Saturday
11:30 A.M., 12:30 P.M., and 1:30 P.M.; Sunday 12:30 and
1:30 P.M.; Monday through Wednesday 12:30 P.M. Short
Saturday programs offer opportunities to explore basic
structural principles along with building tools and materials. The museum's monthly calendar lists hands-on educational activities appropriate for the whole family.

Call in advance for details on special events or to receive the
monthly calendar.

Donation

202-272-2448

# Lillian and Albert Small Jewish Museum (Jewish Historical Society)

**For Teens...** Dedicated in 1876 as the original Adas Israel Synagogue, this is the oldest synagogue building in Washington, D.C.; the Jewish Historical Society now operates the Lillian and Albert Small Museum here. It includes a restored sanctuary and a permanent exhibit on Washington's Jewish community, as well as changing temporary exhibits.

> Metro: Judiciary Square or Gallery Place/Chinatown
> 701 3rd Street, NW, at G Street
> Sunday through Thursday 10 A.M.–4 P.M.; closed holidays.
> Guided tours by appointment.
> Donations
> 202-789-0900

In the middle of Gompers Square (really a little trapezoid of land on Massachusetts Avenue at 10th Street, NW), stands a **memorial** to an English cigar maker. **Samuel Gompers** immigrated to New York City in 1863, at age 13, and within a year of landing a job as a cigar-maker, formed the Cigar-Maker's International Union. In 1896, he organized the American Federation of Labor (AFL) and was its president until his death in 1924. He was a strong believer in collective bargaining and a diligent proponent of labor and antitrust laws. The U.S. Department of Labor owes its existence, in part, to his influence. President Franklin Roosevelt, a friend to American workers, was present at the statue's dedication in 1933. Behind the seated Gompers are figures representing industrial exploitation, the unity of unions, justice, and home. The base is inscribed with his writings. Youngsters whose parents work in a "union shop" know the value of his legacy.

# Mary McLeod Bethune Council House National Historic Site

**For Tweens and Teens...** Also in this part of the city, you can visit the former home of educator Mary McLeod Bethune, founder of the National Council of Negro Women. The little girl, the fifteenth of seventeen children, had to walk ten miles each way to school, and grew up to found Bethune-Cookman College (Dayton, Florida), the first African American women's college in the U.S. The first black woman to become a presidential advisor, Bethune was head of Negro Affairs of the National Youth Administration, appointed to this position by President Franklin D. Roosevelt. Bethune's Victorian townhouse, now a museum and archives, contains the largest collection of original documents chronicling the achievements of African American women in the United States. Through videos, lectures, art exhibits, concerts, and workshops here, visitors can learn about the remarkable achievements of contemporary African American women.

> Metro: McPherson Square and walk northeast on Vermont Avenue, NW
>
> 1318 Vermont Avenue, NW
>
> Open Monday through Friday 10 A.M.–4 P.M.; tours (fee) on weekends; also, films, concerts, workshops (call for schedule)
>
> Call to arrange for group tours of ten or more.
>
> 202-332-1233 or 202-673-2402

# African American Civil War Memorial

**For All Ages...** A new memorial commemorating the more than 209,000 African American soldiers who fought in the Civil War is located right at the U Street-Cardozo Metro station, between Howard University Hospital and the Lincoln Theatre. At its center is an eleven-foot-tall bronze statue, "The Spirit of Freedom," with armed black soldiers. Names of all African American Civil War troops are etched into plates of gray steel encircling the rose garden that frames the statue. The Museum and Visitors Center provides computers linking visitors to Internet sites where they can find further information on the soldiers. War medals, photographs, documents, and paintings are included in exhibits throughout the museum.

This section of the District is called the Shaw neighborhood, honoring Robert Gould Shaw. He was the white colonel of the first African American regiment to fight in the Civil War, the Fifty-fourth Regiment featured in the film *Glory*.

So many books have been written about the Civil War period. For tikes, start with *Follow the Drinking Gourd*, by Jeanette Winter (this one is also an animated movie, read by Morgan Freeman), and *Sweet Clara and the Freedom Quilt*, by Deborah Hopkinson, also for tweens. A few other suggestions for interesting reading include: *Dear Austin: Letters from the Underground Railroad*, by Elvira Woodruff (tweens), *The Last Safe House: A Story of the Underground Railroad*, by Barbara Greenwood (tweens), and *A Different Kind of Christmas*, by Alex Haley (teens/adults). A wonderful movie about part of the African American experience in the Civil War is *Glory!* (tweens and teens)—the story of a heroic black regiment in a fateful battle. The History Channel presented *Underground Railroad*, an interesting historic account now available on video. *A House Divided* (teens) is a Ken Burns PBS film.

Metro: U Street-Cardozo (Vermont Street exit)
1000 U Street, NW
Open Monday through Friday 10 A.M.–5 P.M., Saturday
    through Sunday 2–5 P.M.
Tours by appointment.
202-667-2667
www.afroamcivilwarmemorial.org

# Howard University

**For Teens...** If you're traveling with high school students, some may want to take a brief side trip in this part of the city to see this famous university. A video presentation, campus tours, and a question-answer session are available; call ahead.

Historically one of the nation's most prestigious black universities, Howard was founded in 1867 to educate newly freed slaves. It was named for General Oliver Otis Howard, who headed the Freedmen's Bureau after the Civil War. The large majority of students here are African American; famous graduates include the late Supreme Court Justice Thurgood Marshall; New York's former mayor, David Dinkins; former Atlanta mayor, Andrew Young; the late Patricia Roberts Harris, Secretary of the U.S. Department of Health and Human Services; and novelist, Toni Morrison. Parts of the university library are open to the public; the Moorland-Spingarn Research center has the largest collection of black literature in the country. On one of the capital's highest elevations, Howard offers great views of the city. **Howard University Hospital** is at 2041 Georgia Avenue, NW (202-865-1471), and houses the **Freedmen's Hall Gallery of Art.** In addition to describing the hospital's history, the gallery is a permanent educational and cultural site that provides visitors with an opportunity to explore African American contributions to medicine, health care, and research.

> Metro: Shaw-Howard Univ. and walk north along 7th Street, NW (becomes Georgia Avenue). Don't walk alone here or at night unless you're with a group.
> 2400 6th Street, NW
> 1-800-822-6363 or 202-806-6100
> www.howard.edu/

# Lincoln Theater

**For Teens...** Cab Calloway, Louis Armstrong, Duke Ellington, Count Basie, Ella Fitzgerald, Billie Holiday, and Pearl Bailey were among the black stars who performed here in earlier days. Built in 1920, the Lincoln offered movies, vaudeville, and nightclub acts, and was the first D.C. theater to accept an integrated audience. It closed in the 1970s, but reopened in 1994, restored to its former Georgian Revival elegance. Today, it features special events like the D.C. Film Festival, along with jazz, gospel, comedy, and pop shows. (See Appendix I for details.)

The theater is in the "U Street Corridor," an area significant in the African American renaissance of art, music, and entertainment in Washington. Nightclubs and bars come alive here in the evening. Careful in this area after dark; come with a group.

Metro: U Street-Cardozo
1215 U Street, NW
202-328-6000

# Where to Stay in the Chinatown/ Gallery Place Area

While filled with tourist attractions, this area is limited in its accommodations. It turns out to be a better place to explore in the daytime anyway. We do have a few places you can look into. Be sure to look these specific locations up on your trusty Washington map before you make reservations.

### Red Roof Inn
500 H Street, NW
202-289-5959 or 1-800-843-7663
Metro: Gallery Place-Chinatown

### Hotel Harrington
436 11th Street, NW (at E Street)
202-628-8140 or 1-800-424-8532
Metro: Metro Center

### Grand Hyatt Washington
1000 H Street, NW
202-582-1234 or 1-800-233-1234
Metro: Metro Center

# Answers to Smart Stuff Questions

**A.** Benjamin Franklin's oldest son was the Royal Governor of New Jersey, and, given the circumstances, found it prudent to leave the country.

**B.** Franklin D. Roosevelt, John F. Kennedy, Richard Nixon, Gerald Ford, Jimmy Carter, and George Bush were all in the navy. Theodore Roosevelt and Franklin D. Roosevelt each served as Assistant Secretary of the Navy.

**C.** The FBI handles crimes that cross state lines and crimes that are committed against the United States itself.

**D.** The FBI can do all of the above!

**E.** It might be instructive to do some reading on the Reconstruction Period and the impeachment of Andrew Johnson (especially since our country has recently lived through another such trial). Terms like "carpetbagger" and "Jim Crow laws" are tied to the aftermath of the Civil War and Lincoln's death.

CHAPTER

9

Uptown

**N**ot all the heavy-duty sites are in the city's center. The area known as "upper Northwest" (Uptown) is well worth exploring. From high culture to wildlife, treasures of Czarist Russia to cuddly looking pandas, from an Amazon rain forest to the world's sixth-largest cathedral, Uptown abounds with variety. Just eat breakfast before you come, because you'll have to look hard to find restaurants near these sites.

## ★National Zoological Park

**For All Ages...** If you reside in this 163-acre park (along with about 4,999 other animals), it's okay to act wild. (Inhabitants of other notable D.C. locations don't have the same excuse.) Because of the vastness of this Smithsonian Institution site, it's a good idea to visit the National Zoo at a time of day when you have lots of energy and with a workable "battle plan." There are walking tour maps and animal feeding schedules available at the Visitor Center, near the Connecticut Avenue entrance, and there are clear signs in many strategic spots along the way. For the most enjoyable visit, try to narrow your choices to a few specific areas; you won't feel rushed or exhausted afterward, and you will still have covered a lot of ground. *This* is one of the days when you'll need the most comfortable shoes you have ever worn.

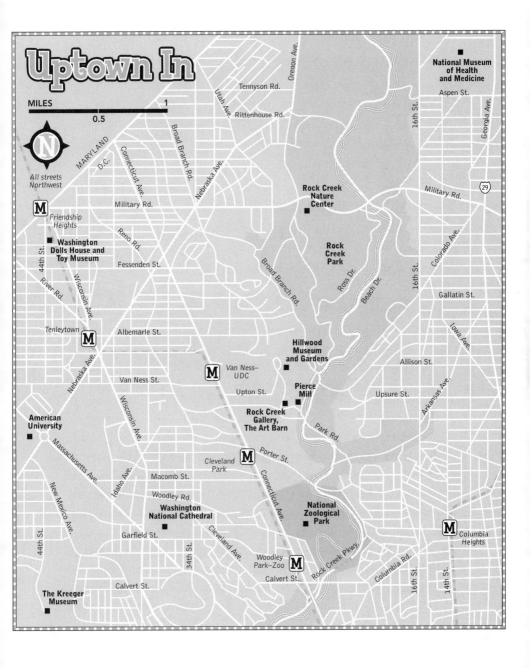

Uptown In

MILES
0.5    1

N

All streets
Northwest

Oregon Ave.

Tennyson Rd.

Utah Ave.
Rittenhouse Rd.

16th St.

Georgia Ave.

National Museum
of Health
and Medicine

Aspen St.

MARYLAND
D.C.

Broad Branch Rd.

Nebraska Ave.

Connecticut Ave.

Rock Creek
Nature
Center

Military Rd.

29

M Friendship
Heights

Military Rd.

Reno Rd.

Rock
Creek
Park

Ross Dr.

Beach Dr.

16th St.

Colorado Ave.

Washington
Dolls House and
Toy Museum

44th St.

Fessenden St.

Wisconsin Ave.

River Rd.

Gallatin St.

Tenleytown M

Albemarle St.

Nebraska Ave.

Hillwood
Museum
and Gardens

Allison St.

Iowa Ave.

Van Ness–
UDC

Van Ness St.

Upton St.

Pierce
Mill

Upsure St.

Arkansas Ave.

Wisconsin Ave.

American
University

Massachusetts Ave.

Idaho Ave.

Rock Creek
Gallery,
The Art Barn

Park Rd.

New Mexico Ave.

Cleveland
Park

Porter St.

Macomb St.

Woodley Rd.

Connecticut Ave.

Washington
National Cathedral

National
Zoological
Park

M Columbia
Heights

44th St.

Garfield St.

34th St.

Cleveland Ave.

Woodley
Park–Zoo M

Calvert St.

Rock Creek Pkwy.

Columbia Rd.

16th St.

14th St.

The Kreeger
Museum

Calvert St.

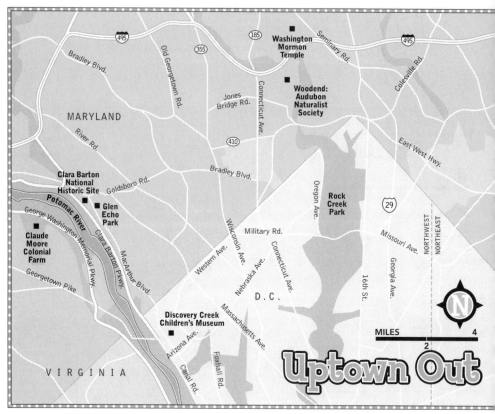

One group *not* in need of shoes is the orangutans, making their way on an overhead line from their habitat to the "Think Tank," where they play with computers. To see the "real thing," they can visit the soaring, net-covered aviary and the state-of-the-art Amazonia rain-forest ecosystem, or watch the graceful sea lions play, through an underwater window. Speaking of going beneath the surface, the zoo's bat cave—complete with bats—is an eerie favorite with youngsters. They may squeal, but they stay glued to their places, watching these dark and mysterious creatures. From the mischievous, barking prairie dogs in an exhibit close enough for animals and humans to become quite friendly *(don't!)* to the lumbering majesty of the huge Kodiak bears (imagine *their* summers in the capital's heat), there is literally a site to fit everyone's fancy. And now that the U.S. government has made a $10,000,000 rental arrangement with the government of China, there

*Looking for a "group rate" at the National Zoo*

are again delightful pandas (Mei Xiang and Tian Tian) to ooh and aah over in their own custom-designed quarters.

If all that oohing and aahing has made your gang ravenous, the zoo does have remedies. In addition to the ice cream stands and snack bars scattered throughout the grounds, the zoo has two restaurants: the fast-food-oriented **Panda Café** (guess where you can find it) and, down the hill a bit, the larger **Mane Restaurant.** The grounds are also a beautiful place for picnicking, and the only animals you'll find in those grassy areas will be the small buzzing, crawling, or flying ones (you know, the usual picnic "guests.") Keep your drinks covered in warm weather unless one of your group is an entomologist-in-training.

During the summer, there are free sunset serenade concerts on Thursday evenings on **Lion/Tiger Hill,** with a wide range of musical selections; bring supper. Fortunately

## Smart Stuff

**For Tweens and Teens...** After a visit to the Amazonia exhibit, talk about ecosystems and why their balance is so fragile. What are some ramifications of deforestation in places like the Amazon (in Brazil)? (A.)

## Smart Stuff

**For Tikes...** Since Batman has already been invented, what animal would you use to create a super hero? Draw a picture of your creation.

# Quick Guide to

| Attraction | Location |
|---|---|
| ★National Zoological Park | 3000 block of Connecticut Avenue, NW (entrances also on Harvard Street, NW and Beach Drive) |
| ★Washington National Cathedral | Mount St. Alban at Massachusetts and Wisconsin Avenues, NW |
| American University | 4400 Massachusetts Avenue, NW (between Ward and Wesley Circles) |
| Hillwood Museum and Gardens | 4155 Linnean Avenue, NW |
| Rock Creek Nature Center | 5200 Glover Road, NW |
| Pierce Mill | 3545 Williamsburg Lane, NW (at the corner of Tilden Street and Beach Drive, NW) |
| Rock Creek Gallery, The Art Barn | 2401 Tilden Street, NW |
| National Museum of Health and Medicine (Walter Reed Army Medical Center) | 6900 Georgia Avenue, NW (at Elder Street (south end of Building 54)) |
| The Kreeger Museum | 2401 Foxhall Road, NW |
| Glen Echo Park | 7300 MacArthur Blvd, Glen Echo, Maryland |
| Discovery Creek Children's Museum of Washington | 4954 MacArthur Boulevard, NW |
| The Clara Barton National Historic Site | 5801 Oxford Road, Glen Echo, Maryland |
| Woodend: The Audubon Naturalist Society | 8940 Jones Mill Road, Chevy Chase, Maryland |
| The Washington Temple and Visitors Center of the Church of Jesus Christ of Latter-Day Saints | Stoneybrook Drive in Kensington, Maryland, off Beach Drive |
| Washington Dolls House and Toy Museum | 5236 44th Street, NW |

# Uptown Attractions

| Age Range | Hours | Details on |
| --- | --- | --- |
| All Ages | Grounds: 6 A.M.–8 P.M. (May–Sept. 15), 6 A.M.–6 P.M. (rest of year) Buildings: 10 A.M.–6 P.M.(May–Sept. 15), 10 A.M.–4:30 P.M. (rest of year) | Page 220 |
| All Ages | Mon.–Fri. 10 A.M.–9 P.M. (May–Labor Day), 10 A.M.–4:30 P.M. (rest of year) | Page 226 |
| Teens | | Page 230 |
| Teens | Tues.–Sat. 9 A.M.–5 P.M. Some evenings and Sundays | Page 230 |
| All Ages | Wed.–Sun. 9 A.M.–5 P.M. | Page 232 |
| All Ages | Wed.–Sun. 9 A.M.–5 P.M. | Page 234 |
| Tweens and Teens | Thurs.–Sun. 11 A.M.–4:30 P.M. | Page 235 |
| Tweens and Teens | 10 A.M.–5:30 P.M. daily | Page 236 |
| Teens | Tours: Tues.–Sat. 10:30 A.M. and 1:30 P.M. | Page 237 |
| All Ages | Mon.–Thurs. 9 A.M.–5 P.M.; Fri.–Sat. 9 A.M.–12 A.M.; Sun. 9 A.M.–6 P.M. | Page 237 |
| Tikes and Tweens | Sat. 10 A.M.–3 P.M., Sun. 12 P.M.–3 P.M. | Page 239 |
| All Ages | 10 A.M.–5 P.M. daily | Page 240 |
| All Ages | Mon.–Fri. 9 A.M.–5 P.M. Grounds: Dawn to dusk daily | Page 241 |
| All Ages | 10 A.M.–9 P.M. daily | Page 242 |
| All Ages | Tues.–Sat. 10 A.M.–5 P.M. Sun. 12 P.M.–5 P.M. | Page 243 |

**Smart Stuff**

**For Tikes...** The National Zoo is the proud home of two pandas. What is the only country where they can be found in the wild?

(B.)

for the kids, and unfortunately for you, well- marked gift shops are scattered throughout the zoo grounds. Here you can stock up on yet another stuffed animal, postcards, key chains, posters, and all the souvenir items you need to fill up the teensy empty space you thought you had in your suitcase. **The National Zoo Bookstore** is located in the **Education Building** (across from 3001 Connecticut Avenue); phone 202-673-4967. A whole range of selections is available here, from picture books for the youngest readers to research-level works on conservation and animal behavior.

Metro: Woodley Park–Zoo

Connecticut Avenue bus lines L2 and L4 stop at the zoo's main entrance

3000 block of Connecticut Avenue, NW (entrances also on Harvard Street, NW and Beach Drive)

Grounds open daily 6 A.M.–8 P.M., and buildings 10 A.M.– 6 P.M., May 1 through September 15; grounds 6 A.M.– 6 P.M. and buildings 10 A.M.–4:30 P.M. rest of year. Closed December 25.

Guided tour information, 202-673-4954. (These tours not recommended for children under four.) FONZ (Friends of the National Zoo) volunteers conduct tours, weekends only, mid-March to May; 202-673-4956.

202-673-4717

http://Natzoo.si.edu

# ★Washington National Cathedral

**For All Ages...** Though the country professes not to have a national religion, the United States has always used the Cathedral Church of St. Peter and St. Paul (better known as the Washington

*Inside
Washington
National Cathedral*

National Cathedral) for official events. Services for the endings of both World Wars were celebrated here; the funerals of Presidents Wilson and Eisenhower were held in this building; and many famous people have spoken from its pulpit, including the Rev. Martin Luther King Jr., Archbishop Desmond Tutu, and the Dalai Lama. Perhaps one of the most moving moments occurred when Col. Thomas Shaefer, released from captivity as one of the Iranian hostages, greeted the congregation: "Good morning, my fellow Americans. You don't know how long I've been waiting to say those words."

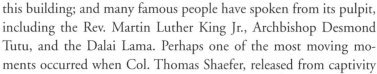

All ages are welcome here. But it is a religious facility, so reminders for quiet behavior are essential. Children under five might find it difficult.

**For All Ages...** As far back as 1701, Pierre L'Enfant had planned for the city to have its own cathedral as a focus for the nation, but as in most federal undertakings, a great of deal of time elapsed before the deed was under way. Taking a mere eighty-three years from President Theodore Roosevelt's laying of the cornerstone until its completion in1990, the "Cathedral," as it is affectionately called in D.C., is a beautiful place to tour. This Gothic style cathedral, the sixth largest in the world (and one of the few in the world to have both heat and air conditioning) is built in the shape of a cross. The building contains no steel

## Smart Stuff

**For Tikes and Tweens...** Look at David Macaulay's book, *Cathedral*. Medieval buildings frequently had *gargoyles* (strange-looking creatures often used as water spouts from gutters) decorating the eaves. How many can you find? Draw a picture of one you'd like to put on the roof of your school. (C.)

framework; only the stone flying buttresses support the vaulted ceilings. All of the artwork, both interior and exterior, is hand-made; of particular note are the stone carvings—children especially love discovering the gargoyles perched high above. The stained glass windows depict both Biblical and modern themes. Kids might also appreciate the **Children's Chapel,** complete with child-sized chairs and pipe organ.

## Smart Stuff

**For Tweens and Teens...** The Washington Cathedral was begun in 1907 and completed in 1990. Medieval cathedrals frequently took a century or more to construct. A project so massive usually involved the entire community. What kinds of skills do you think were needed for this undertaking? (D.)

The highest point in Washington (its address is officially Mount St. Alban), the **Gloria in Excelsis Central Tower,** is said to be among the last towers in the world that contains both a carillon and a ten-bell peal. Push the seventh floor button in the elevator to get to the **Pilgrim Observation Gallery,** where you can see a film about the cathedral's history and enjoy extraordinary panoramic views from seventy windows that overlook Washington and Virginia.

Also sharing the Cathedral's landscaped acreage are two attractive gardens, including the medieval-style **Bishop's garden** (complete with a maze); its herbs and teas, along with books and gifts, are sold in the adjacent **Herb Cottage.** At the greenhouse, you can purchase growing plants. The Cathedral also has a gift shop, in which you can even purchase snacks to enjoy on the grounds.

"Children's Guides" are available at the front door; pick one up as you enter the Cathedral. Medieval Workshops for families are held here every Saturday from 10 A.M.–2 P.M. (as well as on summer weekdays) on a first-come, first-served basis. Children under twelve must be accompanied by an adult. Activities include: creating a "stained glass" window, needlework, limestone carving, and making brass rubbings. A treat for the more refined in your group would be the afternoon teas on Tuesday and Wednesday afternoons; reservations are required a week in advance; phone 202-537-8993.

**Smart Stuff**

For Tweens and Teens...
Who is the only president buried in the National Cathedral? (E.)

Several restaurants are within easy walking distance. North along Wisconsin Avenue is **Cactus Cantina** (3300 Wisconsin Avenue, NW; 202-686-7222), a popular restaurant for Mexican food in colorful surroundings. **Café Deluxe** (3228 Wisconsin Avenue, NW; 202-686-2233) serves excellent American food (including some vegetarian offerings) in very plain surroundings.

Metro: Tenleytown and a 20-minute walk south on Connecticut Avenue, NW; better yet, take any N bus up Massachusetts Avenue, NW from Dupont Circle or a 30 series bus on Wisconsin Avenue.

Call Metro Bus 202-637-7000 for details.

Mount St. Alban at Massachusetts and Wisconsin Avenues, NW

Open Monday through Friday 10 A.M.–9 P.M., first Monday in May through Labor Day; daily 10 A.M.–4:30 P.M., rest of year.

Guided tours and special interest tours of varying lengths; call for details: 202-537-6207; fee.

Cathedral services: Call for times.
Pipe organ demonstrations Wednesday 12:30 P.M. Peal Bell
    recitals Sunday 12:15 P.M. Carillon recitals Saturday
    12:30 P.M.. Choir practices Monday, Tuesday, Wednesday
    4 P.M. during school year.
Donations
202-537-6200 or 202-537-6230
www.cathedral.org/cathedral

## American University

**For Teens...** Set on a seventy-five acre campus that was once a
Civil War Army post, American University draws students from all
over the country and around the world. Its suburban-style campus
is really located within Washington's city limits, with access to
downtown and Georgetown (a favorite student haunt). Many
come here to take advantage of the government internship programs nearby; the school has connections with nearly a thousand
private, nonprofit, or government institutions. Although it was
founded under Methodist auspices, by an 1893 act of Congress,
American University is a comfortable environment for students of
all faiths and cultures.

Metro: Tenleytown
4400 Massachusetts Avenue, NW, between Ward and Wesley
    Circles
202-885-6000
www.american.edu/

## Hillwood Museum and Gardens

**For Teens...** Not only did Battle Creek, Michigan, bring us some
of our most famous cereals, but it also gave us the redoubtable General Foods heiress, Marjorie Merriweather Post. Hillwood Museum,
the 41-room mansion built to house her incredible collection of
decorative arts, was her home until she died in 1973. Representing

priceless objets d'art, prima-
rily from France and Russia,
Hillwood is perhaps best
known for its treasures from
the Czarist era, purchased
when Post's husband, Joseph
Davies, was ambassador to

> Adults, of course, will es-
> pecially enjoy this lovely
> museum and its grounds.
> Children under twelve are
> not admitted.

Russia in the 1930s. Her youngest daughter, actress Dina Merrill,
described how these unwanted remnants from royalty were stacked
in warehouses and how Marjorie climbed through the piles to select
her choices. Collections of china place settings, French Sèvres
porcelain, masterpieces by Carl Fabergé, oil paintings and furniture
from Catherine the Great, tapestries, and gilded French provincial
furniture fill this Rock Creek Park mansion.

## Smart Stuff

**For Teens...** The impressive collection of Imperial Russian
state treasures was bought by Mrs. Post during and after
her stay in the country as the wife of a diplomat. How do
you feel about private ownership of another country's national treasures? (Should there be international conditions
of such ownership or prohibitions against specific kinds of
purchases?) Today, Russia prohibits taking "antiques" out
of the country. Do you agree with this rule?

The twenty-five acres of elegant grounds include an assortment
of lovely gardens and an American Indian Building as well; it holds
artifacts Mrs. Post had displayed at her home in the Adirondacks.
This collection includes baskets, beaded items, moccasins, pottery
and blankets, from the Navajo, Hopi, Acoma, and Santa Clara tribes.

In the old stables is a café that serves Russian lunch specialties
and English afternoon tea; the menu changes during the year, but
Russian delicacies such as blintzes, borscht, or stuffed cabbage are
usually offered. Call for a reservation: 202-686-5807.

Books and movies provide background for all the beautiful and interesting items seen at Hillwood. For example, the classic movie *Dr. Zhivago* (from the bestseller by Boris Pasternak) is still unparalleled in its user-friendly portrayal of a turbulent time in Russia (teens); and *Reds* (with Warren Beatty) gives more of a political view (teens).

### Helpful Hint

Hillwood also has a gift shop, but don't expect to scoop up deals on pricey antiques.

Metro: Van Ness–UDC—but it's a long walk from here; call
Metro Bus 202-637-7000 for directions.
4155 Linnean Avenue, NW
Open Tuesday through Saturday 9 A.M.–5 P.M. and some
evenings and Sundays
Reservations required. Fee, to be paid in advance.
Two-hour guided tours; call for times.
202-686-5807

## Rock Creek Nature Center

**For All Ages...** Take a break from tall buildings and rushing people, and come to the tall trees and rushing water. Rock Creek Park, 2100 acres of parkland running through the center of Washington, has something for everyone. Here, kids can handle animal pelts, feathers, and bones, and watch a beehive in action. The reptiles, amphibians, and fish are fed at 4 P.M. daily. Programs run by the park rangers include nature talks, hikes, live animal programs, craft demonstrations, and workshops. The Discovery Room is set up for hands-on activities for youngsters from preschool through elementary school. The 75-seat planetarium offers free weekend and Wednesday afternoon

These Rock Creek Park sites are less accessible by public transportation and easiest to enjoy by car, private bus, or taxi.

shows (children over four are welcome). The National Capital Astronomers pair up with the National Park Service to offer "Exploring the Sky," a program about the night sky once a month (April through November).

For the Daniel Boone in some of us, there are self-guided nature trails. First pick up a Discovery Pack at the front desk for each child in your group. The binoculars, field microscope, and magnifying lens included in the kit will make the walk more interesting. For the more enterprising youngsters (ages 6–12), ask for the Junior Ranger Activity Book; when a child completes five of eight activities, he earns a Junior Ranger certificate and patch.

### Smart Stuff

**For Tikes...** Look for the live lizards and frogs. Do you know what a chameleon is? If you had a lizard of your own, what would you name it? Where would it live? What would it need from you?

### Smart Stuff

**For Tweens...** Animals, plants and people have lived in this area of what is now the city of Washington long before European colonists came to America. Ask the ranger about the Native American civilization here. Can you find some stone arrowheads by the nature trail?

Several kid-friendly nature books we've liked include: *Kids Camp!: Activities for the Backyard or Wilderness,* by Laurie Carlson (tikes); *Nibble, Nibble: Poems for Children,* by Margaret Wise Brown (tikes); *Backyard Birds (Peterson Field Guides for Young Naturalists),* by Jonathan P. Latimer et al. (tweens); *Backyard Stars: A Guide for Home and the Road* (Klutz Guides; tweens); *Glow-In-the-Dark Constellations: A Field Guide for Young Stargazers,* by C. E. Thompson and Randy Chewning (tweens); *The Insect Book: A Basic Guide to the Collection and Care of Common Insects for Young Children,* by

Connie Zakowski (tweens); *Talking to Fireflies, Shrinking the Moon: Nature Activities for All Ages,* by Edward Duensing (all ages); and *The Lorax,* by Dr. Seuss (also available as an audiotape, with Ted Danson)—all ages *need* this one. As for movies, check out the animated version of *Johnny Appleseed,* read by Garrison Keillor (tweens); *Willy the Sparrow* (tweens); and *Bambi* (tikes and tweens—but prepare them for the sad parts). Kids' reactions can really surprise you. We know of one instance when a young child was totally distraught during *Bambi,* because she thought the young deer had disappeared when he had, in fact, merely grown up.

> No Metro stop; call Metro Bus 202-637-7000 or come by car or taxi—but do come!
> 5200 Glover Road, NW
> Wednesday through Sunday 9 A.M.–5 P.M.; closed federal holidays
> Special programs: call for schedule; ask for a calendar in advance.
> 202-426-6829

## Pierce Mill

**For All Ages…** Take a trip back in time to see the best thing since *before* sliced bread: how corn and wheat become the flour that kids

are used to seeing in the bakery. The restored nineteenth century stone building houses the gristmill, complete with its enormous water wheel outside and ponderous millstone inside. Pierce Mill presents a real-life example of the way an important agricultural process worked in the 1820s. Renovation is currently under way to restore the last running mill in the

*Historic Pierce Mill in Rock Creek Park*

## Smart Stuff

**For Tweens...** Colonial mills like Pierce Mill depended on water power to grind their grain. What other power sources can you think of for this job? (F.)

District to working order. Kids can watch as individual craftsmen carefully use their skills to bring this slice of history back to life.

## Smart Stuff

**For Teens...** Areas of the U.S. were developed specifically because of their proximity to power sources. Can you single out some places where economic progress has come on the heels of the development of an industrial power source? (G.)

Bus (call 202-637-
7000), taxi, or car
3545 Williamsburg
Lane, NW, at the
corner of Tilden
Street and Beach
Drive, NW
Wednesday through
Sunday 9 A.M.–5 P.M.; self-guiding tours; closed holidays
Group tours require reservations. Educational programs for
school age kids; guided hikes and activities
202-426-6908

# Rock Creek Gallery, The Art Barn

**For Tweens and Teens...** Formerly the carriage house belonging to Isaac Pierce (who built Pierce Mill), the Art Barn is now home to the works of local artists. Exhibits include photographs, paintings, prints, sculptures, and ceramics.

Bus (call 202-637-7000), taxi, or car
2401 Tilden Street, NW
Open Thursday through Sunday 11 A.M.–4:30 P.M.; closed
federal holidays and one summer month (call to check)
202-244-2482

# National Museum of Health and Medicine (Walter Reed Army Medical Center)

**For Older Tweens and Teens...** During the Civil War, this museum was established to explore causes of the diseases that killed more soldiers than bullets did. Military and civilian medical history from then to the present are documented in the displays. Diagnostic and surgical instruments and an extensive microscope collection share space with a bone from Abraham Lincoln's skull and one from President Garfield's spine, diseased organs and body parts, and an exhibit focusing on biology and anatomy. A computer program that allows students to "treat" the mortally wounded Abraham Lincoln might be of interest to those with a medical bent. The modern world is not exempt from troubles: An exhibit to educate visitors about HIV is called "Living in a World with AIDS." Sometimes temporary exhibits are also on display.

## Smart Stuff

**For Teens...** It is widely acknowledged that more Civil War soldiers died of disease than were killed on battlefields. If you were a doctor on staff in a Civil War hospital, what medical breakthrough do you think you would have wanted most?

The Bell Telephone Science Series of films includes a classic on the circulatory system, *Hemo the Magnificent,* written and directed by Oscar-winning director Frank Capra (tweens and teens). *Fantastic Voyage* (tweens and teens) is another classic movie that focuses on the human body and how it works; it *is* fantastic.

> Metro: Takoma Park or Silver Spring, *plus* a short taxi ride
> 6900 Georgia Avenue, NW, at Elder Street (south end of
>     Building 54)
> Daily 10 A.M.–5:30 P.M.; closed December 25
> 202-782-2200

# The Kreeger Museum

**For Teens...** Set among the mansions of Foxhall Road is this contemporary house-turned-museum, filled with modern art. Carmen and David Lloyd Kreeger built this as their home, though they always intended it to become a museum to hold their collection. The 22-foot square marble modules contain works by Van Gogh, Chagall, Monet, Cezanne, and Picasso. An entire room is devoted to artists from the Washington Color School. Out back is a wonderful sculpture terrace; every room in the building (including the bathrooms) is filled with original artwork.

## Smart Stuff

**For Teens...** This museum was originally a twentieth-century family home. If you were the curator, what guidelines would you use for the kinds of art to be placed in each room? What kinds of art would you want in your bedroom, if you could choose anything you wanted?

No Metro; call Metro Bus 202-637-7000
2401 Foxhall Rd., NW
Tours Tuesday through Saturday 10:30 A.M. and 1:30 P.M.,
    September through July; closed January 1, Thanksgiving
    and the day after, and December 25
Fee
Reservations required; children under 12 not permitted.
202-337-3050 or 202-338-3552

# Glen Echo Park

**For All Ages...** Glen Echo has quite a history, which native Washingtonians who grew up here as late as the 1960s will remember. What began as a cultural and educational center in the 1800s (by the National Chautauqua Assembly) later metamorphosed into a colorful, full-service amusement park, complete with swimming pool and ballroom. Owned by the Washington Railway and Electric Company, it closed for financial reasons in 1968 and was acquired by the federal government in 1970, when it was turned over to the National Park Service.

Continuing under the stewardship of the National Park Service, Glen Echo emphasizes the arts and cultural education, offering more than a hundred different classes in theater, art, dance, music, and gardening. Many of the historic buildings have become dilapidated over the years, but hardy volunteer fund raisers and workers are helping to restore some of them. Housed here are art studios for pottery, glass-making, quilting, jewelry-making, painting, and metal work; beautiful handmade pieces can be purchased. Some studios are in primitive-looking, thatched-roof huts called yurts, built as overflow facilities for some of the artists and their work. The old stone tower is now the **Glen Echo Gallery,** where you can see (and purchase) some creations of the artists who work and teach classes here; books, postcards, and souvenirs are also available.

> There is a lot of walking here, some uphill, but there's plenty of room to run and play.

Since 1921, the beautiful antique carousel has run regularly; it is one of only twenty-seven Dentzel-made carousels remaining in the United States and Canada. (Always call ahead to be sure it is running if you are going to Glen Echo *just* for the carousel.) Sometimes park rangers can tell you more about this lovely carousel, if you ask.

The **Snack Bar** (open when the carousel runs), sells ice cream, popcorn, snacks, and drinks; the nearby picnic grove has plenty of tables. This is a great place to enjoy your picnic lunch *al fresco.*

No Metro; try Metro Bus 202-637-7000 or private transportation
7300 MacArthur Blvd, Glen Echo, Maryland
Open Monday through Thursday 9 A.M.–5 P.M., Friday and
 Saturday 9 A.M. to midnight; Sunday 9 A.M.–6 P.M.;
 closed January 1, Thanksgiving, and December 25

Tours with rangers Sunday 2 P.M.; Carousel rides Wednesday
and Thursday 10 A.M.–2 P.M., Saturday and Sunday noon
to 6 P.M., May through September; fee
301-492-6229

# Discovery Creek
# Children's Museum of Washington

**For Tikes and Tweens...** A real discovery on the museum scene is
the Discovery Creek Children's Museum. A dedicated staff and
many volunteers, including teenagers, make it possible for groups of
kids to have an incredible va-
riety of hands-on experiences
with nature. Children produce rainstorms (complete
with clouds), get down and
dirty to explore a termite
mound, experience life *inside*
a tree, meet live animals, hike
to a local creek to learn about
the water cycle, and create
myriad art projects. Ideas and
activities are above and beyond any other nature programs we've
seen. Beautiful educational materials are available even before your
visit to Discovery Creek. Call and ask for details.

> ## Helpful Hint
> Definitely get in touch
> with the Discovery Creek
> people before you come
> to the area, to make
> arrangements to enjoy
> whatever is available for
> your group.

Along MacArthur Boulevard, the food pickin's are slim, but
there are some restaurants worth a visit. One old favorite is **Listrani's**
(5100 MacArthur Boulevard, NW; 202-363-0619). A neighborhood
Italian restaurant that is kid-friendly, Listrani's serves pizza, salads,
and various pasta dishes as well as larger main courses and desserts.

No Metro; try Metro Bus 202-637-7000; come by private
transportation if you can
Museum at 4954 MacArthur Boulevard, NW, and Stable at
Glen Echo Park, 7300 MacArthur Boulevard, Glen Echo,
Maryland

Open 10 A.M.–3 P.M. Saturday; noon–3 P.M. Sunday; weekdays for school groups only; call two months in advance
to schedule
202-364-3111
www.discoverycreek.org

# The Clara Barton National Historic Site

**For All Ages...** Adjacent to Glen Echo Park, the last home of
Clara Barton, founder of the American Red Cross, now serves as a
museum. From 1897 to 1904, it was also the headquarters for the
organization; remaining fur-
nishings belonged to Barton
during this period. Known as
the "angel of the battlefield,"
Clara Barton (the only woman whose pay was equal to
that of a comparable male
employee) left her government job in Washington,
D.C., to bring supplies and medical care to Union soldiers on the
battlefield. Although she had no formal training as a nurse, she had
natural nursing and organizational skills, and a great deal of bravery.
At one point, she was asked to supervise all the Union Army's
nurses. Following the Civil War, she gave lectures on her experiences; during this time, she learned about the Red Cross that had
been founded in Switzerland
in 1864. She spent years lobbying for federal government
support to found an American chapter of the Red Cross,
which was finally accom-
plished in 1881.

Humanity, impartiality,
neutrality, independence, vol-
untary service, unity, and uni-

## Smart Stuff

**For Tikes...** Pretend you
were a nurse during war-
time. Draw pictures of
the kinds of supplies you
think you would need.

## Smart Stuff

**For Tweens and Teens...**
The Red Cross has chap-
ters all over the world.
What health issues do you
see worldwide today?
What kinds of remedies
would you suggest?

versality are the seven guiding beliefs of the American Red Cross. It helps victims of natural disasters, including earthquakes, floods, and storms, as well as medical disasters. Clara Barton didn't retire until she was 83 years old; her life is an example of selfless public service— a good example for children.

Some of the books about Clara Barton focus on different aspects of her life. *Clara Barton: Red Cross Pioneer,* by Matthew G. Grant (tikes and tweens); *The Story of Clara Barton,* by Zachary Kent (tweens); and *Clara Barton: Angel of the Battlefield,* by Rae Bains (tweens). A "readers' theater script" that casts fourteen characters (and lots of sound effects) for play-reading is available in *Our Nation's Capital: Activities and Projects for Learning About Washington, D.C.,* by Elizabeth F. Russell.

> No Metro; call Metro Bus 202-637-7000; private transportation is easiest
>
> 5801 Oxford Road, Glen Echo, Maryland
>
> Daily 10 A.M.–5 P.M.; closed January 1, Thanksgiving, and December 25
>
> Call in advance to arrange for your group to tour. Guided tours every hour until 4 P.M.
>
> 301-492-6245

# Woodend: The Audubon Naturalist Society

[**All Ages**] The Audubon Naturalist Society's peaceful 40-acre estate, Woodend, is a wildlife sanctuary as well as the society's headquarters. Children can explore the meadows and woods here, and follow a self-guided nature trail. Inside the main building, formerly a residence, visit the **Wilbur Fisk Banks Memorial Collection of Birds,** with 594 different kinds of bird specimens on display. The bookstore has animal-friendly gifts, such as birdfeeders and animal treats, as well as a wide selection of nature books and related educational toys. Picnicking is allowed on the grounds, but in the true spirit of conservation, visitors are responsible for taking their trash with them when they leave.

Many books on related subjects are available here and in other bookstores and libraries. Tweens and teens might find *The National Audubon Society Field Guide to North American Weather,* by David M. Ludlum, of interest; they usually are especially interested in snow (and "snow days"). *The Audubon Backyard Birdwatcher: Bird-feeders and Bird Gardens,* by Robert Burton, appeals to teens and adults who hope to lure more varieties of birds to their own turf.

No Metro; call Metro Bus 202-637-7000; private transportation is easiest

8940 Jones Mill Road, Chevy Chase, Maryland

Grounds open dawn-dusk daily; building 9 A.M.–5 P.M. weekdays; closed weekends. The bookstore is open Monday through Friday 10 A.M.–6 P.M., Saturday 9 A.M.–5 P.M., and Sunday noon to 5 P.M.

Call for information on special programs and classes on conservation and environmental issues. Also special family events. 301-652-9188; bookshop 301-652-3606

# The Washington Temple and Visitors Center of the Church of Jesus Christ of Latter-Day Saints

**For All Ages...** Like the spires of a far-away castle, the striking white marble steeples of the Washington Temple of Jesus Christ of Latter-Day Saints serve as a special landmark in the Washington suburbs. The Temple and Visitors Center are just off Exit 33 on the Washington Beltway (I–495), and about a thirty-minute drive from the center of the city. They offer a glimpse into the only non-Native American religion founded in America. With a missionary component of worldwide volunteers, the Church of Jesus Christ of Latter-Day Saints has become truly international.

In a visitor-friendly setting that seems like someone's home, the Visitors Center provides multimedia presentations and videos, as well as hands-on displays and seasonal events and programs, in-

**Smart Stuff**

**For Tweens and Teens...** Read some background information about the history of the Mormon Church in the U.S. As a religious community, the Mormons faced frequent discrimination and persecution for their beliefs and lifestyle. Yet an American, Joseph Smith, had a vision of a religion that would eventually take his band of believers across the country to settle what would become the forty-fifth state. If *you* were destined to found a religion that would incorporate the most significant principles of American life, what would it be like?

cluding a festival of lights outdoors and a lighted nativity scene for Christmas. The Temple itself is not open to the public.

In preparation for or follow-up to a visit here, an explanatory book might be helpful. *What Mormons Believe,* by Rex E. Lee (teens and adults) is a good source. A very old but informative film about the history of the Mormons in the U.S. is *Brigham Young, Frontiersman.*

> No Metro; call Metro Bus 202-637-7000; private transportation is easiest
>
> On Stoneybrook Drive in Kensington, Maryland, off Beach Drive
>
> Visitors center open daily 10 A.M.–9 P.M.; phone 301-587-0144
> 301-588-0650 (Temple)

# Washington Dolls House and Toy Museum

**For All Ages...** Tucked away behind the shopping centers and restaurants in this busy section of Washington is a real treat. Housing only part of the original collection of Flora Gill Jacobs, together with many gifts from Jacobs and other donors, the Washington Dolls House and Toy Museum provides visitors with a glimpse of affluent life in earlier times. Travel back into time as you enjoy the delightful display of antique miniatures that fill this small row house. Included with the intricately detailed replicas of homes from a variety of periods are: stage sets (like the one featuring Teddy Roosevelt on a safari); tiny versions of Noah's Ark, complete with a parade of animals; a houseboat; a model railroad; and a store window full of nineteenth century specialty shops. In addition, there are dolls, dolls, dolls of all kinds, shapes, and sizes, and rooms filled with dollhouse paraphernalia like miniature chandeliers that actually light, teeny little books with actual printed pages, tapestries, and hand-painted china.

The second floor offers you a chance to spend every cent in your pocket on the tiniest souvenirs of your trip. In addition to every conceivable miniature, there is a selection of magazines and books; if you want to *make* some miniatures, kits are available for furniture, accessories, and even quilts.

An old-fashioned tearoom makes a fabulous setting for a child's birthday party, with its potted plants and Edwardian furnishings. But unfortunately you can't just drop in for tea. If creative sandwiches are more your cup of tea anyway, you're in luck. **Booeymonger's** has a second location, at the corner of Wisconsin Avenue and Jenifer Streets, NW, just around the corner (5252 Wisconsin Avenue, NW; 202-686-5805). Open Monday though Thursday 7:30 A.M.–1 A.M., Friday through Sunday 7:30 P.M.–2 A.M.

Everywhere you turn in this area, there are restaurants, cafés, and fast food places. If you don't mind waiting in line or eating at a really odd time to avoid the lines, the **Cheesecake Factory** (5335 Wisconsin Avenue, NW; 202-364-0500) has super meal choices and desserts to die for. If you work things like we do, you can always share a salad and go straight to the dessert menu. Open Monday through Thursday 11:15 A.M.–11:30 P.M., Friday 11:15 A.M.–12:30 A.M., Saturday 11:30 A.M.–12:30 A.M., Sunday 10 A.M.–11 P.M. **Bambulé** (5225 Wisconsin Avenue, NW; phone: 202-966-0300) has a scrumptious Sunday brunch, 10 A.M.–3 P.M.; open Monday through Wednesday 11:30 A.M.–10 P.M., Thursday through Saturday 11:30 A.M.–11:30 P.M., Sunday 10 A.M.–3 P.M. and then 4–10 P.M.

Metro: Friendship Heights

5236 44th Street, NW

Open Tuesday through Saturday 10 A.M.–5 P.M., Sunday noon to 5 P.M.; closed Thanksgiving, December 25, January 1

Reservations can be made for birthday parties, with sandwiches and sweets, for groups of 12 or more.

Admission fee

202-244-0024 or 202-363-6400

## Where to Stay in the Uptown Area

The good news is that this is generally a safe area, with restaurants and shops and easily accessible subway stops. The bad news is that it can be a little pricey. Do your arithmetic as you plan.

### Days Inn Connecticut Avenue

4400 Connecticut Avenue, NW

202-244-5600 or 1-800-325-7466

Metro: Van Ness–UDC

### Embassy Suites at the Chevy Chase Pavilion

4300 Military Road., NW

202-362-9300 or 1-800-362-2779

Metro: Friendship Heights

### Marriott Wardman Park Hotel

2660 Woodley Road, NW

202-328-2000 or 1-800-228-9290

Metro: Woodley Park–Zoo

# Answers to Smart Stuff Questions

**A.** Kids might be surprised to learn that many everyday products have their origins in the rain forest (rubber, medicines). A debate between the "industrialists" and the "conservationists" might be fun also.

**B.** China

**C.** Some especially amusing gargoyles found on the Cathedral are: a bearded hippy with a protest sign, Darth Vader (from *Star Wars*), a weeping sea turtle (it's too cold up there?), and the eerie-looking skeleton of a horse (no food up there, either).

**D.** Included in a community-wide effort would have been church officials, architects, builders, stonecutters, painters, calligraphers, sculptors, patrons, and even serfs to do the manual labor. Instead of unions, there were craft-based guilds for artisans. Frequently, those who began such a project did not live long enough to see its completion, and that wasn't due to labor negotiations.

**E.** Woodrow Wilson

**F.** Some other power sources are: mules or horses or oxen; air/wind (windmill); electricity or batteries

**G.** For example, New England mill towns, Hoover Dam, and the Tennessee Valley Authority.

# CHAPTER 10

# Northeast & Southeast

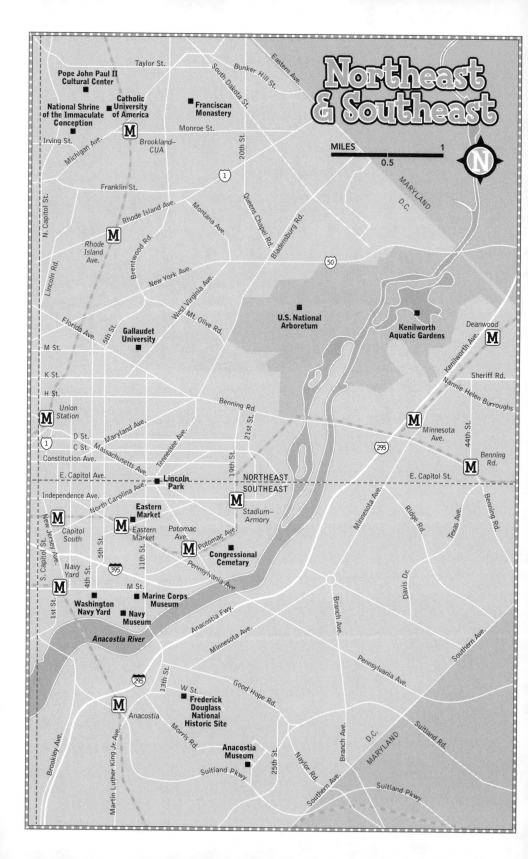

# Northeast & Southeast

MILES
0.5        1

**N**

Taylor St.

Bunker Hill St.

Eastern Ave.

South Dakota St.

Pope John Paul II
Cultural Center

Catholic
University
of America

Franciscan
Monastery

National Shrine
of the Immaculate
Conception

Monroe St.

M Brookland–
CUA

Irving St.

20th St.

Michigan Ave.

Franklin St.

1

MARYLAND
D.C.

N. Capitol St.

Rhode Island Ave.

Montana Ave.

Queens Chapel Rd.

Bladensburg Rd.

Rhode
Island
Ave.

M

Brentwood Rd.

50

Lincoln Rd.

New York Ave.

West Virginia Ave.

Florida Ave.

Mt. Olive Rd.

U.S. National
Arboretum

Kenilworth
Aquatic Gardens

Deanwood

M

5th St.

Gallaudet
University

Kenilworth Ave.

M St.

Sheriff Rd.

K St.

Nannie Helen Burroughs

H St.

Benning Rd.

M Union
Station

21st St.

M

Minnesota
Ave.

44th St.

D St.

Maryland Ave.

1

C St.

Massachusetts Ave.

Tennessee Ave.

19th St.

295

Benning
Rd.

Constitution Ave.

Lincoln
Park

M

E. Capitol St.

E. Capitol Ave.

NORTHEAST
SOUTHEAST

Independence Ave.

North Carolina Ave.

M

Capitol
South

M

Eastern
Market

Stadium–
Armory

New Jersey Ave.

Eastern
Market

Potomac
Ave.

M

Potomac Ave.

M

Minnesota Ave.

Ridge Rd.

Texas Ave.

Benning Rd.

5th St.

11th St.

Congressional
Cemetary

Navy
Yard

395

Pennsylvania Ave.

Davis Dr.

M

4th St.

M St.

S. Capitol St.

1st St.

M

Washington
Navy Yard

Marine Corps
Museum

Navy
Museum

Anacostia Fwy.

Branch Rd.

Pennsylvania Ave.

Southern Ave.

Anacostia River

Minnesota Ave.

295

13th St.

Good Hope Rd.

Brookley Ave.

M

Anacostia

W St.

Frederick
Douglass
National
Historic Site

Morris Rd.

Branch Ave.

D.C.
MARYLAND

Suitland Rd.

Martin Luther King Jr. Ave.

25th St.

Anacostia
Museum

Naylor Rd.

Southern Ave.

Suitland Pkwy.

Suitland Pkwy.

**F**rom the beauty of nature to the beauty of the spirit, Northeast and Southeast Washington have treasures to discover. **The National Arboretum** and **Kenilworth Aquatic Gardens,** overflowing with color and fragrance in the warm months, complement the exotic aromas wafting from the **Eastern Market.** From the **Basilica of the National Shrine of the Immaculate Conception** to the **Emancipation Statue** in **Lincoln Park,** this section of the city commemorates the strivings of man's spirit.

## ★The Basilica of the National Shrine of the Immaculate Conception

**For Tweens and Teens...** The largest Catholic church in the Western Hemisphere is a beautiful site. Featuring the Latin cross design, the Shrine was built of granite, brick, tile, and concrete, without a steel frame. Architecturally, Byzantine and Romanesque styles (of 1,500 and 1,000 years ago) combine to effect a major change from the Gothic styles so frequently used in the United States. Outside, the blue, red, and gold-leaf mosaic dome is a landmark in the city.

# Quick Guide to

| Attraction | Location |
|---|---|
| ★The Basilica of the National Shrine of the Immaculate Conception | Michigan Avenue at 4th Street, NE (on the campus of the Catholic University of America) |
| Pope John Paul II Cultural Center | 3900 Harewood Road, NE |
| Catholic University of America | 620 Michigan Avenue, NE |
| Franciscan Monastery | 1400 Quincy Street, NE |
| Gallaudet University | 800 Florida Avenue, NE |
| U.S. National Arboretum | 3501 New York Avenue, NE (another entrance on R Street, NE) |
| Lincoln Park | E. Capitol Street between 11th and 13th Streets, NE |
| Eastern Market | 7th Street (between North Carolina and C Streets, SE) |
| Washington Navy Yard | M Street (between 1st and 11th Streets, SE) |
| Marine Corps Museum | Building 58 in the Washington Navy Yard at 9th and M Streets, SE |
| Navy Museum | Building 76 in the Washington Navy Yard, 9th and M Streets, SE |
| Anacostia Museum | 1901 Fort Place, SE |
| ★Frederick Douglass National Historic Site (Cedar Hill) | 1411 W Street, SE |
| Kenilworth Aquatic Gardens | Anacostia Avenue and Douglass Street, NE; 2 miles south of Jct. U.S. 50 |

# Northeast/Southeast Attractions

| Age Range | Hours | Details on |
| --- | --- | --- |
| Tweens and Teens | 7 A.M.–7 P.M. daily (Apr.–Oct.) 7 A.M.–6 P.M. (rest of year) | Page 249 |
| All Ages | Tues.–Sat. 10 A.M.–5 P.M. Sun. 12 P.M.–5 P.M. | Page 253 |
| Teens | Tours: Mon., Wed., Fri. 10:30 A.M. | Page 254 |
| Tweens and Teens | 9 A.M.–5 P.M. daily | Page 255 |
| Teens | See page 255 for details | Page 255 |
| All Ages | 8 A.M.–5 P.M. daily | Page 256 |
| All Ages | 24 hours, daily | Page 258 |
| All Ages | See page 260 for complete details | Page 260 |
| All Ages | Mon.–Fri. 9 A.M.–4 P.M. Sat.–Sun. 10 A.M.–5 P.M. | Page 261 |
| All Ages | See page 263 for complete details | Page 263 |
| All Ages | See page 264 for complete details | Page 264 |
| All Ages | 10 A.M.–5 P.M. daily | Page 265 |
| Tweens and Teens | Call in advance to reserve tour time | Page 267 |
| All Ages | 8 A.M.–4 P.M. daily | Page 269 |

Visitors can explore sixty chapels throughout the building, representing different ethnic groups. Altars in thirty-two chapels are devoted to the worship of the Virgin Mary, who, by Papal decree, became the patron saint of America. Two hundred stained glass windows provide brilliant color. A striking mosaic, "Christ in Majesty," adorns the main altar; "The Descent of the Holy Spirit," the largest mosaic, is in the dome. Vatican City presented two mosaic reproductions as gifts to the United States, also housed in the National Shrine: "Immaculate Conception" and "Assumption of the Virgin." The addition of artwork continues. In 1999, a local Washington area artist's thirty-eight-ton, 750-square-foot marble relief, "The Universal Call to Holiness," was installed on the basilica wall. The artist, George Carr, used local residents as his models for the figures. The 329-foot-high Knights' Bell Tower is home to a fifty-six-bell carillon, topped with a large gilded cross.

> This might be a difficult place for younger children to visit because of the respectful and reverential behavior necessary. The tour is long; pick up a map at the ground (crypt) level information desk.

While the upper building with its vaulted ceilings gives a feeling of spaciousness and serenity, the crypt is constructed in the spirit of the Roman catacombs. A gallery in the crypt displays the crown of Pope Paul VI, from his coronation.

Snack-alert: There is a small cafeteria (daily 8 A.M.–2 P.M.) on the Shrine's crypt level; hot meals as well as sandwiches, drinks, and desserts are available. Vending machines also offer snacks, soft drinks, and desserts.

Daytime visits are recommended, to appreciate the beauty of the facility as well as *for personal safety.* Also, you have to walk through Catholic University to get to the Shrine, so wear your comfortable shoes.

For general information about Catholicism, look at *American Catholicism,* by John Tracy Ellis (teens). An interesting movie to watch before or after a visit here is *A Man for All Seasons* (tweens and teens). Also enjoyable would be *The Nun's Story,* starring the young Audrey Hepburn (teens), and *Heaven Knows, Mr. Allison,* starring Robert Mitchum and Deborah Kerr (teens).

**Smart Stuff**

Who is the only American saint canonized by the Catholic Church? (A.)

Metro: Brookland-
    CUA
Michigan Avenue at
    4th Street, NE (on
    the campus of the
    Catholic University of America)
Daily 7 A.M.–7 P.M., April through October; 7 A.M.–6 P.M.,
    rest of year
Guided tours Monday through Saturday 9 A.M.–3 P.M., Sun-
    day 1:30–4 P.M.
Carillon recitals Sunday 2:30 P.M.; guest organists' recitals
    Sunday 6 P.M., preceded by carillon recital at 5:30, June
    August.
202-526-8300
www.nationalshrine.com

# Pope John Paul II Cultural Center

**For All Ages...** This newly completed Catholic museum occupies a dramatic, new building, with a copper roof resembling angel wings and a soaring rotunda, set into a wooded twelve-acre site adjacent to Catholic University. Upon entry, visitors receive a bar-coded "smart card" they will use to access the exhibits. With five interactive galleries that hold thirty-four different activities, the museum brings together information on religion and faith from a global perspective. Some exhibits will also rotate from the Vatican Museums. A small chapel provides a quiet setting for peaceful reflection. The center also houses two gift shops; one offers fine art, religious icons, art of the Vatican Museum, and jewelry; the second has educational items as well as books and music, and a children's section with toys, books, and videos.

Metro: Brookland-CUA
3900 Harewood Road, NE
Tuesday through Saturday 10 A.M.–5 P.M., Sunday noon to
5 P.M.; closed Monday (except holidays)
Admission fee
202-635-5400
www.jp2cc.org

# Catholic University of America

**For Teens...** Talk about a campus with a landmark! The **Basilica of the Shrine of the Immaculate Conception** is located on the campus of the Catholic University of America. Particularly known for its outstanding drama and music departments (the training ground for some famous stage and film stars), Catholic University is the only U.S. university operating under specific papal authority. The gothic buildings, set on a lush green campus, might make an interesting stop for college-bound young people.

Metro: Brookland-CUA
620 Michigan Avenue, NE
Tours Monday, Wednesday, Friday at 10:30 A.M.
202-319-5305

A favorite hangout for Catholic U. folks is **Colonel Brooks Tavern** (901 Monroe Street, NE; 202-529-4002). The friendly waitstaff can guide you through a menu filled with enormous and mouth-watering sandwiches, such as "The Colonel's Favorite," a triple-decker affair of turkey, cheese, pastrami, and coleslaw, or grilled, marinated chicken with Jack cheese, smoked bacon, and jalapeño mayonnaise. Grilled vegetable enchiladas make a tasty appetizer.

# Franciscan Monastery

**For Tweens and Teens...** It's not every day you get an opportunity to tour a working monastery (unless you live there), so here's your chance. The Franciscan Monastery, near Catholic University, offers some interesting contrasts. The church is modeled after the famous Hagia Sophia in Istanbul. On the grounds are replicas of various shrines and sites from the Holy Land: the Stations of the Cross, the Manger in Bethlehem, the Garden of Gethsemane, the Holy Sepulcher, and a statue of St. Francis of Assisi (whose order runs this monastery). These sites are surrounded by famed rose gardens, among the largest in the country; some of the roses here even bloom in early winter. For a change from this peaceful environment, take a tour of the catacombs, which replicate those used in Rome by early Christians, who hid there to avoid persecution. The dark passageways with their steep stairs lend themselves to some of the harrowing stories of early martyrs; if you're lucky, you will have a guide who relishes sharing some of these tales.

A classic book by St. Francis is *The Little Flowers of St. Francis of Assisi,* edited by Ugolino and W. Heywood (tweens and teens); also check out *God's Fool: The Life and Times of Francis of Assisi,* by Julien Green and Peter Heinegg (teens).

> Metro: Brookland-CUA
> 1400 Quincy Street, NE
> Tours on the hour, Monday through Saturday 9–11 A.M., 1–4 P.M., Sunday 1–4 P.M.
> Church and gardens open daily 9 A.M.–5 P.M.
> Contributions welcome
> 202-526-6800

# Gallaudet University

**For Teens...** The world's *only* university for the deaf was established in 1864. It sits on a 99-acre campus with buildings in Victorian Gothic- and Queen Anne–style architecture. Its 2,200 students are quite modern, however, and made big news in 1988 by insisting that the school be headed by a *deaf* president. Dr. I. King Jordan became the first non-hearing president of Gallaudet University.

Known for its fine complement of offerings in academics, sports, and the arts, Gallaudet is especially recognized for its unique drama department. Three shows are produced annually in American Sign Language, with voice interpretation available for the hearing (frequently a minority of *this* audience).

Because of the specialized nature of this university, it might be the perfect stop if a young person or family member in your group is hearing disabled.

> Metro: not accessible; take a bus, cab, or car
> 800 Florida Avenue, NE
> Visitors Center Monday through Friday 9 A.M.–5 P.M.; tours 10 A.M. and 1 P.M., conducted in American Sign Language; if an interpreter is needed, call 202-651-5505.
> 202-651-5000 or 202-651-5050 (tours); TDD 202-651-5050
> www.gallaudet.edu

# U.S. National Arboretum

**For All Ages...** A world-class collection of trees, bushes, ornamental grasses, flowering annuals and perennials, and herbs, this 444-acre site was originally established (1927) for research and educational purposes. From the R Street entrance, visitors can access the Information Center, restrooms, the Arbor House Gift Shop, and the Administration Building. In this same area is the aquatic garden, with pond lilies and large koi (colorful Japanese carp). All sorts of interesting details are available in a little brochure about the koi, who are fed from the back terrace at 12:30 P.M. from April to November. Be sure kids do not attempt to feed them *anything* except the special food provided here.

A network of trails leads visitors through various gardens of specialty plants. Teak benches are placed here and there for rest and contemplation. The **National Bonsai and Penjing Museum Collection** showcases American, Chinese, and Japanese artistically dwarfed trees and miniature landscapes. The **Herb Garden** is not only delightful to your nose but practical as well (no, you *may not* pick the herbs here to take home). From medicines to fuel, from dyes to beverages, from the delicious scents of licorice and English lavender to the unmistakable pungency of ginger, kids can learn how useful plants can be. In the **National Grove of State Trees** (ask for a State Tree List at the Administration Building), kids can hunt for their state's official tree.

Money jangling in your pockets as you peruse the beauty here? There's a gift shop! The **Arbor House Gift Shop** has souvenirs, soap, stuffed animal toys, artwork, and postcards, as well as books about plants and their care, and a complete guidebook for the gardens. Soda provides the only sustenance for the tummy, however. You can bring a picnic, and enjoy it in the Arboretum's beautiful settings.

**Smart Stuff**

For Tikes... Look for the fish in the aquatic garden. What are these fish called? Draw a picture of your favorite.

Books that might be of interest are: *Tom Brown's Field Guide to Nature and Survival for Children,* by Judy Brown, Heather Bolyn, and Tom Brown Jr. (tweens); *Nature's Wonders: For the Young at Art: Creative Activities for Ages Six and Up Using the Please Touch Philosophy,* by Susan Striker and Sally Schaedler (tweens); *Silent Spring,* by Rachel Carson (teens); *My First Summer*

**Smart Stuff**

For Teens... Find your state tree in the National Grove of State Trees. Why do you think this particular kind of tree was chosen? What is it usually used for? What are the state trees of Alaska and Hawaii? Could they be grown where *you* live? How about in each other's climates? (B.)

> The *Franklinia altamaha* is a tree. Named for Benjamin Franklin, a man who seemed to have an interest in everything, it now grows nowhere else, apparently extinct.

*in the Sierra,* by John Muir (teens); and *Walden,* by Henry David Thoreau (teens).

> Metro: complicated; call Metro Bus 202-637-7000, but if you can, come by bus or car (the easiest way); there's plenty of parking
>
> 3501 New York Avenue, NE (another entrance on R Street, NE)
>
> Grounds open daily 8 A.M.–5 P.M.; closed December 25
>
> Administration Building open Monday through Friday 8 A.M.–4:30 P.M. (Saturday and Sunday 9 A.M.–5 P.M., March 1 to mid-November)
>
> National Bonsai and Penjing Museum Collection open daily 10 A.M.–3:30 P.M.
>
> Groups can book the tram tour in advance; each tram can hold up to 48 people. Tram tour (40 minutes) Saturday and Sunday 10:30 A.M., 11:30 A.M., 1 P.M., 2 P.M., 3 P.M. (and 4 P.M. in summer); fee
>
> Arbor House Gift Shop, open daily March through December, 10 A.M.–3:30 P.M.; phone: 202-399-5958
>
> 202-245-2726 (recording)
>
> www.usha.usda.gov

# Lincoln Park

**For All Ages...** Memorializing the abolition of slavery in Washington, D.C., Lincoln Park is home to two historic statues. Dedicated in 1876, the **Emancipation Statue, "Freedom's Memorial,"** represents Abraham Lincoln in a life-size statue (who stood over six feet tall), with the Emancipation Proclamation in one hand as he liberates a slave. At Lincoln's feet is the likeness of Archer Alexander, the last man to be captured under the Fugitive Slave Law. The statue took its name from the president, who was called "the great emancipator." All the funds for this project came from freed slaves, some of whom also served in the Union Army during the Civil War.

**Helpful Hint**

Call to request the National Park Service brochure for the Black History National Recreation Trail: 202-619-7222.

Also located here is the **Mary McLeod Bethune Memorial,** the first **statue** to honor a black American woman in the nation's capital. The National Council of Negro Women, founded by Bethune in 1935, erected this statue in her honor in 1974. This 12-

**Smart Stuff**

**For Tikes...** If you were a slave, you would have to do just what your master or mistress told you *every* day. Try this with a friend: Have him boss you around for one hour; then change places and you be the boss. Suppose your master told you to do a really *bad* thing—what would you do? (C.)

foot-tall monument features an elderly Bethune, complete with cane, reaching out to black children, exemplifying her focus on learning and self-respect for African Americans.

**Smart Stuff**

**For Tweens and Teens...** With the end of the Civil War came the end of slavery in the U.S. You probably know about the American Civil Rights struggle. In what ways were black Americans still not free one hundred years after the Civil War? What kinds of discrimination do you think minorities face today?

Lincoln Park is included in the **Black History National Recreation Trail.** A pamphlet/guide for these sites is available through the National Park Service. Several movies and books are worth investigating before or after your visit. We suggest *A Picture of Freedom: The Diary of Clotee, A Slave Girl,* by Patricia McKissack (tweens and teens); *To Be A Slave,* by Julius Lester (tweens and teens); *Malcolm X* (a film, teens); *Uncle Tom's Cabin,* by Harriet Beecher Stowe (teens); *Black Like Me,* by John H. Griffin (teens), which is also available as a film (inspired by the movie, *Gentleman's Agreement*); and *King: A Filmed Record . . . Montgomery to Memphis* (a film for tweens and teens).

> It took until 1977 for an African American woman to serve as a cabinet secretary. President Jimmy Carter named Patricia Roberts Harris to be secretary of Housing and Urban Development.

Metro: Eastern Market

E. Capitol Street between 11th and 13th Streets, NE

**Congressional Cemetery** (from 17th between E and H Streets, SE, to the river) set on a 30-acre hillside by the Anacostia River, is the final resting place for a variety of celebrities. Founded in 1807, this spot is where Civil War photographer Matthew Brady; Washington resident and "March King" John Philip Sousa; former FBI Director J. Edgar Hoover; and the less-known former vice president, Eldridge Gerry (who left us "gerrymandering" as his legacy) are all buried. Take a taxi, if you're interested in looking around here, and go in the daytime.

# Eastern Market

**For All Ages...** The butcher, the baker, and the candlestick maker are all alive and well and selling their wares at the Eastern Market, seven blocks behind the U.S. Capitol building. Built in 1871, and designed by the same architect as the Smithsonian Arts and Industries Building, the Eastern Market is the last remaining public market in the city. Children love the colorful array of produce, clothing, toys, arts and crafts, and flowers; on Saturdays, extra vendors set up stands, with products from all over the world. This is one place you can visit without worrying about where to get a snack.

Nearby is the **Fairy Godmother** (319 7th Street, SE), a bookstore for families, filled with children's books and toys; call for story time schedule: 202-547-5474. There's other shopping here, too, so allow some time to explore after visiting the market itself. Known for its wonderful selection of secondhand books, **Capitol Hill Books** (657 C Street, SE) is another find. Interested in clothes instead? Try **Clothes Encounters of A Second Kind** (202 7th Street, SE), where you'll probably rub elbows with Capitol Hill staffers vying for the same outfits you like.

Hankerin' for a hamburger (or have a whole string of kids who are)? You're in luck. **Capitol Hill Jimmy T's** (501 East Capitol Street at 5th Street; 202-546-3646) has sandwiches and hamburgers of all varieties, all in a retro-'50s setting.

Metro: Eastern Market (walk north on 7th Street until you get there)

7th Street between North Carolina and C Streets, SE

Open Tuesday through Thursday 7 A.M.–6 P.M., Friday and Saturday 6 A.M.–7 P.M.; Sundays, outdoor flea market 9 A.M.–4 P.M.

Try 202-724-4400 (D.C. Office of Property Management). There is currently no central phone number for Eastern Market itself.

www.easternmarket.net

# Washington Navy Yard

**For All Ages…** Some *yard!* The oldest naval installation still in use in the U.S., the Washington Navy Yard opened in 1799 as a shipyard

There's something here for everyone, but the Navy Yard requires a lot of walking to get to what you want to see.

for the navy. Later it was used as a plant for manufacturing weapons and munitions. In recent years, it has been used for offices. The old buildings, built between 1800 and 1900, are interesting, and the outdoor military history park has cannons and naval artifacts to discover. The **U.S. Navy Combat Art Center** (Building 67; 8 A.M.–4 P.M. daily; 202-433-3815) features paintings of military action, exploration, and ship launchings; changing exhibits are on display all year. A retired Navy destroyer, the USS *Barry* (in service from 1956 to 1982, and used in the Cuban Missile Crisis and in the Vietnam War), is at Pier 2 at the dock, and you can explore its cramped quarters if you are feeling particularly nimble. Kids think it's a great adventure; they love the mess hall, the narrow hallways, the bunk beds, and even the homing torpedo; they can even take the captain's wheel and "steer" for a bit.

## Helpful Hint

Call in advance to request the generous educational packet of materials about the Washington Navy Yard and the museums on its grounds: 202-433-6826.

While the Navy Yard itself is perfectly fine to explore during the daytime, the surrounding neighborhood is *not*. Take a cab, or better yet, go by car, if you can, and stay *in* the yard. Inside the gates there is plenty of free parking, especially on weekends.

You and your landlubbers might (or might not!) be happy to know that **McDonald's, Subway,** and **Dunkin' Donuts** are all open in the Navy Yard on weekdays. On weekends, only McDonald's remains open, but there's also a **Catering and Conference Center cafeteria** (202-433-3041).

Metro: Navy Yard or Eastern Market ( the Navy Yard neighborhood is *not* a safe place to walk around; take a bus, cab, or car if you possibly can).

M Street between 1st and 11th Streets, SE

Monday through Friday 9 A.M.–4 P.M., Saturday and Sunday 10 A.M.–5 P.M.

USS *Barry* self-guided tours 10 A.M.–5 P.M. daily March through October; 10 A.M.–4 P.M. rest of year; 202-433-3377

202-433-2218

# Marine Corps Museum

**For All Ages...** If hearing "The Marine Corps Hymn" sends chills down your back, this is the place for you. Guns, swords, uniforms, flags, models, dioramas, an interactive video kiosk, and memorabilia all portray the Marine Corps history from the American Revolution to the present. The actual flags that were raised on Mt. Suribachi,

## Smart Stuff

What is the Marine Corps Latin motto? What does it mean? (D.)

## Smart Stuff

**For Tweens and Teens...** The Marine Corps has always prided itself on being a special, small service within the military. What is its unique function? (E.)

Iwo Jima, are displayed here, bullet holes and all. A special collection of military music exhibits mementos of John Philip Sousa, once the Marine Corps Bandmaster.

Metro: Navy Yard or Eastern Market (this is *not* a safe neighborhood to walk around; if you can, take a bus, cab, or car).

Building 58 in the Washington Navy Yard at 9th and M Streets, SE

Monday, Wednesday, Thursday, Saturday 10 A.M.–4 P.M.; Friday 10 A.M.–8 P.M., May 1 through Labor Day; Sunday, and holidays noon to 5 P.M.; closed January 1 and December 25

202-433-3840

## Smart Stuff

**For Tikes...** How many kinds of ships can you find in this museum? Can you find one that carries airplanes? What is it called? (F.)

# Navy Museum

**For All Ages...** Ahoy, mates! Welcome aboard a place where war and peace are both treated with honor. The Visitor Center in the Navy Museum presents an audio-visual introduction, and the front desk has free brochures listing all the activities available for kids. In a refreshing hands-on style, kids can peek through real submarine periscopes, "operate" antiaircraft weapons, climb into a space capsule, and perch on a real cannon. They can view a *hand*-propelled submarine, "The Intelligent Whale," from 1869. The Navy's peacetime successes, including space flight, diplomacy, and charitable service, are all featured as well.

## Smart Stuff

**For Tweens...** Who is considered "the father of the U.S. Navy?" What is his famous quote? (G.)

If your youngster wants to spend a few minutes before the mast, he will be awed by the fully rigged foremast fighting top from the frigate USS *Constitution* and the replica of a gun deck, too. "In Harm's Way" highlights the U.S. Navy in World War II. Videotapes, a Corsair fighter plane, and an interactive game are all part of this exhibit. All hands on deck!

Metro: Navy Yard or Eastern Market (*don't* walk around in this neighborhood; take a bus, cab, or car).

Building 76 in the Washington Navy Yard, 9th and M Streets, SE

> **Helpful Hint**
>
> It's a good idea to call ahead and request a guided tour for your group before you come to town. Ask for the educational materials for your particular age group.

Monday through Friday 9 A.M.–4 P.M., Saturday, Sunday, and holidays 10 A.M.–5 P.M., March 21 through July 4; Monday through Friday 9 A.M.–5 P.M., Saturday, Sunday, and holidays 10 A.M.–5 P.M., rest of year; closed January 1, Thanksgiving, and December 24–25.

Navy Band performances on some summer evenings; call for details.

Guided tours available. Self-guiding information is available for children. Pre-visit materials for different ages can be provided, including activities that go with the tours.

202-433-6897 or 202-433-4882

www.history.navy.mil

# Anacostia Museum

**For All Ages...** The Smithsonian Institution established the Anacostia Museum in 1967 to concentrate on African American history and culture, research, and historical documentation. Originally a storefront museum, the Anacostia focused on programs and exhibits reflecting its surrounding community, and involved community members in training and development of the exhibitions. The goal of its founder, John Kinard, was to train young people in museum work and build pride in their own history and cultural experience.

In a setting of changing exhibits, music, art, photography, and historic documents reflect the rich cultural heritage of the black experience in America. A small museum shop offers postcards, note paper, posters, and books by and about African Americans. Talks, workshops, educational programs, as well as free concerts, poetry readings, plays, and dance programs all take place here; call for details and schedules.

Visitors can take a guided tour of the museum grounds, on the **George Washington Carver Nature Trail,** less than one-third of a mile long (doable even for young museum-goers). Take the trail *only* with a guide, however; the rest of the neighborhood is *not* a safe place to explore on your own.

Named for its original inhabitants, recorded as Nacothtant or Anaquashtank, the name of this area became Anacostia. Home to a large free black community before the Civil War, Anacostia developed into a middle class African American community by the early 1900s. The city is trying to revitalize this area, after years of decline, bringing in government offices, improving roads, and creating affordable housing, with new town houses and single-family residences. Negotiations are under way for new retail shopping centers to be built here as well, and the mayor is placing emphasis on improving the neighborhood schools. For now, however, Anacostia is *not* a place to explore on foot or at night.

Many books and films can enrich the experience of visiting the Anacostia Museum. *The Drinking Gourd (I Can Read Series),* by F. N. Monjo (tikes) is also available on audiocassette. Worthwhile book choices include: *Benjamin Banneker: The Man Who Saved Washington,* by Claude Lewis (tweens); *Dear Benjamin Banneker,* by Andrea Davis Pinkney (tweens); *Our Nation's Capital: Activities and Projects for Learning About Washington, D.C.,* by Elizabeth F. Russell (tweens), which includes a little make-your-own book about Banneker; *Roll of Thunder, Hear My Cry,* by Mildred D. Taylor (tweens and teens) is a beautiful story, available as a film as well; *Five Smooth Stones* (teens), by Ann Fairbairn, is an especially sensitive story about the activist life of a young black man from New Orleans; *Selected Poems of Langston Hughes* (tweens and teens)—or any books of his poetry; *The Collected Poems of Sterling A. Brown,* by Sterling A. Brown (some of his poems are set in D.C.); *The Negro in the*

*Making of America,* by Benjamin Quarles (teens); *Black Voices: An Anthology of Afro-American Literature,* edited by Abraham Chapman (teens); *Manchild in the Promised Land,* by Claude Brown (teens); *Native Son,* by Richard Wright (now a real classic, for teens); *Race Matters,* by Cornel West (teens); and *Colored People: A Memoir,* by Henry Louis Gates Jr. (teens). Movies include: *Perfect Harmony* (tweens and teens); *A Raisin in the Sun* (tweens and teens); *Home of the Brave* (tweens and teens); *A Soldier's Story* (teens); and *In the Heat of the Night* (teens).

> Metro: Take a bus, cab, or car to this location (for safety and
>     convenience)
> 1901 Fort Place, SE
> Daily 10 A.M.–5 P.M.; closed December 25
> Note: This museum is closed until late 2001, so be sure to
>     call before scheduling your visit.
> Reservations needed for exhibition tours
> 202-357-2700 or 202-287-3369

# ★Frederick Douglass National Historic Site (Cedar Hill)

**For Tweens and Teens...** Opened to the public in 1972, this was the last home of Frederick Douglass, former slave, statesman, and activist for human rights; it still contains many of the original Victorian furnishings. To this day, it still has no electricity. Douglass's life is portrayed in exhibits and a film in the visitor center here.

Named for the cedar trees that graced the nine-acre lot, Cedar Hill was originally part of a 237-acre plot being subdivided for development. When Douglass purchased it in 1877, the real estate deed restriction, in addition to preventing "soap-boiling, piggeries, and slaughterhouses," forbade ownership except to "white persons only." After his first wife, Anna, died in 1882, he brought his second wife, Helen Pitts, to live there. She was white.

Having taught himself to read and write while still a slave, Douglass escaped from his captivity in 1838, at the age of 21. A tall, handsome man, and an excellent speaker, he published his first autobiography *(The Narrative of the Life of Frederick Douglass: An American Slave)* in 1845. In it, he identified his former master, effectively jeopardizing his own life. He fled to England, and friends purchased his freedom. Returning to the U.S., he published his own newspaper, *The North Star,* in Rochester, New York, and was stationmaster for the Underground Railroad there. A well-known abolitionist, he recruited black soldiers for the Union Army, and after the war, supported Reconstruction.

## Smart Stuff

**For Tweens and Teens...**
What do you think enabled Frederick Douglass to be such a *powerful* advocate for abolition? Do you think it helped or hurt his cause that he was a former slave?

In addition to other federal appointments, Douglass was secretary of the Santo Domingo Commission, marshal and recorder of the Deeds of the District of Columbia, and minister of the United States to Haiti. The house was dedicated as a memorial to Douglass in 1922, to serve, as his wife Helen wished, as a "Mount Vernon to the black community."

Among the many books about this famous man and his times are: *Frederick Douglass: Portrait of a Freedom Fighter,* by Sheila Keenan (tikes); *Escape From Slavery: The Boyhood of Frederick Douglass in His Own Words,* edited by Michael McCurdy (tweens); and his three autobiographies, *The Narrative of the Life of Frederick Douglass: An American Slave, My Bondage and My Freedom,* and *Life and Times of Frederick Douglass* (teens). A wonderful book (*and* movie) is *Having Our Say: The Delany Sisters' First 100 Years,* by Sarah Louise Delany and Annie Elizabeth Delany (tweens and teens). Among other movies that would be enlightening about the times of Frederick Douglass are: *The Autobiography of Miss Jane Pitman* (tweens and teens); and *Roots* (teens), from the classic by Alex Haley.

Metro: *Don't* use Metro for this area. Take a bus, cab, or car.
1411 W Street, SE
Guided house tours available with reservations; call *way* in
advance (even weeks or, better yet, months) of your visit.
1-800-967-2283. Run by the National Park Service.
202-426-5961
www.nps.gov/frdo/freddoug.html

# Kenilworth Aquatic Gardens

**For All Ages...** The last natural marsh in Washington,
D.C., and the largest group
of water lilies and aquatic
plants in the world, the Kenilworth Aquatic Gardens are
also known for bird-watching
opportunities. Water lilies,
lotuses, water hyacinths, and

## Smart Stuff

**For Tikes...** There are lots
of stories of make-believe
people so small they can fit
into tiny spaces. Make up a
story about a person or animal that lives inside a lotus
flower. What happens to
the flower at night?

rare, exotic varieties of other water plants all flourish here, in the
forty-four ponds over the twelve acres that make up the gardens.
These ponds and marshes, along with the Anacostia estuary, provide
natural habitats for waterfowl, turtles, frogs, and small mammals,
including muskrats, raccoons, and opossums. A ¾-mile trail leads
past the marshland to an outlook across the Anacostia River.

Possibly the oldest
flower seeds ever cultivated,
those from the stunning,
pink East Indian Lotus, were
transported from a Man-
churian lakebed in 1951.
They are believed to have
been between 350 and 960

## Smart Stuff

**For Tweens and Teens...**
What ancient civilization
depicted the lotus flower
as a crown for their kings
and queens? (H.)

years old! This gives a whole new meaning to the term "late bloomer!"

The Visitors Center has a map of the ponds, as well as pamphlets and brochures, an aquarium exhibit, artwork, and a display on the Gardens' history. Picnic tables are available, and National Park Service naturalists lead nature walks in the Gardens on summer weekends.

Begun inauspiciously on his property, the gardens were a hobby of Walter B. Shaw, a Civil War veteran. In 1882, he planted some water lilies from his original home in Maine near his new house by the Anacostia River. His water plants multiplied so rapidly that his hobby became a commercial venture. The gardens became a popular spot for Washingtonians' Sunday outings in the 1920s.

> Metro: Deanwood, *but* don't come by Metro. For safety's sake, come by bus, cab, or car; the surrounding area is definitely *not* a safe place to be walking
>
> Anacostia Avenue and Douglass Street, NE; .2 miles south of Jct. US 50 (New York Avenue) and Kenilworth Avenue, NE
>
> Open daily 8 A.M.–4 P.M.; closed January 1, Thanksgiving, and December 25
>
> Operated by the National Park Service
>
> Special environmental education programs offered; call for details.
>
> Most plants in bloom May through September; go before 1 P.M. for best view
>
> 202-426-6905

# Where to Stay in Northeast and Southeast D.C.

While much of this area requires real caution, there are places to stay, some with restaurants and pools, and even group-rate bargains to be found. But for safety's sake, use the Metro shuttle services offered free with your stay.

### Capitol Hill Suites
200 C Street, SE
202-543-6000 or 1-800-537-8483
Metro: Capitol South

### Days Inn-Gateway
2700 New York Avenue, NE
202-832-5800 or 1-800-832-0012
Metro: Union Station, with free shuttle bus six times a day

### Gallaudet University Kellogg Conference Center
800 Florida Avenue, NE, on campus at Gallaudet University
202-651-6000
Metro: Union Station, with shuttle service (Monday through
    Friday)

### Travelodge Gateway
1917 Bladensburg Road, NE
202-832-8600 or 1-800-231-4270
Metro: Union Station, with shuttle service

# Answers to Smart Stuff Questions

**A.** Saint Elizabeth Ann Bayley Seton was born in 1774 to a Protestant family, and was both a wife and mother before she turned to Catholicism. Entering the novitiate as a widow, she rose to become mother superior of her convent. After her death, she was credited with the miraculous healing of several people with incurable diseases. This native-born American woman was canonized in 1975.

**B.** The state tree of Alaska is the Sitka spruce. The state tree of Hawaii is the kukui tree.

**C.** If a child brings up the idea of running away, you might talk a bit about the Underground Railroad.

**D.** The Latin motto is *Semper fidelis,* which means "Always faithful."

**E.** The Marines always go first; they are the official amphibious landing force of the United States armed services, and are thus in great personal danger.

**F.** A ship that can carry planes on its decks is called an aircraft carrier.

**G.** Often considered the "father of the U.S. Navy," John Paul Jones, aboard his ship, *The Bonhomme Richard,* refused to surrender to the British (during the Revolutionary War), declaring: "I have not yet begun to fight!"

**H.** The lotus flower was pictured by the ancient Egyptians in its closed, or nighttime, form, as the tall white crown for royalty. In both India and ancient Egypt, the lotus played an important role in religion. In one legend, it was said to be the birthplace and residence of the sun god, Atum or Ra. Closing at night, the flower's petals hid the sunlight from the earth.

CHAPTER
11

# Northern Virginia

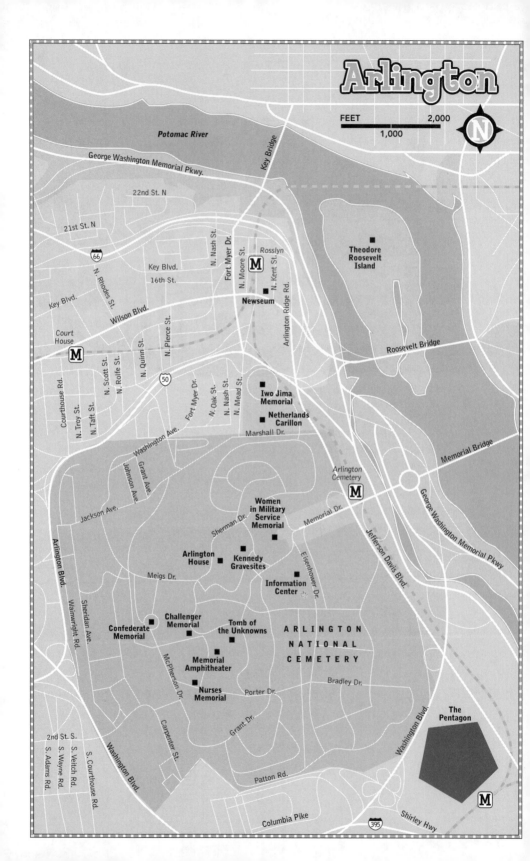

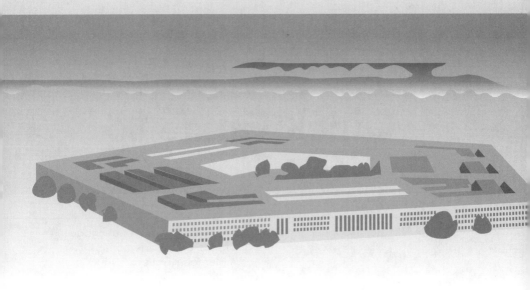

I f you like sightseeing outdoors, here's an opportunity to spend time in some beautiful and meaningful settings. From **Arlington National Cemetery**'s many different kinds of monuments and memorials, to **Theodore Roosevelt Island**'s idyllic setting, Northern Virginia offers opportunities for enjoyment of nature and reflection on man. The **Newseum** and the **Pentagon** afford different opportunities, for a look at the fast-paced worlds of journalism and the military. Whatever stops are of interest to you, it's worth a trip, as the natives say, "across the bridge."

## ★Arlington National Cemetery

**For All Ages...** It is rare that a tourist site is also a place with emotional impact, but

### Smart Stuff

**For Tikes...** This is a cemetery mostly for famous soldiers. If you could design a soldier's uniform for *yourself*, what would it look like? What would your rank be? If you like to draw, make a picture of yourself in your make-believe uniform.

# Quick Guide to

| Attraction | Location |
| --- | --- |
| ★Arlington National Cemetery | Directly across Memorial Bridge from the Lincoln Memorial, just off Memorial Drive |
| Iwo Jima Memorial, Marine Corps War Memorial | Fort Myer Drive (just outside the Arlington National Cemetery, near the Netherlands Carillon) |
| Netherlands Carillon | Off U.S. Route 50, just outside Arlington National Cemetery, and near the Marine Corps War Memorial |
| ★Newseum | 1101 Wilson Boulevard, Arlington, Virginia |
| Theodore Roosevelt Island | Between the District and Virginia, on the Potomac River, just north of the Theodore Roosevelt Bridge |
| The Pentagon | In northern Virginia, across the Potomac River from Washington, D.C. |

# Northern Virginia Attractions

| Age Range | Hours | Details on |
|---|---|---|
| All Ages | 8 A.M.–7 P.M. daily (April–Sept.), 8 A.M.–5 P.M. (rest of year); see individual sites for details | Page 275 |
| All Ages | Sunset Parade the last Tuesday in May; third Tuesday in August, 7 P.M. | Page 294 |
| All Ages | Bells: Sat. 6 P.M.–8 P.M. (June–August); Sat. 2 P.M.–4 P.M. (May, July 4, and September) | Page 295 |
| All Ages | Wed.–Sun. 10 A.M.–5 P.M. | Page 296 |
| All Ages | Dawn to dusk, daily | Page 299 |
| Teens | Guided tours only: Mon.–Fri. 9 A.M.–3 P.M. | Page 300 |

this is one. Set high on hills overlooking the city, Arlington National Cemetery is the final resting place of over 230,000 of our

Of course everyone can visit here, but it is important to recognize that some visitors here are *not* tourists; they are family and friends visiting loved ones. Every week there are 90 to 100 burials here. Demeanor and voices must be appropriate during the visit to Arlington National Cemetery.

nation's veterans, statesmen, and national heroes, and their dependents. Participants in all our nation's wars, even some from the Confederacy, can be identified by clearly marked headstones. Sections of the cemetery are dedicated to astronauts, chaplains, and nurses who were veterans. Until 1948, interment locations were determined by race and rank; now, however, a private and a general might lie side by side.

In addition to the Tomb of the Unknowns, from our four major wars, the cemetery has poignant memorials to those who have served the United States from the battlefield to space flight to the White House. The sound of *Taps,* gracing even the most standard funeral here, can be overwhelming.

## Helpful Hint

Don't come here without eating first, and eating well. First, there is no food sold here at all, nor can you even eat snacks you might have hidden in your pockets while you are on the cemetery's grounds. Also, it can get pretty hot in the middle of a summer day, so plan to make your cemetery visit *early* or *late* in the day.

Metro: Arlington Cemetery
Directly across Memorial Bridge from the Lincoln Memorial,
    just off Memorial Drive

Open daily 8 A.M.–7 P.M. April through September; 8 A.M.–
5 P.M. rest of year

Tourmobiles from the visitor center are the only vehicular
transportation through the cemetery (relatives visiting
gravesites request temporary passes to drive in).

Tourmobile offers the only *guided* tours here.

Tourmobile: 202-554-5100

Visitor Center phone: 703-607-8052

http://xroads.virginia.edu/~CAP/ARLINGTON/arlington.html

## Information Center

A visit to Arlington National Cemetery involves a great deal of
walking, whether you are heading for a specific gravesite or wandering among many. Tourmobile also offers guided tours throughout
the cemetery, leaving the Information Center every fifteen to twenty
minutes; you can get on and off at various stopping points along the
way. Bathrooms are located here and *only* here (until you get to the
Arlington House), so remember to take advantage of the facilities.

First, pick up a map; then you can plan the cemetery sites you
would like to visit. The location of any specific person's burial site is
available here. Exhibits clarify what there is to see; informative
brochures, as well as books and videos, are all offered in the Information Center.

## Arlington House, The Robert E. Lee Memorial

On a June day in 1831, a young couple got married in the front
parlor of this house, and were destined to live in it for thirty years.
Mary Anna Randolph Custis, great-granddaughter of Martha
Washington, married her teenaged love, a dashing young military
officer named Robert E. Lee. They lived in the house with her parents, and inherited the estate. Six of their seven children were born
here. As a colonel in the United States Army, Lee wrote one of his
sons as late as January 1861, "Secession is nothing but revolution."
Yet, in the end, he felt obligated to fight with his region. On April
22, 1861, U.S. Army Col. Robert E. Lee accepted the command of
the Confederate forces when his home state of Virginia joined the

## Smart Stuff

**For Tweens and Teens...** Robert E. Lee gave up his commission in the U.S. military, and President Lincoln's offer to head the Union army, to accept command of the Confederate forces. He said that he could not bear arms against his own state. His father, "Lighthorse Harry" Lee, was a famous patriot in the American Revolution. If *you* had been a Lee family member in 1861, what course of action would you have advocated? Why?

Confederacy. One month later, Union troops quartered officers in the house and soldiers on the surrounding property. Lee's long-time friend, fellow Southerner and Quartermaster General Montgomery Meigs, retaliated for Lee's desertion of the Union Army and chose Lee's estate as the home for the National Cemetery. With war dead buried in their yard, the Lee family never returned to live in this home, and sold it to the U.S. government in 1882.

## Smart Stuff

**For Tikes...** Can you find a picture of a Civil War soldier? Can you tell by the color in which army he fought? Why do you think neither side chose red, yellow, or orange?

## Smart Stuff

**For Tweens...** What was the name of General Lee's famous horse? (It never shied away from battle, and even had bullets whiz beneath its belly.) (A.)

Interestingly, his own family mirrored the upheaval that confounded even the closest of ties: His cousin, also named Robert E. Lee, was a Union officer. Still revered in the South as a man of integrity and valor,

Robert E. Lee's memory is preserved here, on the grounds he once called home.

In one of history's ironies, Congress dedicated Arlington House in Robert E. Lee's honor in 1925, and in 1955, made it a permanent memorial. Today, park rangers in period costumes answer questions and assist visitors on self-guided tours. Some of the furnishings are original to the house. Note Lee's bedroom upstairs, where he signed his resignation from the U.S. Army. Slave quarters and a small museum are adjacent to the house. Both Mrs. Lee and her mother, Mrs. Custis, taught their slaves to read and write in this house, and Robert E. Lee officially freed all his slaves at Arlington House in 1863, even though the Confederacy was still fighting to preserve the institution of slavery.

> Open daily 9:30 A.M.–4:30 P.M.; closed January 1 and December 25
> Run by the National Park Service
> 703-557-0613

## Gravesite of General Omar Bradley

The last American five-star general, Omar Bradley commanded the Twelfth Army Group in World War II, the largest single command ever held by an American officer. He is only one of five people ever to hold that rank.

## Challenger Memorial

This memorial honors the crew of the space shuttle

**Smart Stuff**

For Tweens and Teens...
Who was called the "soldiers' soldier?" Why? (B.)

*Challenger,* which exploded just after its lift-off in 1986. The vertical monument depicts the crew on the front and the poem "High Flight," by John G. Magee Jr. (quoted by President Ronald Reagan in memoriam) on the reverse. The remains of crew members Dick Scobee and Michael Smith, as well as the unidentified remains of others, are buried in the cemetery.

*Challenger* was the first space flight to have a private citizen aboard, the public school teacher, Christa McAuliffe. The crew: Mission Commander Dick Scobee, Mike Smith, Greg Jarvis, Ron McNair, Judy Resnick, and Ellison Onizuka, was also representative of some American minorities; McNair was African American, Resnick was Jewish, and Onizuka was Asian American. The *Challenger* explosion marked the only American space shuttle disaster in the twentieth century.

## The Confederate Memorial

Confederate soldiers are also buried in Arlington National Cemetery. Life-size figures of soldiers (both white and black), sweethearts separating, parents and children, Roman goddesses, and women representing Bible verses are featured in the Confederate Memorial. A statue of a war-like goddess supports a wounded woman clinging to a shield, the sculptor's emotional portrayal of his region's losses. The frieze in bronze at the base depicts Southern troops departing for battle and then returning in defeat. The monument's designer, Moses Jacob Ezekiel, is buried at its base, himself a Confederate veteran.

Commissioned in 1900 to commemorate the sacrifices of the men fighting for the Confederacy, the monument was erected in 1914 on the birthday of Jefferson Davis, the only president of the Confederacy. It was dedicated by President Woodrow Wilson, a native of Virginia, who said, " turn your faces to the future. . .as we have shed our blood upon opposite sides, we now face and admire one another."

Arranged in concentric circles around the monument, the gravestones of the Confederate soldiers have pointed tops. Some say it's to keep Yankees from sitting on them.

An interesting view of the Confederacy is presented in *Military Memoirs of a Confederate: A Critical Narrative* (teens), by General Edward Porter Alexander.

## Gravesite of Justice William O. Douglas

Appointed to the Supreme Court by Franklin Delano Roosevelt in 1939 at the extraordinarily young age of 41, Justice William O.

Douglas was an outspoken advocate for individual rights. He served for thirty-six years. A native of Washington state, he was also a staunch conservationist and made a lasting contribution to Washington, D.C., by helping to preserve the historic C & O Canal (now a popular recreation site) from destruction by developers.

It is interesting to read about complex people like Justice Douglas. Two books Douglas wrote are about different aspects of his life: *Go East, Young Man: The Early Years (Autobiography)* (teens), by William O. Douglas; and *Nature's Justice: Writings of William O. Douglas* (teens), by William O. Douglas.

## Gravesite of Medgar Evers

A towering figure in the American Civil Rights struggle, Medgar Evers was assassinated for his efforts. But his dream of equal rights for African Americans continued; only one year after his death, Congress enacted the Civil Rights Act of 1964, prohibiting public, employment, and union discrimination. Since then, African Americans have assumed the posts of mayor (including Evers' brother Charles, in his home state of Mississippi), governor, members of Congress, ambassador to the United Nations, and to numerous foreign countries, and a wide variety of cabinet positions, including secretary of state. The legacy of Medgar Evers continues.

The movie story about Medgar Evers, *Ghosts of Mississippi* (teens) is also told in a book, *The Ghosts of Medgar Evers: A Tale of Race, Murder, Mississippi, and Hollywood* (teens), by Willie Morris. Also, the film *Mississippi Burning* (teens) paints, in graphic detail, the racism prevalent at the time.

## Gravesite of Justice Oliver Wendell Holmes

Son of the famous author of *The Autocrat of the Breakfast Table*, Oliver Wendell Holmes Jr. spent a lifetime trying to measure up to his accomplished father. Eventually, he succeeded. Known as "the great dissenter," he became a justice of the United States Supreme Court in 1902 (appointed by Theodore Roosevelt). He helped Theodore's cousin, Franklin Delano Roosevelt, select his successor to the Court. Holmes was renowned for his learning and wisdom, and was a brilliant advocate of individual rights.

## Iran Rescue Mission Memorial

Sometimes heroes have to rescue other heroes. In 1980, the soldiers sent to free the fifty-three U.S. hostages held by the fanatic Iranian government, died in an aircraft accident in the attempt; this is a memorial to those men. Sometimes the price we pay for liberty is high.

## Gravesites of President John F. Kennedy and Jacqueline Kennedy Onassis

When President Kennedy visited Arlington, twelve days before his assassination in November 1963, he was heard to remark, "It's so peaceful here, I could stay here forever." This president, long on grace and ideals, but short on time to accomplish his goals, sent a nation and a generation into mourning at his death. A young husband, father, and charismatic leader, Kennedy strode onto the national stage as the personification of a dynamic, progressive era in America. An entire generation gauged their dreams by his, and many chose their life's work as a result of his call to public service. His death punctuated a time of turbulence seared into the consciousness of all who lived through it, and barely believable to later generations.

**Smart Stuff**

**For Tweens and Teens...**
When President Kennedy was assassinated, his widow decided on an eternal flame as his memorial. Why do you think Mrs. Kennedy used this symbol? Do you feel it is effective? Why or why not?

Marked by an eternal flame, President Kennedy's marble, slate, and Cape Cod fieldstone gravesite also includes a low wall with quotes from his speeches. How apt that the torch he spoke of being "passed to a new generation" is echoed in the flame above his grave and can be seen at night from many points around the city.

Next to him lie his wife, former first lady Jacqueline Bouvier Kennedy Onassis, and two of their children who died in infancy.

Kennedy family books abound, but here are some of particular interest: *When John and Caroline Lived in the White House* (tweens), by Laurie Coulter; *The John F. Kennedys: A Family Album* (tweens and teens), by Mark Show and Richard Reeves; *Jackie: Her Life in Pictures* (tweens and teens), by James Spada; *President Kennedy: Profile of Power* (teens), by Richard Reeves (a behind-the-scenes view of the Kennedy administration); and *Conversations with Kennedy* (teens), by Benjamin Bradlee. A movie about the 1962 Cuban missile crisis came out early in 2001: *Thirteen Days* (teens).

## Gravesite of Senator Robert F. Kennedy

This was the Kennedy who tended to evoke both the greatest adoration and the strongest animosity. As a young man, he worked on the notorious Senator Joseph McCarthy's House Un-American Activities Committee, which used hearsay and fabrication to brand hundreds of innocent Americans as communists in the 1950s, frequently ruining their lives. In public life on his own, he authorized numerous projects for underprivileged families, and worked tirelessly for those America had forgotten.

His assassination on the eve of his nomination as the Democratic Party's presidential candidate in June 1968 was a major event in the turmoil of the Vietnam and Civil Rights eras. Many of his bereaved, youthful followers lost faith in the efficacy of government as the engine to repair social ills. His absence is still mourned by advocates for the poor, the hungry, and the disenfranchised in America.

Robert F. Kennedy evoked controversy when he was named attorney general in his brother President Kennedy's Cabinet. He turned out to be a thoughtful and restrained counselor, and his brother's most trusted advisor. What do you think about a national leader bringing a family member into his or her administration?

Two books teens might enjoy are: *Robert Kennedy: His Life,* by Evan Thomas (even though it is very lengthy); and *85 Days: The Last Campaign of Robert Kennedy,* by Jules Witcover (out of print, but worth finding in your library).

## Tomb of Pierre L'Enfant

The original planner of the District of Columbia, French engineer Pierre L'Enfant had to wait over a hundred years to be recognized for his genius. True to his name, L'Enfant often behaved in a juvenile fashion, and managed to alienate everyone he worked with, finally incurring the displeasure of the man who hired him, General George Washington. After L'Enfant was fired, it fell to his remarkable assistant, Benjamin Banneker, to bring the work to fruition. Pierre L'Enfant died practically penniless, and was buried in a pauper's grave in nearby Prince George's County, Maryland.

### Smart Stuff
**For Tweens and Teens...** Pierre L'Enfant provided the broad tree-lined avenues and open green spaces reminiscent of what city? Compared to other cities you know, how pedestrian-friendly is D.C.'s downtown area? (C.)

In 1908, the city's Board of Commissioners realized the debt owed to this talented man, and requested the secretary of war to make a burial site available in Arlington. In 1909, after lying in state in the Capitol Rotunda, L'Enfant's body was re-interred in Arlington National Cemetery. His original design for the city is depicted on the top of the monument at his gravesite, located in front of Arlington House (the Robert E. Lee Memorial). The view of the city he designed is breathtaking.

## Gravesite of Joe Louis

Known affectionately as "the Brown Bomber," Joseph Louis Barrow avenged his 1936 loss to German boxer Max Schmeling to gain the title of Heavyweight Champion of the World in 1938, a title he retained for twelve years. He brought special pride to African Americans living in a less tolerant time.

Two books we can suggest for teens are: *Champion Joe Louis: A Biography*, by Chris Mead; and *Joe Louis: The Great Black Hope*, by Richard Bak. A movie classic, starring James Earl Jones, is *The Great White Hope* (teens).

## Gravesite of Justice Thurgood Marshall

The nation's first black Supreme Court Justice, Thurgood Marshall, gained renown when he argued on behalf of the National Association for the Advancement of Colored People (NAACP) for desegregation of America's public schools in the landmark case, *Brown v. (Topeka, Kansas) Board of Education*. The successful outcome effectively ended the practice of mandating two unequal school systems in the U.S.—one for blacks and one for whites. In one of history's delightful twists, the African American lawyer who asked the land's highest court to ensure the educational rights of black children rose to become the first black member of that court.

A *Look Magazine* cover that appeared January 14, 1964, brought the school desegregation issue dramatically to life. Artist Norman Rockwell depicted in "The Problem We All Live With" a little girl in a starched white dress being escorted to school by federal marshals; this was a portrait of six-year-old Ruby Bridges, in her poignant attempt to enter her elementary school in New Orleans—the first black child to attend. On the wall behind

**Smart Stuff**

For Tweens and Teens...
What governor vowed to "stand in the schoolhouse door" to prevent integration of his state's public schools? What happened? (D.)

her are the splattered remains of a thrown tomato. Find this picture in your library. In a collection of Rockwell's paintings, two others also deal with integration: the *Look Magazine* cover of May 16, 1967, bears the picture titled "New Kids in the Neighborhood," and his Boy Scout Calendar of 1961 shows a black Cub Scout in a sea of white scouting faces.

Some books to consider are: *A Picture Book of Thurgood Marshall (Picture Book Biography)* (tikes and tweens), by David A. Adler and Robert Casilla; and *Thurgood Marshall: American Revolutionary* (teens), by Juan Williams.

## Nurses Memorial

A white stone statue of a nurse in uniform surveys the army, navy, and air force nurses buried with their service brothers in Arlington National Cemetery. Sculpted by Frances Rich, this monument originally honored the nurses who served so valiantly in World War I. In 1971, the monument was rededicated to commemorate "devoted service to country and humanity by Army, Navy, and Air Force Nurses."

**Col. Anita Newcomb McGee,** founder of the Army Nurse Corps in 1901, was the only woman with the rank of assistant surgeon of the U.S. Army. A veteran of the Spanish-American War, she was instrumental in the establishment of this memorial. Dr. McGee was buried with full military honors in the cemetery in 1940.

Several books on nursing that are of interest here are: *Angels of Mercy: The Army Nurses of World War II* (tweens), by Betsy Kuhn; and *G.I. Nightingales: The Army Nurse Corps in World War II* (teens), by Barbara Brooks Tomblin.

## Memorial Amphitheater; Mast of USS *Maine*

The Grand Army of the Republic, a Civil War group, spearheaded the idea for a ceremonial spot appropriate to the nation's military cemetery. Woodrow Wilson laid the cornerstone in 1915; it was dedicated on Memorial Day in 1920. There are crowds here for memorial services on Memorial Day, Veterans Day, and Easter Sunday; it is quite a colorful spectacle to see the miniature American flags on all the graves on Memorial Day weekend.

The mast of the USS *Maine,* the ship blown up in Havana harbor in 1898, brought to this spot in 1912, serves as a memorial to the 229 crewmen who died. This incident at sea precipitated U.S. entry into the Spanish-American War. Located behind the amphitheater and just across Memorial Drive, the mast rests on a battle-ship-style turret, with the names of the dead inscribed around it. It is a dramatic monument to a bygone era of American imperialism.

## Memorial to I. J. Paderewski

This Polish pianist, composer, and statesman (who died in 1941) had requested that he be buried in Arlington until his homeland became a free country. In 1992, his remains were re-interred in his native Poland.

To learn more about this renowned musician, listen to music he played; some accessible examples are: *Paderewski Plays Chopin, Vol. 2, Great Pianists of the 20th Century,* and *Grand Piano—Ignaz Jan Paderewski.*

## Gravesite of Robert Edwin Peary

A tireless explorer of the northern reaches of the planet (he proved Greenland was an island rather than a continent), Robert Edwin Peary contributed to our scientific knowledge of the peoples he encountered. He adapted Inuit survival skills to his arctic travel. After several unsuccessful attempts, he reached the North Pole on April 6, 1909. A civil engineer in the U.S. Navy, Peary retired from exploration in 1911. In recognition of his achievement, Congress bestowed on him the rank of rear admiral before he retired.

Some books that treat Peary's adventures are: *Robert Peary and the Quest for North Pole (World Explorers)* (tweens), by Christopher Dwyer; and *Robert E. Peary and the Fight for the North Pole* (tweens and teens), by Madalyn Klein Anderson.

It is now disputed whether Peary's assistant, Matthew Henson (an African American), reached the North Pole ahead of him. Henson wrote *A Black Explorer at the North Pole: An Autobiographical Report by the Negro Who Conquered the Top of the World with Admiral Robert E. Peary* (teens), an interesting view of this history.

## Gravesite of John Joseph Pershing

The only American six-star general gained renown as the leader of the American Expeditionary Force in Europe during World War I.

He was also General of the Armies of the United States, a rank he shared only with George Washington.

His memoirs, *My Experiences in the World War (Military Classics Series)* (teens), give a vivid firsthand account of his experiences. *Until the Last Trumpet Sounds: The Life of General of the Armies John J. Pershing* (teens), by Gene A. Smith, is another view.

## Rough Riders Monument

Also known as the Spanish-American War Memorial, the Rough Riders Monument commemorates the Spanish-American War fought in Cuba at the end of the nineteenth century. President Theodore Roosevelt, brought to prominence through his battlefield adventures at that time, dedicated the monument in 1902. Resigning his post as secretary of the navy in 1898, Lt. Col. Roosevelt organized the Rough Riders (a band of enthusiastic recruits) in order to get in on the military action in this brief war.

For young readers (and listeners), the Step-Up Book Series offers *Meet Theodore Roosevelt,* by Ormonde De Kay Jr. an appealing overview of the life of our nation's youngest president. Tweens might enjoy *Bully for You, Teddy Roosevelt,* by Jean Fritz; and teens can explore *The Boys of '98: Theodore Roosevelt and the Rough Riders,* by Dale L. Walker; and *Carry a Big Stick: The Uncommon Heroism of Theodore Roosevelt (Leaders in Action Series),* by George E. Grant.

### Smart Stuff

**For Tweens and Teens...**
Not exactly a major conflict, the Spanish-American War included Theodore Roosevelt's much-publicized "charge up San Juan Hill." (Actually, his men captured Kettle Hill, but don't be dismayed by the discrepancies—that's history.) As the result of clever publicity, Roosevelt emerged from his military adventure as a "war hero," and later became U.S. president.

What part do you feel "advertising" plays in our perceptions of public figures?

## Gravesite of Albert Sabin, M.D.

Albert Sabin, lieutenant colonel in the U.S. Army Medical Corps, served more than the armed forces when he developed the first oral polio vaccine. It is estimated that his work prevented millions of cases of paralytic polio and hundreds of thousands of deaths in the years since the vaccine became available in 1961.

Polio, a forgotten disease for today's youth, comes graphically to life in: *Close to Home: A Story of the Polio Epidemic (Once Upon America Series)* (tweens), by Lydia Weaver; and *Small Steps: The Year I Got Polio* (tweens), by Peg Kehrret and Denise Shanahan.

## Gravesite of President William Howard Taft

An enormous person with a resume to match, William Howard Taft, weighing in at 300 pounds, definitely made a mark on his times. As governor of the Philippines, secretary of war, the president of the United States, and chief justice of the Supreme Court, Taft was the *only* person to have held *both* of the latter two positions. Not bad to be chief justice in your retirement from the White House!

> All of Taft's personal settings had to allow for his large girth. There is a tale that he even got stuck in the White House bathtub. Subsequently, a huge new tub replaced it.

Tweens can get some of the flavor of the Taft era in *Lost at the White House: A 1909 Easter Story,* by Lisa Griest and Andrea Shine, and teens can get a feel for Taft in his professional life in *William Howard Taft, Chief Justice,* by Alpheus Thomas Mason.

## Tomb of the Unknown Dead of the Civil War

The 2,111 unidentified soldiers who died on nearby Virginia battlefields in the Civil War are memorialized by a huge granite marker over their mass grave. The war with the greatest number of casualties in proportion to our population in our nation's history, the Civil War left over half a million soldiers dead from a population of

31.5 million (1860). By contrast, the American death toll from World War II numbered just over one million from a population of between 132 and 150 million, and the War in Vietnam claimed only 211,556 from a population of between 179 and 203 million.

*Soldiers' Heart: Being the Story of the Enlistment and Due Service of the Boy Charley Goddard in the First Minnesota Volunteers* (tweens and teens), by Gary Paulsen, is a coming-of-age tale of a 15-year-old volunteer in the Minnesota militia of the Union Army.

## Tomb of the Unknowns

"Here rests in honored glory an American soldier known but to God" is the inscription on the Tomb of the Unknowns, one of Arlington National Cemetery's most visited sites. Troops from the Third U.S. Infantry Regiment (known as the "Old Guard") stand as sentinels here twenty-four hours a day. Children are especially fascinated by the drills these troops carry out, facing the tomb, marching, and shifting their M-14 rifles in precision time.

The secret to the sharp sound of the sentinels' clicking heels is taps on the bottoms of their shoes. If their hands look cold in the winter, it's because they are required to wet their gloves in order to have a firmer grip on their custom-made guns. To see the ceremony of the changing of the guard, visit on the half-hour (from April 1 to September 30, 8 A.M.–7 P.M.) or on the hour (from October 1 to March 31, 8 A.M.–5 P.M.); the guard is changed every two hours at night.

*At the Tomb of the Unknowns*

There is *no* soldier buried in the Tomb of the Unknowns from the Vietnam War. DNA tests identified the soldier buried there as Lieutenant Michael Blassie, who was shot down in his A-37 plane in 1962. He was subsequently buried in his hometown, at the request of his family.

## Women in Military Service for America Memorial

Finally, a little attention for the distaff side. Completed in 1997, the Women in Military Service for America Memorial commemorates the service of the 1.8 million women who served the nation from the American Revolution through the present. In nearly every American war, women have played a military role, frequently as spies, but occasionally as soldiers disguised as men, in addition to serving as soldiers in uniform for their country. It took many years for the United States to commission women as officially acknowledged members of our armed forces. But, by the turn of the twenty-first century, women had earned commanding positions in all branches of the armed services.

Even the marines finally commissioned women. In 1943, Oveta Culp Hobby was sworn in by President Franklin Delano Roosevelt as the first female American marine.

Set into the side of a hill, an **Education Center** with a **Hall of Honor** exhibits photographs and artifacts that depict the history of U.S. servicewomen. There is also a computer register to trace specific history and individuals, as well as informative films, a gift shop, and bookstore. A brochure offers a self-guided tour through the memorial.

The site itself affords a spectacular view of Washington. Constructed of reinforced concrete and several colors of granite, a semicircular wall (Hemicycle), glass tablets of etched quotations, and a Court of Honor, with a fountain in front, the memorial is a dramatic

A sign of the times: a 1979 recruitment ad for the U.S. Army read, "Some of our best men are women."

tribute to the individual and collective efforts of women in service to the military.

Located at the entrance to the cemetery
Daily 8 A.M.–7 A.M., April through September; 8 A.M.–5 P.M. rest of year; closed December 25
703-533-1155 or 1-800-222-2294

# Iwo Jima Memorial, Marine Corps War Memorial

**For All Ages...** Appropriately situated on a promontory at the north end of Arlington National Cemetery, overlooking the city, the Marine Corps War Memorial commemorates the battle at Mount Suribachi in 1945, where 6,321 U.S. soldiers died. It is an image etched in our national memory—six American Marines struggling to raise the flag on a rocky hilltop their comrades died

## Smart Stuff

**For Tikes...** When you salute the flag, where do you put your hand? Where does a soldier put his? Try "standing at attention." What do you do with your feet? (E.)

## Smart Stuff

**For Tweens and Teens...** The U.S. Military knew that taking Japan was going to involve massive casualties, especially in initial landings. President Harry S. Truman justified using the first atomic bomb as a way of bringing Japan to surrender, while saving the lives of thousands of American troops. If you were an officer ordered to land in that first wave of attack on the Japanese mainland, what would *you* have advised? Why?

*Iwo Jima
Memorial*

trying to secure. Sculpted by Felix W. de Weldon and based on the Pulitzer Prize-winning photograph by Joe Rosenthal, the statue is inscribed with a comment from Admiral Chester Nimitz: "Uncommon valor was a common virtue."

> Metro: Rosslyn; a five-minute walk east on Ft. Myer Drive
> Sunset Parade: the last Tuesday in May through the third Tuesday in August, 7 P.M. (free shuttle bus service from the cemetery); for information, phone: 202-433-4073 202-208-4748 or 202-433-6060, for parade reservations

# Netherlands Carillon

**For All Ages...** Commemorating Holland's liberation from the Nazis on May 5, 1945, the Netherlands Carillon holds a set of forty-nine bells, each given by a different segment of that country's population. Housed in a 127-foot tower, the Carillon was a gift in gratitude for United States aid during and after World War II. Park rangers give a brief explanation half an hour before each concert; sometimes visitors can climb the tower and watch the bell-ringers perform: an a-pealing experience.

> Off U.S. Route 50, just outside Arlington National Cemetery, and near the Marine Corps War Memorial
> Bells play June through August, Saturday 6–8 P.M.; May, July 4, and September, Saturday 2–4 P.M.
> 703-289-2530

# ★Newseum

**For All Ages...** It's not news that a museum devoted to stories that captured the nation would be a "hot item" on the tourist circuit. What is newsworthy is the way this particular museum works. In a multilevel setting (and at a currently out-of-the-way location), the Newseum brings the viewer into the role of journalistic participant.

## Smart Stuff

**For Tikes...** What is the biggest news that ever happened in your family? Try "broadcasting" your news on the Newseum's television. What could you do to make your audience excited about your story? (F.)

Through interactive exhibits, memory-dredging film clips, and a series of imaginative displays, this museum reminds us that we are *all* participants in history—and some of it is, indeed, historic. Take the escalator up to the theater to watch the 13-minute film that explains the Newseum's functions. There is even a broadcast studio on site, and viewers can watch through a glass window to see television programs in production. (Check the posted schedule for a list of daily programs.) An enormous 126-foot-long **Video News Wall** offers a dramatic view of historic broadcasts as well as late-breaking current news. This is definitely a pulse-quickening place, and children love to visit. One of the favorite activities for all ages is the **Interactive Newsroom,** where you can try your hand at being a news reporter, editor, photographer or on-camera newscaster—and see yourself on screen. After you have had your five minutes of fame, you can visit the **Ethics Center,** which focuses on journalists' frequently difficult choices, and evaluate your own biases.

Your own hometown newspaper might be featured on the **News Globe,** which includes 1,841 newspaper nameplates from around the world. The monitors nearby will respond to your instructions and print a Birthday Banner, with news from the month

## Smart Stuff

**For Tweens and Teens...** Journalists frequently make tough choices: Editors, publishers, the story "source" and even the government of the location where the story is taking place may exert pressure to "kill" a story or slant it in a specific direction. Assume you were covering a story about worker abuse (intolerable working conditions, unacceptably low pay, discrimination against particular categories of worker, or any combination of your choosing) in a factory located in a distant country (the Far East or South America, for example) and you found your publisher was part of a conglomerate that owns the plant. Your editor wants you to "kill" the story and the foreign government is beginning to harass you for your "interference" in their workplaces. You have just been told that your passport will be confiscated until you agree to leave the country, and you realize that your next visit to the factory will likely land you in a foreign jail. What would you do? (PS: You are *not* Clark Kent.)

that you were born. Proving that time *is* money, these souvenirs are available for purchase.

On a more somber note, older kids should spend a minute of reflection in adjacent **Freedom Park.** The **Freedom Forum Journalists Memorial,** in memory of journalists who gave their lives in pursuit of their calling, reminds us that a free press, like a free society, often has a high price. Replicas of the Goddess of Democracy from Tiananmen Square, a model of a Cuban refugee kayak, and a sculpture of the door from Martin Luther King Jr.'s Birmingham, Alabama, jail cell are all tangible reminders of some of freedom's milestones in the second half of the twentieth century.

The gift shop is on the same level as the entrance, and is well worth a visit. There are wonderfully historic newspapers, books, and photographs available here, as well as the usual souvenir mugs, jewelry, and pens. And the bright silver-colored bags your items will go home in make your purchase really shine.

Journalism makes interesting reading. Teens might enjoy wrestling with the questions posed in *Media Ethics: Where Do You Draw the Line,* by Rosalind G. Stark; and *Every Four Years: Presidential Campaign Coverage 1896–2000,* by Doris Kearns Goodwin. Offered by Close Up Publishing, two videos would also intrigue teens: *Press and the Presidency* and *Close Up Conversations: Reporting from Hot Spots.*

If all this excitement has made your natives restless and hungry, the **News Byte Café** on the lowest level provides light snacks and a variety of drinks. When the weather is welcoming, you can use Freedom Park for a picnic.

If you're in search of an actual place for lunch or a big snack, across the street is the **Wall Street Deli** (1100 Wilson Boulevard; 703-276-3353). Farther west on Wilson Boulevard, in the 1700 block, is **Pho 75** (1711 Wilson Boulevard; 703-525-7355). Here you can try every imaginable variation of beef-noodle stews, in a cafeteria-style setting. The **Lynn Street Café** (1735 N. Lynn Street; 703-525-0384) has great turkey sandwiches. You can reserve the lunchroom at the **Newseum's Education Center Building** in advance (one to three months in advance, through the Education Department), and then you can bring in carry-out from some of these small restaurants; seats ninety people.

Metro: Rosslyn

1101 Wilson Boulevard, Arlington, Virginia

Wednesday through Sunday 10 A.M.–5 P.M.; closed Thanksgiving, December 25 and January 1

Audio tours available in English, French, Spanish, and Japanese for rent at the Audio Tour Desk

Free activity guides are offered at the Level I Information Desk.

A monthly Family Day includes hands-on opportunities for young children.

Educational programs are tailored to school groups. Call the Education Department: 703-284-3545.

Daily schedule of special programs for the public available on the Web or by phone 703-284-3544 or 888-NEWSEUM (toll free)

www.newseum.org

# Theodore Roosevelt Island

**For All Ages...** How appropriate it is that our nation's first "environmental" president should be memorialized on his own island, an oasis of greenery devoid of the trappings of business, government, and even of human habitation. Two-and-a-half miles of (sometimes challenging) hiking trails diverge off into the woods. On a wide plaza, an imposing statue of "T. R.," emphasizing his characteristic vigor, stands guard over this pastoral eighty-eight-acre setting. It was primarily from his prior initiatives that the National Park Service, which oversees many of the outdoor settings in Washington, D.C., (as well as the White House

**Smart Stuff**

**For Tikes...** If you could have your very own island, what would be on it? Draw a picture of your make-believe island. What kind of house would you have?

**Smart Stuff**

**For Tweens...** Theodore Roosevelt was known as our first "environmental" president. One of his legacies is our series of national parks. If you had to name a special area to preserve in *your* home state, what would it be and why would you choose it? (Would you have to "fight" any "special interests" to get this place protected?)

## Smart Stuff

**For Teens...** In Theodore Roosevelt's day, there were fewer industry/ conservationist clashes. What do you see today as our country's biggest environmental danger? If you were president, what course of action would you advocate?

building and grounds, and both the Kennedy Center and Wolf Trap Center for the Performing Arts) was established in 1916. Near the larger-than-life statue, four massive stone tablets carry quotations from his speeches. Roosevelt's eternal "bully pulpit" continues in the National Parks he initiated across the country.

*Theodore Roosevelt: A Life* (teens), by Nathan Miller is a lengthy but interesting story; the movie *The Indomitable Teddy Roosevelt* (teens) brings T. R. to life.

> Metro: Rosslyn, but a long walk from there; most easily reached by car, bus, or taxi.
>
> Between the District and Virginia, on the Potomac River, just north of the Theodore Roosevelt Bridge
>
> Daily dawn to dusk
>
> No bicycles or camping
>
> Park Service rangers give nature and history tours of the island during summer months. Make an appointment at least seven days in advance.
>
> Restrooms are located only at the southwest corner of the island, near the Theodore Roosevelt Bridge.
>
> 703-285-2530

## The Pentagon

**For Teens...** The only building in the city visible from space, the Pentagon is a fitting symbol of the size of the nation's military. In July 1941, with another World War looming, the War Department required larger quarters, so demanded that its planners come up with a

### The Pentagon

suitable building. The familiar edifice took only sixteen months and $50 million to build and is overwhelming in its statistics. The six-and-a-half million square feet (with 131 stairways, nineteen escalators, and seventeen-and-a-half miles of corridors) house the offices of the U.S. Army, Navy, Marine Corps, and Air Force under the umbrella of the (since-named) Defense Department. The military establishment here is so mammoth, it even has four zip codes of its own.

The tour here is quite zippy, as well, possibly because it takes a whole hour and runs over one-and-a-half miles. As befits this kind of marathon, prepare yourself (and all those accompanying you): eat and drink before you come, wear comfortable shoes, and *remember to use a bathroom*. The nearest eating places are at Pentagon City, via Metro.

Some books to consider are: *All My Sons* (teens), by Arthur Miller; *The Hollywood Propaganda of World War II* (teens), by Robert Fyne; *Around the World with the U.S. Navy: A Reporter's Travels* (teens), by Bradley Peniston; *Five Days in London, May 1940* (teens), by John Lukacs; and *The Red Badge of Courage* (an oldie but goodie), by Stephen Crane, which is also a wonderful movie starring Richard Thomas (teens). Films include: *The Day the Earth Stood Still* (tweens and teens); *The Right Stuff* (teens); and *A Few Good Men* (teens).

Both shopping and restaurants are prevalent at **Fashion Centre at Pentagon City** (1100 South Hayes Street, Arlington; Metro: Pentagon City), so if you're now ready for either or both, hop back on the Metro. Here you will find both **Nordstrom** and **Macy's,** as well as **The Gap, Disney Store, Abercrombie and Fitch,** bookstores, toy stores, six movie theaters, and all kinds of food from candy to shakes and hamburgers to seafood to the **Grill at the Ritz-Carlton.** Open Monday through Saturday 10 A.M.–9:30 P.M., Sunday 11 A.M.–6 P.M.

At the next Metro Stop, Crystal City (only one stop from Reagan Washington National Airport), is the **Crystal Underground.** This huge underground mall, with many more stores and restaurants, even has a small museum, the **Patent and Trademark Museum,** worth investigating if you want to explore this area. (Open Monday through Friday 8:30 A.M.–4:30 P.M. and by appointment; 703-305-8341.) There's also a **Days Inn at Crystal City,** a short distance from the Metro and thus a short distance from the airport as well, in case you want to check in near the airport and take the Metro daily to sightseeing.

> Metro: Pentagon
> In northern Virginia, across the Potomac River from Washington, D.C.
> No visits to the Pentagon are permitted *except with early sign-up.*
> Guided tours (1.5 hours) Monday through Friday 9 A.M.–3 P.M.; closed holidays. Tour sign-ups begin 8:45 A.M., limited to 30 per tour. Film presentation. Photo ID required. Children under sixteen must be accompanied by an adult.
> No public restrooms
> 703-695-1776

# Where to Stay in Arlington

For a whole different flavor from the downtown Washington, D.C., areas, maybe you'll want to stay in Arlington near the Newseum.

> ### The Virginian Suites
> 1500 Arlington Boulevard
> 703-522-9600 or 1-800-275-2866
> A suite hotel
> Metro: Rosslyn (free shuttle service to hotel)

### Days Inn Crystal City
2000 Jefferson Davis Hwy. (U.S. 1)
703-920-8600 or 1-800-DAYS INN
One stop from National Airport
Metro: Crystal City

# Answers to Smart Stuff Questions

**A.** Traveler. This horse was the stuff of legends.

**B.** General Omar Bradley was an unpretentious, straightforward leader whose concern for his troops made him a beloved figure in World War II. The present-day Bradley fighting vehicle (tank) is named in his honor.

**C.** L'Enfant wanted the capital of his adopted country to look much like Paris, capital of his native country, France.

**D.** In 1957, Arkansas Governor Orville Faubus brought state troopers to the door of Little Rock High School, forcing a reluctant President Dwight D. Eisenhower to send federal troops to escort embattled black students to school. News photos of the day show Little Rock citizens, old and young, hurling taunts and jeers as the frightened teenagers walked through the crowd.

**E.** We place our right hand over our hearts when saluting the American flag. Soldiers place their right hands to the right sides of their foreheads. Standing at attention includes placing your feet together, side-by-side and touching.

**F.** Some hints to give kids: Using different voice pitches and volumes, beginning with a question, varieties of facial expressions, a dramatic change of mood (angry, happy, scared) will all change a viewer's attitude toward a "broadcast" story.

CHAPTER

12

Olde Virginia

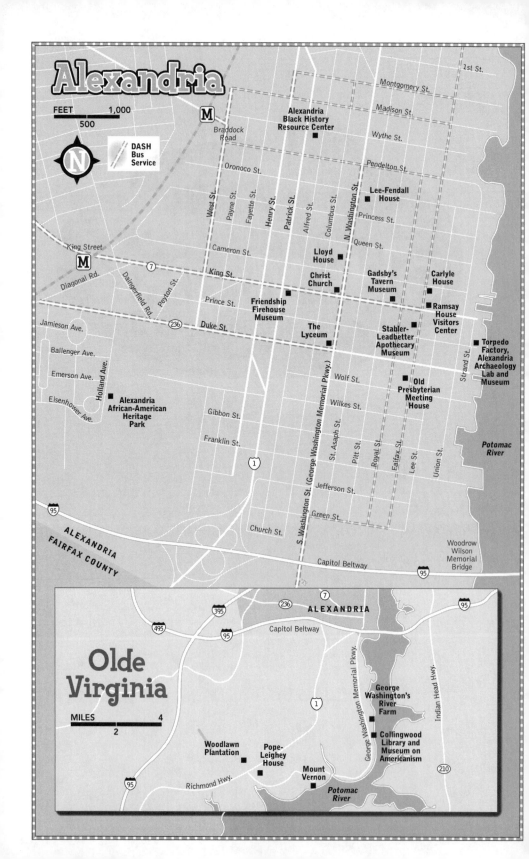

**A** beautiful time warp on the Potomac, Alexandria, Virginia and its Old Town neighborhood exemplify the graciousness of colonial America. From the quiet elegance of **Carlyle House,** to the lively environment of the restored **Gadsby's Tavern,** from the modern handcrafts at the **Torpedo Factory Art Center** to the archaeological artifacts at the **Alexandria Archaeology Lab,** from the rustic setting of **Claude Moore Colonial Farm,** to the timeless grace of George Washington's **Mount Vernon,** there's no shortage of interesting sites to explore. Calling herself "Washington's older sister," Alexandria (and its surroundings) reminds us in our modern society to have respect for age. Authors' note: Many places in this area are closed on Mondays, no doubt the effect of the gracious living of a bygone era.

# ★Old Town Alexandria

**For All Ages...** So why are all those guys marching down the street in *skirts* in the middle of December? It's the annual Scottish Christmas Walk, a Yuletide parade held here because of Alexandria's Scottish roots. It was a group of Scottish tobacco merchants who

# Quick Guide to

| Attraction | Location |
|---|---|
| ★Old Town Alexandria | Metro: King Street (plus a 15-minute walk; take a shuttle bus, or take a DASH bus down King Street) |
| ★Claude Moore Colonial Farm at Turkey Run | Route 495 (Beltway) to Route 193 (Georgetown Pike) East, to access Road, ½ mile on left |
| ★Mount Vernon | 6th and Water Streets, SW |
| George Washington's River Farm | 7932 East Boulevard Drive, Alexandria; off the George Washington Memorial Parkway, 4 miles south of Old Town, Alexandria |
| Collingwood Library and Museum on Americanism | 8301 East Boulevard Drive, Alexandria, off George Washington Parkway |
| Woodlawn Plantation | 7.5 miles south of D.C. on U.S. Route 1 (enter opposite the turnoff for Route 235) |
| Frank Lloyd Wright's Pope–Leighey House | 7.5 miles south of D.C. on U.S. Route 1 (enter opposite the turnoff for Route 235) |

# Olde Virginia Attractions

| Age Range | Hours | Details on |
| --- | --- | --- |
| All Ages | See individual sites for their hours | Page 307 |
| All Ages | Wed.–Sun. 10 A.M.–4:30 P.M. (April–mid-December) | Page 324 |
| All Ages | 8 A.M.–5 P.M. daily (April–August); 9 A.M.–5 P.M. (March, Sept., Oct.), 9 A.M.–4 P.M. (rest of year) | Page 325 |
| All Ages | Mon.–Fri. 8:30 A.M.–5 P.M. | Page 329 |
| Teens | Mon., Wed.–Sat. 10 A.M.–4 P.M.; Sun. 1 P.M.–4 P.M. | Page 331 |
| Tweens and Teens | Guided tours only: 10 A.M.–4 P.M. daily (March–Dec.); Weekends only (Jan.–Feb.) | Page 331 |
| Tweens and Teens | 10 A.M.–4 P.M. daily (March–Dec.); weekends only (Jan.–Feb.) | Page 332 |

founded the town in 1749. Named for a tobacco merchant (not for a city in Egypt), John Alexander, who purchased the site from its English owner in 1669, Alexandria was a major colonial port, as well as a trade, social, and political center, during Revolutionary times. During the Civil War, Alexandria was occupied by Federal troops and used as a base for Union campaigns in Virginia. In 1801, Congress officially accepted Alexandria as a part of the District of Columbia, but by 1846, Alexandria residents were disillusioned with their disenfranchisement as citizens of the District; they incorporated themselves back into the County of Alexandria. (Current D.C. residents, still disenfranchised, would consider this a smart move.) The now-restored historic area of Old Town Alexandria still looks like it is part of an earlier century.

**Smart Stuff**

**For Tikes...** Alexandria began as a colonial town growing up around a port. In the early days of America, many items had to be imported from other countries. If you lived in Alexandria in colonial times, what would you want to receive by ship?

> Metro: King Street (plus a 15-minute walk; take a shuttle bus, or take a DASH bus down King Street; DASH info: 703-370-3274)
>
> Parking is at a real premium; you need a pass from Ramsay House (see below), so if you're driving, stop here first.
>
> Located in Virginia, eight miles south of Washington, extending west from the Potomac River into Alexandria
> www.dashbus.com

## Ramsay House Visitors Center

In this port city, even the buildings sometimes come from elsewhere. This yellow clapboard house came up the river from Dumfries, Virginia, in 1749 (not all by itself, of course!), to be the home of Lord Mayor (and Scottish merchant) William Ramsay. Cigars were manufactured here after the Civil War; now it's a visitors center and convention bureau, offering free maps, brochures, parking passes for the area, and directions, all more useful here than cigars.

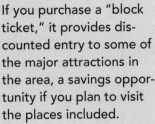

**Money-Saving Tip**

If you purchase a "block ticket," it provides discounted entry to some of the major attractions in the area, a savings opportunity if you plan to visit the places included.

> Metro: King Street
>
> 221 King Street
>
> Self-guiding tour brochures and maps; bicycle trail maps; 24-hour parking passes
>
> Be sure to pick up the *Alexandria, VA Official Visitors Guide;* it even has coupons for good deals inside; or call and request an information packet in advance.
>
> 703-838-4200 or 1-800-388-9119
>
> www.funside.com
>
> http://seewashingtondc.net/nvaattr.htm

## ★Torpedo Factory Art Center; Alexandria Archaeology Lab and Museum

**For All Ages…** Talk about recycling! This World War I munitions plant is now home to artists and archeologists. Over 160 professional artists are at work here: sculptors, painters, photographers, weavers, potters, glass-blowers, stained-glass designers, jewelry designers, and printmakers display and sell their original creations. Kids of all ages enjoy watching the artists, and frequently engage them with questions. Because the building faces the waterfront, this is also a pretty place to picnic or stroll. The **Food Pavilion** (daily 8 A.M. to midnight) behind the building offers several different selections and a pretty outdoor seating area.

Headquartered in the Torpedo Factory is **Alexandria Archaeology,** a working urban archaeology lab and museum. Organized to

preserve and interpret information about the city of Alexandria, **Alexandria Archaeology** (for Tweens and Teens) involves children and families in its work. Visitors observe volunteers at work, cleaning and cataloging artifacts found in the local area, and can explore the exhibit area. Kids are astonished to learn firsthand that these relics of another time were found by digging right within what are now the city limits. This might lend new meaning and value to that old collection of baseball cards or bottle caps. Volunteers are happy to answer questions, and there are videos to see as well.

> Metro: King Street
> 105 N Union, between King and Cameron Streets (waterfront)
> Daily 10 A.M.–5 P.M.; closed January 1, Easter, July 4, Thanksgiving, December 25
> Tours through Friends of the Torpedo Factory arranged in advance for different age groups; call at least two weeks ahead.
> 703-838-4565
> Groups can arrange in advance to visit the lab/museum for an Alexandria Archaeology Adventure Lesson; programs can be specifically designed for children in grades three through twelve. Phone: 703-838-4399.
> Archaeology Museum open Tuesday through Friday 10 A.M.–3 P.M., Saturday 10 A.M.–5 P.M., Sunday 1–5 P.M.; closed January 1, Easter, July 4, Thanksgiving, December 25; 703-838-4399.

## Carlyle House

**For Tweens and Teens...** Where the Old World meets the new, this Palladian-style stone mansion was patterned after English and Scottish manor houses, and built between 1751 and 1753, by Scottish merchant John Carlyle. A man of substantial means, he imported the finest furnishings from Europe and hired the most skilled local craftsmen to produce the beautiful woodwork found throughout the house. Unfortunately, most of the original furnishings have been replaced with similar period pieces, and the original people, including slaves, have been replaced by mannequins in period dress. You can hear some recorded conversations, and also pick up a twenty-two-pound bucket of water, similar to those that slaves were expected to carry. Construction of this eighteenth century house is demonstrated in one unrestored room upstairs, with its exposed beams, handwrought nails, and unplastered walls.

## Smart Stuff

**For Tweens...** If you were building a home in colonial times, what materials would you have wanted to import from England? What would you most likely have used from local sources? (A.)

Of all the historic encounters in this house, where George Washington was a frequent visitor, the most notable was likely the 1755 meeting between Major General Edward Braddock, Commander-in-Chief of the King's Forces in North America, and five colonial governors, whom he asked to financially support Britain's war with the French and Indians. The five colonial legislatures refused, exercising the colonies' newfound feelings of separation from their mother country. The buck started here.

Behind the Carlyle House, a gazebo and a garden function as a public historic park. Picnickers are welcome; BYO.

Metro: King Street
121 N. Fairfax Street, at Cameron Street
Open Tuesday through Saturday 10 A.M.–4:30 P.M., Sunday
    noon to 4:30 P.M.
Tours every half-hour.
Special programs and tours can be arranged for if you call in
    advance: 703-549-2997.
Admission fee; free under age 10
703-549-2997

## Gadsby's Tavern Museum

**For Tweens and Teens...** The "in" place for the fun bunch, Gadsby's Tavern was the social center for eighteenth-century Alexandria. The innkeeper, John Gadsby, who purchased the original tavern from John Wise, joined two buildings (one a tavern and one a tavern/hotel) to provide guests with food, lodging, entertainment, the wares of itinerant merchants, and even the services of doctors and dentists. George Washington might not have slept here (his kitchenless town house was nearby), but he and Martha certainly ate and partied here a great deal. Other visiting notables included James Madison, John Adams, John Quincy Adams, the Marquis de Lafayette, and Thomas Jefferson. Overnight stays meant paying for a *space* in a bed or on the floor; your roommate or bedmate was entirely up to chance. Because this was also the scene for numerous political meetings, it was likely the origin of the phrase "politics makes strange bedfellows." These days, most travelers choose their *own* bedfellows, regardless of their politics.

Thanks to archaeological excavations and inventories of colonial furnishings, the rooms have been painstakingly restored. The tour includes a sampling of the different kinds of entertainment and meeting rooms, as well as bedrooms; it also visits the underground icehouse (talk about water in the basement).

**Gadsby's Tavern Restaurant** (11:30 A.M.–3 P.M. and 5:30–10 P.M., with Sunday brunch 11 A.M.–3 P.M.; 703-548-1288; reservations are a good idea) hearkens back to those thrilling days of yesteryear, when entertainment came with your meal and everybody dressed for dinner. Don't worry—the food is *not* genuinely antique, and includes delicious homemade soups, sandwiches, fresh Virginia ham, roasted turkey and duckling, Sally Lunn bread, English trifle, and buttermilk custard pie; selection of half-priced children's entrees. A good-sized helping of modern-day dough is essential here, but strolling musicians (Sunday and Monday evenings and Sunday brunch) are free; so is the "gentleman" who brings news of 200 years ago on Tuesday through Saturday nights.

Metro: King Street

134 N. Royal Street at Cameron Street

Open Tuesday through Saturday 10 A.M.–5 P.M., Sunday
1–5 P.M., April through September; Tuesday through Saturday 11 A.M.–4 P.M., Sunday 1–4 P.M., rest of year;
closed all federal holidays except Veterans Day

Guided tours quarter before and quarter after the hour; last
tour starts 45 minutes before closing.

Special programs offered; ask about Time Travels, Young
Ladies' Tea, and children's activities.

Admission fee

703-838-4242

## Lloyd House

**For Tweens and Teens...** Although some of us might feel that our
houses are overrun with books, here's a house that actually became a
library. Built in 1797, by the same wise fellow (John Wise, actually)
who established Gadsby's Tavern, the house is an appealing example
of the late Georgian style. A Quaker schoolteacher of Robert E. Lee
lived here for a time, as well as yet another set of Lees.

The house functioned as a subscription library as early as
1794, and displays books and papers from that period. Lloyd
House became a formal part of the Alexandria public library
system in 1976, and its Virginia Research Collection on the second floor focuses on Alexandria and Virginia history and genealogy. For research about the family, guess there's no place
like a home.

Metro: King Street

220 N. Washington Street

Open Monday through Saturday 9 A.M.–5 P.M.; closed major
holidays

Guided tours (20 minutes) available

703-838-4577

www.alexandria.lib.va.us/exhibit.htm

## Lee–Fendall House

**For Teens…** Though this house was built by a civic leader, Philip Richard Fendall, the Lees far outnumbered the Fendalls in residency; thirty-seven of them called this place home between 1785 and 1903. Actually, even Fendall was a distant Lee relative, and, marrying at various times, three different Lee wives, certainly an in-law. From 1937 to 1969, ironically, it was the residence of someone anathema to Virginia conservatism: labor leader John L. Lewis.

The house, originally Federal white clapboard, was treated to a revival of a different sort during the 1850s. The house was renovated in the Greek classical Revival style, and was accentuated with ornate woodwork and decorations, some of which remain. A treat for miniaturists is the third floor, with its exhibit of antique dollhouses.

On display in the Lee–Fendall House is an original copy of the newspaper eulogy written by Harry Lee for George Washington. Look for the famous phrase, "First in war, first in peace, and first in the hearts of his countrymen." This family did have a way with words. As Alexandria was taken over by the government to give the capital more security during the Civil War, the Union forces appropriated the house for use as a Union hospital. The beautiful colonial garden includes a 200-year-old magnolia tree and boxwood-lined paths.

## Smart Stuff

**For Teens…** During the eight years of the American Revolution, imports from England were nearly nil. If you were a colonial merchant, what kinds of goods would you be lacking? (B.)

Metro: King Street
614 Oronoco Street
Open Tuesday through Saturday 10 A.M.–4 P.M., Sunday
    1–4 P.M.; closed Thanksgiving and mid-December until
    February 1; call regarding weekend visits (sometimes used
    for private events and closed to the public)

Guided tours on the hour
Admission fee (some exhibits require additional special fee);
    free for children under 10
703-548-1789

Only one pair of brothers signed the Declaration of Independence, both Lees. Richard Henry Lee and Francis Lightfoot Lee were, ironically, ancestors of Robert E. Lee, who served as leader of the Confederate forces attempting to separate from the Union.

## Alexandria Black History Resource Center

**For Tweens and Teens...** A change of era, this twentieth-century building was the product of a sit-in. Located in the Parker-Gray Historical District, the building was originally built in 1940 as a library for black Americans after a sit-in was staged to protest the segregation of the Alexandria library system. In two rooms, photographs, paintings, books, and ethnic memorabilia depict the black experience in this area from 1749 to the present day. One gallery has the permanent display that tells the history of the Parker-Gray District; the other hosts changing exhibits. The annex, referred to as the **Watson Reading Room,** holds

Because this site is basically a research center, there is not much here for small children. African American children of all ages, however, will take great pride in the accomplishments of black Americans that are highlighted in the displays.

## Helpful Hint

For convenience when taking a group, call ahead to ask for copies of this tour and any other relevant information.

many books and documents on African American topics; while the references do not circulate, the public is welcome to come here to do research. Historical sites connected with black history are listed on a printed walking tour; pick one up at the Information Desk. Of note on this tour are the **Franklin and Armfield Slave Market** and the **house** of a free black master carpenter, **George Seaton,** elected to the City Council and the Virginia legislature during Reconstruction.

> Metro: King Street
> 638 N. Alfred Street
> Tuesday through Saturday 10 A.M.–4 P.M.; closed major holidays
> Call in advance if bringing a group; reservations needed for a
> guided tour.
> Donations
> 703-838-4356
> http://ci/alexandria.va.us/oha/bhrc.html

A number of blocks south and west of the Resource Center, on Holland Lane, between Duke Street and Eisenhower Avenue, the **Alexandria African-American Heritage Park** is an eight-acre cemetery, preserved wetland, and memorial site. If you have a chance to wander through, you will find numerous memorial sculptures.

## Christ Church

When Franklin Delano Roosevelt brought Winston Churchill to attend services here on the World Day of Prayer, January 1, 1942, he was maintaining a tradition. Twentieth-century presidents attended services here, usually on a Sunday close to George Washington's birthday, sitting in his pew, #60. The Lee family also had pews here; Robert E.'s was #46. In continuous use since 1773, the church has been restored to its original Georgian-style beauty. Some parts are original to the structure: the hand-blown glass windows, for example, and the cut-glass chandelier that was one of the most advanced types of light fixtures available in the early nineteenth century. In the early 1800s, the galleries, organ, bell tower, and church bell were added, but, of course, modern heating, which came later, was probably the most appreciated innovation.

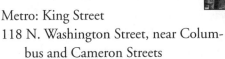

*The gates to historic
Christ Church*

The old **Parish Hall** is now a gift shop and houses an exhibit on the church's history. The graveyard was Alexandria's only burial ground until 1805; thirty-four Confederate soldiers, among others, are buried here.

Metro: King Street
118 N. Washington Street, near Colum-
    bus and Cameron Streets
Open Monday through Saturday 9 A.M.–4 P.M., Sunday
    2–4 P.M., except during services; closed holidays and after
    services January 1, Thanksgiving, and December 25
Guided tours (20 minutes) available, but *call before visiting.*
Donations
703-549-1450

## Friendship Firehouse Museum

**For All Ages...** It is always nice to know people in high places, and this firehouse had an auspicious start. When the Friendship Fire Company was organized in 1774, it had an impressive list of "honorary" volunteers, including high ranking political figures, governors, and even George Washington. Before they had a building, the fire company met in taverns, with its equipment stored in members' barns. Ironically, the original building was destroyed by fire and rebuilt in the 1850s. The first floor exhibit room of this restored Italianate building houses fire-fighting equipment, such as leather buckets, speaking trumpets, and an ornate hand-drawn fire "engine," from the eighteenth and nineteenth centuries.

On the second floor, furnished in Victorian style, is the firemen's meeting room, testifying to the fraternal character of its organization in the community. Although it ceased fire fighting in the 1870s, the current Friendship Veterans Fire Engine Association continues as an historic and ceremonial organization.

Metro: King Street
107 S. Alfred Street, between King and Prince Streets
Friday and Saturday 10 A.M.–4 P.M., Sunday 1–4 P.M.; closed
    January 1 and December 25
703-838-3891

## The Lyceum

**For Teens…** In addition to serving as Robert E. Lee's schoolteacher, Benjamin Hallowell was the prime motivator for establishing a cultural center in the city of Alexandria. In 1839, this Greek Revival building boasted a library, lecture rooms, natural history exhibits, and programs with guest speakers such as Daniel Webster. Despite a slight hiatus during the Civil War, when it was used by both Confederate and Union troops, the Lyceum continues in Hallowell's vision to host lectures, concerts, and educational programs on local and state history, serving as Alexandria's history museum. Exhibits include photographs, prints, silver, period furniture, ceramics, and memorabilia from the Civil War.

Adjacent to the Lyceum is a gift shop, with reproductions of early pewter, silver, brass, glassware, prints, posters, toys and games for kids, needlepoint patterns, books, exhibit catalogs, and regional food items to select from as Old Town mementos. You can also stock up on Alexandria and Virginia maps and brochures, and consult the knowledgeable staff if you have any questions.

Metro: King Street
201 S. Washington Street
Monday through Saturday 10 A.M.–5 P.M., Sunday 1–5 P.M.;
    closed January 1, Thanksgiving, and December 25
703-838-4994

## Old Presbyterian Meeting House

Reverend Alexander Whitaker evidently converted Pocahontas in 1614 in Jamestown, and ever since, Presbyterians have been worshipping in Virginia. Alexandria, with its Scottish heritage, was an obvious spot for this brick church built in the mid-1770s. George Washington's memorial service was held here in 1799, and in the graveyard, lies, among others, Dr. James Craik, Washington's doctor, and the surgeon general of the Continental army. The tomb of an Unknown Revolutionary War Soldier is enclosed in a sarcophagus, marked by a wrought-iron rail. An active church until 1889, the Meeting House again opened its doors in 1949 and, fully restored, still uses its old-fashioned gate pews in its original building.

> Metro: King Street
> 321 S. Fairfax Street, between Wolfe and Duke Streets
> To visit the sanctuary, stop at the church office first, Monday through Friday 9 A.M.–5 P.M.
> 703-549-6670

## Stabler-Leadbetter Apothecary Museum

**For Tweens and Teens…** The family that sells together sometimes stays in business 141 years; that's what happened to the Stabler family, who founded the Apothecary Shop in 1792, Alexandria's oldest mercantile establishment. Of course, it helped to have high-class patrons like Henry Clay, John C. Calhoun, Robert E. Lee, James Monroe, George Mason, and of course, the father of our country, George

### Smart Stuff

**For Tweens and Teens…** Several of our modern-day medicinal and food products come from herbs and plants. Ginger ale, a popular drink and aid for calming upset stomachs, is made from ginger root, said to quell nausea. What present-day herbal products can you name?

Washington. Martha was a good customer, too; her letter requesting a quart of castor oil still hangs in a glass case in the shop. Looking similar to its appearance in colonial days, the Stabler-Leadbetter Apothecary Museum displays its original collection of 900 colorful hand-blown medicinal bottles, with gold-leaf labels, as well as other antique items including old-fashioned scales, account books, prescriptions, and medical wares such as equipment for blood-letting.

The adjoining gift shop sells antique books on medicine, antique medicine bottles, and candy (*not* antique). All proceeds help support the museum.

> Metro: King Street
> 105 S. Fairfax Street
> Open Monday through Saturday 10 A.M.–4 P.M., Sunday
>      1–5 P.M., April through December; closed Wednesday,
>      November through March; closed January 1, Thanks-
>      giving, and December 25
> Admission fee
> 703-836-3713

If you've been plodding along with us all this time, you *must* be hungry, or at least thirsty, by now. Up and down King Street is a variety of eateries. The **Farmer's Market** (301 King Street; 703-838-4770) is a good stop for fresh fruit and veggies, and for baked goods. **La Madeleine** (500 King Street; Sunday through Thursday 7 A.M.–10 P.M., Friday and Saturday 7 A.M.–11 P.M.; 703-739-2854; near Gadsby's Tavern) serves wonderful baked goods, fresh salads and homemade soups, and delectable entrees from quiche to salmon, with cozy ambience, though in a cafeteria-style setting. **Bread and Chocolate** (611 King Street; 703-548-0992) has sandwiches and delectable desserts; it serves breakfast as well as lunch (so you could *start* the day here) and is a block away from the Lyceum (where you might stop in for tourist maps and brochures). The Vietnamese restaurant, **East Wind** (809 King Street; Monday through Friday 11:30 A.M.–2:30 P.M., Monday through Thursday 5:30–10 P.M., Friday and Saturday 5:30–10:30 P.M., Sunday 5:30–9:30 P.M.; 703-836-1515), will especially appeal to the vegetarians in your crowd with hot soup (pho) and vegetarian entrees, in addition to its fish, chicken, and beef offerings; it's near Christ Church and the Friendship Firehouse Museum. **King Street Blues,** which *isn't* on King Street (112 N. St. Asaph Street; Monday through Thursday 11:30 A.M.–10 P.M., Friday and Saturday 10:30 A.M. to midnight, Sunday 11:30 A.M.–10 P.M.; 703-836-8800), is a southern-style roadhouse diner with music to accompany your meal. Head here for a bargain: chicken, garlic potatoes, beef stew, or meatloaf; or you could try this one for brunch.

Near the King Street Metro is the **Hard Times Café** (1404 King Street; Sunday through Thursday 11 A.M.–10 P.M., Friday and Saturday 11 A.M.–11 P.M.; 703-837-0050), for inexpensive entrees such as chili, Mexican dishes, cornbread, steak fries, onion rings, and, for atmosphere, jeans-and-T-shirted waitstaff, Texas décor, historic Old West photos, and country jukebox music.

**Shopping in Old Town** is an adventure in itself. There's no shortage of ways to spend your money; most of the shops are along King Street and Washington Street. (We start near **Ramsay House Visitors Center,** but if you follow our list backwards, you can start near the King Street Metro.) For music, try **The Record Mart** (second floor, 217 King Street, between Lee and Fairfax Streets) for a huge collection of new, used, and hard-to-find records, CDs, and tapes. **Granny's Place** (303 Cameron Street)—with a name like Granny's, it has to be good—sells dolls, toys, wooden playground equipment, unusual games and puppets, in addition to children's clothing (just in case you haven't spent enough already). **Diversities** (821 King Street) is a showplace of costly treasures to peruse if you send the kids (the older ones) off on their own for a little while, or leave them (with a grown-up) at Granny's Place a little longer. **Women's Work** (1201 King Street) offers handcrafted items from around the world, including charms made from the bones of water buffalo, Japanese puppets from Indonesia, woodcarvings, and other unusual treats. For the comic book collectors, **Aftertime Comics, Inc.** (1304 King Street) stocks not only hard-to-find collectors' items, but also back issues of *MAD* and *Eerie* magazines. **The Tiny Dwelling, Inc.** (1510 King Street) has miniatures adults and teens

will appreciate, more than younger kids will; from tiny college pennants to miniature guns and china, all the accoutrements you could ever want for a dollhouse are available here. Thumbelina would have had a field day. **A Likely Story** (1555 King Street) even has a play area for younger kids while everyone who loves books has a heyday; special programs are also offered, so you might want to check by calling ahead. These are just a few suggestions; please keep us posted when you find gems we can share with other readers.

# ★Claude Moore Colonial Farm at Turkey Run

**For All Ages...** Here's a chance for kids to find out what the good ol' days were *really* like. Although colonial kids didn't have to go to school, wait 'til your youngsters find out what they *did have* to do. Costumed park service guides (and school-age volunteers on weekends) carry out the daily activities of residents in this example of a lower-income farm family of the 1770s. Planting and harvesting tobacco, wheat, and vegetables; tending farm animals; chopping wood; and cooking were all part of the daily routine, demonstrated here with period tools. The orchard, fields, pond, hog pen, and single room farmhouse are accessible via dirt paths that wind around the property. Eighteenth-century Market Days are held the third full weekends in May, July, and October, with live colonial music, puppet shows, crafts, and merchants. Families can participate in colonial craft-making, munch on delicious colonial-style food, and shop for reproductions of eighteenth-century clothing, soap, jewelry, pottery, and toys. A visit here makes a wonderful contrast with Mount Vernon. Maybe after seeing this, kids will think it is better to go to school.

## Smart Stuff

**For Tikes...** Make a toy you would have liked to play with if you lived in colonial times. Toys were extremely simple then, made from sticks, pebbles, corn husks, cloth, and other natural materials.

Remember to use modern restrooms *before* you come to the Colonial Farm; the portable toilets aren't exactly outhouses, but they're today's equivalent.

Metro: not accessible; bus or car only
Route 495 (Beltway) to Route 193 (Georgetown Pike) East,
    to access road, ½ mile on left
6310 Georgetown Pike, McLean, Virginia
Open April through mid-December, Wednesday through
    Sunday 10 A.M.–4:30 P.M.; closed mid-December-March,
    holidays, rainy days
Group visits must be scheduled in advance. Also, call for a
    calendar of special events at different times of the year.
703-442-7557

# ★Mount Vernon

**For All Ages...** While adults are impressed with this beautiful water-front property and its gorgeous views, kids are more interested in the outbuildings that housed the smokehouse, the kitchen, the stables, the blacksmith shop, the cobbler shop, the spinning house, the carriage house, the greenhouse and all the others, on the grounds of George Washington's home planta-tion in Virginia; you can visit the tomb and the gardens as well. Washington believed a

*The mansion at Mount Vernon*

## Helpful Hint

Special activities and tours are offered at Mount Vernon, so it's a good idea to call in advance to make your plans appropriately. Ask for the information on landscape and garden tours, and also "Slave Life at Mount Vernon" tours; these are at certain times of the year, with no extra charge. Wagon rides, hands-on activities, and demonstrations of farm methods and tools, as well as the "Hands-on History" area that lets kids handle eighteenth-century toys and tools, are also scheduled for specific months and times. Be sure to request all the details in advance. Phone: 703-780-2000. Write to: Mount Vernon Education Department, Box 110, Mount Vernon, VA 22121, to ask for additional information.

farm should be completely self-sufficient, so all its needs had to be met on site, even those of the "spirit." His Scottish-born farm manager persuaded him to include a working distillery on his property. (In the process of being reconstructed, the still will *not* actually produce any liquid refreshment). On days when there are no specific demonstrations, youngsters can peer into these various outbuildings and see how food was prepared, how shoes were made, how laundry was done, and how the father of our country got around, since he didn't have a presidential limousine. The **Mount Vernon Forest Trail** provides a quarter-mile hike, which kids enjoy.

Opportunities to learn a wide variety of colonial skills and activities are offered at Mount Vernon, including: carding and spinning wool, digging for archaeological artifacts, learning slave songs, playing with colonial toys, constructing wooden buckets, hiking nature trails, and even popping into a Revolutionary War tent filled with soldiers' gear and an imposing life-size statue of George Washington. An eye-opening contrast to the gracious main building is a visit to the slave quarters. Pick up an Adventure Map to guide your choices of where to go and what to see while exploring George and

*George Washington slept here.*

Martha Washington's estate. Guides in eighteenth-century costumes are stationed at various spots on the grounds and in the mansion.

For somebody who had a war to fight and a young country to run, it is amazing that Washington was able to take out time to run his plantation and entertain nearly 800 guests per year. Obviously, a prerequisite was this lovely mansion, a convenient inheritance from his older brother, Lawrence. In addition to the beautiful period furnishings and accessories (30 to 40 percent of which are original), Mount Vernon holds some interesting curiosities. One is the key to the Bastille (displayed in a glass case), a gift to Washington in 1790, from his wartime buddy, the Marquis de Lafayette. There's a foot-operated fan chair, to keep away the flies when Washington sat down to read (remember, screens hadn't been invented yet). The gracious, formal rooms reflect the Washingtons' focus on entertainment, particularly dancing and dining.

The Georgian mansion, with its tall white columns, is not only a study in elegance, but an example of artifice as well. Its "stone" blocks are really wood coated with sand, edges carefully beveled, and painted white! Since air conditioning was not available in the eighteenth century, George and Martha and their guests enjoyed the cool breezes from the Potomac, sitting out on their large veranda. Nowadays, when navy ships pass the mansion, they offer a salute in tribute to our first president.

Now for the gift shops (yes, that's plural). **The Mount Vernon Gift Shop** is just at the entrance gate (no admission ticket needed

to go into the shop). It sells jewelry, toys, postcards, souvenir items, fine gifts, film, reproductions and furniture, and books, some especially for kids, published by Mount Vernon. There's also a **Christmas Shop** in here, and a Plant Window, with plant seeds for colonial style gardening. Hours are extended slightly during "tourist season," but the shop is open daily 9 A.M.–5:30 P.M. **The Museum Shop,** near the upper garden (next to the Slaves' Quarters), carries the same types of merchandise but in a smaller setting; it's also open 9 A.M.–5:30 P.M. daily. If you happen to arrive by boat, there's also a **Wharf Shop,** on the banks of the Potomac, open 11 A.M.–5 P.M., March through October, Tuesday through Sunday, for souvenirs.

If you get hungry at Mount Vernon, you're in luck. There's a snack bar with breakfast, lunch, and, of course, snacks. **The Mount Vernon Inn,** open daily for lunch, and for dinners every day but Sunday, is a little on the pricey side; reservations are recommended (703-780-0011). Waitstaff are in period costume, and fare is primarily colonial-style.

## Smart Stuff

**For Tikes and Tweens...** The Washington family entertained a great deal, and even George Washington found time to fuss over his menus. If you had lived at Mount Vernon, what kinds of foods would you have had to eat? Look around the dining room for some hints; there were lots and lots of courses. (D.)

## Smart Stuff

**For Teens...** The Washington family, like so many others in the South, relied on numerous slaves to maintain their lifestyles and livelihoods. If you had lived on such a plantation, what changes would you have implemented in order to maintain your farm and home with the employment of (freed) hired hands?

Metro: Huntington, and then bus #11 P; best by bus or car

Riverboat trips on *The Spirit of Mt. Vernon* from Pier 4 at
6th and Water Streets, SW, except in November and December. Fares include admission fee to Mt. Vernon; snack bar;
202-554-8000

South end of the George Washington Memorial Parkway,
overlooking the Potomac River

Open daily 8 A.M.–5 P.M., April through August; 9 A.M.–
5 P.M. in March and September through October; 9 A.M.–
4 P.M. rest of year. To avoid spring and summer crowds,
come before 11 A.M., especially Monday, Friday, and Sunday mornings, or after 3 P.M. (you'll still have to leave by
5:30 P.M., though).

Self-guided tours of home and gardens.

Tourmobile offers Mount Vernon tours April through October; 202-554-5700.

Gray Line also offers tours here and to Old Town; 202-289-
1995.

Admission fee

Gift shops: 703-799-6301

703-780-2000

www.mountvernon.org

# George Washington's River Farm

**For All Ages...** One of George Washington's five farms, purchased
in 1760, and rented out to tenant farmers for tobacco farming,
River Farm is not your average colonial farm, with its elegant main
house and vistas of the Potomac River. Here, there is a special garden area for children. They
can visit a "pizza garden" that
grows basil, thyme, oregano,
and other herbs essential to
this favorite dish. They can
explore a bat cave, with a
fort-like structure covered

**Smart Stuff**
**For Tikes...** Farmers have
to decide what to plant on
their land. What would you
plant if you had a farm?

## Smart Stuff

**For Tweens...** Do you know what tenant farming is? What are some of the differences between being a tenant farmer and owning a farm? (E.)

with plants and vines, and can visit gardens that specifically attract bats, butterflies, birds, and bees. There are even special child-size rocks for sitting in the stone garden. Visitors—both young and grown-up—can enjoy self-guided tours of the 1757 main house, with its period furnishings, and the elaborate gardens with their labeled plants. Today, George Washington's River Farm is owned by the American Horticultural Society, who purchased it in 1973. The Society maintains both display and test gardens on the twenty-seven acre site.

## Smart Stuff

**For Tweens and Teens...** George Washington's first job was as a surveyor. What does a surveyor do? See if you can find out whether the tools used in Washington's day are the same kinds used today. (F.)

## Helpful Hint

Call in advance for the schedule of classes and lectures, and for details on Living Laboratory Tours (for groups) on Wednesdays.

Metro: not accessible; come by bus or car only

7932 East Boulevard Drive, Alexandria; off the George Washington Memorial Parkway, 4 miles south of Old Town, Alexandria

Open Monday through Friday 8:30 A.M.–5 P.M.; closed holidays
703-768-5700 or 1-800-777-7931
www.ahs.org

# Collingwood Library and Museum on Americanism

**For Teens...** Like red, white, and blue? Have we got a place for you
to visit! A research facility devoted to Americanism, the Collingwood Library and Museum was once actually part of George Washington's property at River Farm. Now owned by a nonprofit group,
the Foundation for Collingwood Library and Museum, this white-
columned mansion houses an
extensive collection of books,
slides, and videotapes on patriotic subjects that can be
viewed on site and also taken
out on loan. Flags of all fifty
states, along with those of the

**Helpful Hint**
This is more of a research
facility on patriotism than
a full-fledged museum.

District of Columbia and the five armed services, are on display. Of
special interest is a Sioux Chief's full-length ceremonial headdress of
eighty-seven eagle feathers, along with a collection of American Indian artifacts, basketry, pottery, and beaded belts.

> Metro: not accessible; come by bus or car only
> 8301 East Boulevard Drive, Alexandria, off George Washing-
>     ton Parkway
> Open Monday, Wednesday, Thursday, Friday, Saturday 10 A.M.–
>     4 P.M.; Sunday 1–4 P.M.; closed Tuesdays and holidays
> Call about slide and video shows.
> 703-765-1652

# Woodlawn Plantation

**For Tweens and Teens...** The kind of wedding gift *everyone* would
want, Woodlawn Plantation was given by George and Martha

Washington to their granddaughter Eleanor (Nelly) Park Custis when she married Lawrence Lewis (Washington's nephew and personal secretary) in 1797. At the same time, Washington turned over to the young couple a distillery and a mill, hoping they would thus have a means of employment, he said, because "idleness is disreputable." In the late Georgian style, this typical Virginia plantation home echoes the style of the groom's boyhood home, Kenmore, in Fredericksburg, Virginia. Still decorated with period antique furnishings, including some pieces brought from Mount Vernon, Woodlawn also has a formal garden, with lovely roses in summer. The drawing room still houses the harp and piano that Nelly and her daughters used to give frequent informal musical performances.

> Metro: Huntington, and then take a 9-A bus; come by bus or car
>
> 7.5 miles south of D.C. on U.S. Route 1 (enter opposite the turnoff for Route 235)
>
> Open daily March through December 10 A.M.–4 P.M.; January through February weekends only; closed Thanksgiving and December 25.
>
> Guided tours only, on the half hour
>
> Admission fee. Discounted combination ticket for Woodlawn and Pope–Leighey House.
>
> 703-780-4000

# Frank Lloyd Wright's Pope-Leighey House

**For Tweens and Teens...** A visit to the Pope-Leighey House on the grounds of the Woodlawn Plantation is a study in contrasts. The graciously detailed colonial architecture of the past is only a few minutes' walk from the stark, modernism common in the twentieth century. An example of what its architect Frank Lloyd Wright called his "Usonian" architecture (from author Samuel Butler's abbreviation for "the United States of North America"), the house was to be a "no frills," simply designed home, theoretically affordable for the

American middle class. Built for a Washington area journalist, Loren Pope, in 1941, it was sold to the Leigheys five years later; it was then threatened with demolition by highway construction, when the Leighey family turned it over to the National Trust for Historic Preservation.

The flowing space and strong horizontal lines, typical of Wright's work, take precedence over the potential attic and basement storage; Wright liked living space, not closets. Maybe he never had to store outgrown clothing or toys. An added attraction to this house is the furniture, designed by the architect himself. While the house is built of cypress, glass, concrete, and brick, the furniture is more inviting comfort-wise. Unfortunately, the architect is no longer available to design any for you. Everything about this home is utilitarian but quite attractive.

## Smart Stuff

**For Tweens and Teens...**
Frank Lloyd Wright was one of the twentieth century's foremost architects. His focus was fitting a structure into its natural surroundings, as though it had grown from its environment. In what ways does this house fit that description? (For a surprise tidbit, see Answers list.) (G.)

> Metro: same as for Woodlawn Plantation (above)—this house is on the grounds there
>
> Open daily March through December 10 A.M.–4 P.M.; January through February weekends only; closed Thanksgiving and December 25.
>
> Admission fee. Discounted combination ticket with Woodlawn. 703-780-4000

# Where to Stay in Olde Virginia

These days, visitors don't have to share beds unless they choose to, but there are some bargains to be found in Alexandria.

### Days Inn Alexandria

110 S Bragg Street (Exit 3B off I-395 at Route 236W)
703-354-4950
Metro: King Street

### Radisson Old Town

901 N Fairfax Street
703-683-6000 or 1-800-333-3333
Metro: King Street

### Sheraton Suites Alexandria

801 N St. Asaph Street
703-836-4700 or 1-800-325-3535
Metro: King Street

# Answers to Smart Stuff Questions

**A.** You would have needed to import doorknobs and other hard-ward, perhaps of brass or wrought iron, and some construction tools. If you were prosperous, you might also have ordered fine fabrics and elegant furniture. From local sources, your building materials might have been lumber, stone, or bricks (made from local clay).

**B.** Youngsters might want to consider that England had far greater manufacturing capacity than the colonies, and yet the colonies were home to abundant natural resources, such as wood, and plants like cotton and corn.

**C.** Some herbal products used today are: aloe vera, from aloe plants, for skin irritations and burns; herbal teas from fruits and leaves, such as mint, lemon, or raspberry; dried herbal seasonings for food, such as rosemary, thyme, and basil; and calendula (from marigolds), found in ointments, for healing cuts and bruises.

**D.** The displays here change; some include breakfast foods, such as hoecakes, from cornmeal (like our pancakes), served with butter and honey. The main meal featured smoked ham, fish or shellfish, chicken, duck, game birds, or lamb; fresh vegetables from the garden (such as lettuce, carrots, cucumbers, beans); a variety of potatoes; homemade bread; and desserts such as jellies (like modern gelatin), cakes, and pies from local fruit (peaches, pears, cherries, apples, currants, and figs). No one was expected to eat everything; the presentation was done like a modern smorgasbord.

**E.** Tenant farming is growing produce on land that belongs to someone else. Some of what you grow as a tenant farmer can be used as rent payment for the land; any improvements you make to the property belong to its owner.

**F.** A surveyor studies and measures the topography of land, maps specific areas and boundaries, and might even evaluate the

quality of the land for specific building types. In colonial times, surveyors relied on a 32-point compass card, different lengths of chain for measurements, and markings by tree locations. At some point, the sextant, the telescope, and the leveling rod were developed as well. These tools can still be used, but today we also have cameras, complex technological tools, and global positioning satellite systems to help surveyors with their work.

**G.** The house was actually *moved* from its original site in Falls Church, Virginia, due to highway construction, when Mrs. Leighey donated it to the National Trust for Historic Preservation. This modern structure is nestled on the grounds of the Woodlawn Plantation.

# APPENDIX I
## For the Fun of It

Not usually thought of as fun city U.S.A., D.C. *can* be a really fun place, and we're not just talking about those exciting state dinners in the White House (move along; don't wait for your invitation *there!)* Each season brings its own special events, and almost every imaginable sports and cultural activity is available for the choosing. As with hotels, when you're investigating where to go and when, ask for every conceivable discount. Student? AAA? Senior citizen? Military? Good sports? Birthday? Get creative—who knows *what* might be available—but you have to *ask.*

## Seasonal Events

In addition to the permanent monuments and buildings in Washington, D.C., there are other things to see that depend on *when* you come to town. Each month brings special events and festivities. This being the nation's capital, new and interesting celebrations often evolve. Unless otherwise noted, most events offer something for all ages. Be sure to check the local newspaper for the most up-to-date information, and have a great time.

### Spring

Even before the cherry blossoms decorate the city in pink and white, Washington's spring rituals begin.

## St. Patrick's Day Parade

Bagpipes, floats, and marchers with festive costumes and banners bring in the "green" (no, not money—that's only at the Bureau of Engraving and Printing) in the St. Patrick's Day parade; it winds down Constitution Avenue, from 7th to 17th Streets, NW, traditionally the second Sunday in March. Check local newspaper listings for details.

## Smithsonian Kite Festival

Late in March, usually the last Saturday, while the winds are still impressive, the Smithsonian holds its annual kite festival near the Washington Monument. Adults and kids bring their colorful and creative homemade kites to fly and compete for prizes. Registration 10 A.M. to noon; festival lasts until 4 P.M.

202-357-2700

## Ringling Brothers and Barnum & Bailey Circus

Always a tremendous draw for both adults and children, "the greatest show on Earth" comes to D.C. from late March into early April. You can watch the animals parade from the circus train on the morning before the circus opens.

703-448-4000

## ★National Cherry Blossom Festival

In this city of monuments to war and government, it's nice that there's a special holiday to celebrate natural beauty. At the center of the festivities are the trees themselves, magnificent in bloom, attracting crowds of visitors all day and even after dark, under the huge floodlights. Capping the celebration is the annual Cherry Blossom Parade, with its floats, concerts, celebrity guests, and princesses from all fifty states. Parade information: 202-728-1137; Cherry Blossom events: 202-789-7038 or 202-547-1500. Sometimes the blossoms *do* actually bloom during this two-week celebration.

202-619-7222
www.nps.gov

### ★ *The White House Easter Egg Roll*

**For Tikes...** An event only for youngsters age eight and under, who are not likely to be so hard-boiled yet that they mind the crowds and commotion, the annual Easter Monday roll is really a treasure hunt. Children search for colorful wooden eggs, many with celebrity autographs, hidden on the grounds of the South Lawn of the White House. Puppet and magic shows, dancers, clowns, military drill teams, egg-decorating exhibits, and an egg-rolling contest are all part of the festivities. Besides the tickets (available starting at 7 A.M.—and yes, get there very early—at the Visitor Pavilion on the Ellipse), an accompanying grown-up is the only other requirement for admission. Check to see whether any tickets will be distributed in advance.

202-456-7041

### *The White House Spring Garden Tour/Children's Garden*

In mid-April (check the newspaper), visitors can tour the lovely landscaped Rose Garden and Children's Garden; don't be put off by the lines of people—get into the line. Watch for the bronze impressions of the hands and feet of White House children.

202-456-7041

### *D.C. International Film Festival*

For two weeks in mid- to late April, filmmakers from around the world show their work in movie theaters, embassies, and other screening facilities all over the city. An artistic treat. Some are free; some require admission fees.

202-628-FILM
www.capaccess.org/filmfestdc

### *Shakespeare's Birthday at the Folger*

A birthday by any other name isn't quite the same as this one. On the Saturday closest to April 26, the Bard's real birthday, the Folger Shakespeare Library celebrates in style. Food, Elizabethan music (what else?), theatrical productions, exhibits, and children's events make this a festive day indeed.

202-544-7077 (Box Office)
202-675-0365 (Education Department)

### National Cathedral Flower Mart (and Carnival)

Tra-la, it's May. While adults tiptoe through the tulips (and other plants and herbs), kids can enjoy ethnic food booths, rides, and activities, including an antique carousel and puppet shows. First Friday and Saturday in May.

202-537-6200

### Goodwill Embassy Tour

Travel to other countries without even bringing your passport. Every May, several Washington embassies welcome participants in this annual tour. Tickets include free shuttle bus service. Reservations required. Bon voyage.

202-636-4225

### Air Show at Andrews Air Force Base

The Department of Defense Joint Services holds its annual Open House at Andrews Air Force Base every May. Ground displays and exciting aerial events lure thousands of spectators every year. Up, up, and away.

301-981-4424

### ★Memorial Day

On the Sunday evening (8 P.M.) before Memorial Day, the National Symphony (202-619-7222) performs its memorable concert before thousands on the West Lawn of the Capitol. Music to your ears— bring a blanket.

At the Tomb of the Unknowns in Arlington National Cemetery, a high-ranking government official (or the president) lays a wreath in the 11 A.M. ceremony, which includes military band music, a service, and a speech. The Vietnam Veterans Memorial (202-619-7222) and the U.S. Navy Memorial (202-737-2300) also host commemorative ceremonies. Check the newspaper for additional listings and local events.

202-685-2851

## Summer

What a nice time to have a birthday. In addition to the Fourth of July, this city knows how to celebrate all summer long. Be sure to check local newspaper listings for schedules of the many free musical programs and mid-day entertainment activities around the city.

### *Dupont–Kalorama Museum Walk Day*

**For Teens...** On the first Saturday in June, when the weather is usually gorgeous, go for this walk if you can. Museums and historic houses north of Dupont Circle offer tours, crafts demonstrations, music, and free refreshments. A charming section of the city to explore. Shuttle service provided.

**Helpful hint**
This is not really a kids' activity, but if you can get your teens interested, you'll love it.

202-667-0441

### *DanceAfrica DC*

During the first week in June, Dance Place (8th Street, NE, near Catholic University) hosts a celebration of African culture, with music, dance, visual arts, clothing, crafts, and food.

202-269-1600

### *Alexandria Red Cross Waterfront Festival (Tall Ships)*

The romance of the high seas comes to Alexandria on the second weekend in June. At the Alexandria Red Cross Waterfront Festival, in Old Town (Oronoco Bay Park), you can tour the tall ships, and learn about the seaport through historic reenactments. Food from the local restaurants, music, clowns, children's activities, rides, a petting zoo, canoe rentals, and even fireworks enliven this annual event.

703-549-8300

### Carter Barron Amphitheatre Shakespeare Free For All

[**Tweens/Teens**] The show must go on—and it does, for free. For two to three weeks in June, The Shakespeare Theatre brings the Bard to this venerable northwest amphitheater (16th Street and Colorado Avenue, NW). Check local listings for specifics. At different times during the summer, all kinds of musical performances are also offered here.

202-619-7222

### ★ Smithsonian Festival of American Folklife

Highlighting a specific state each year, this festival incorporates the diverse ethnic traditions that comprise

the U.S.A. Children and adults relish the excitement of discovering the native costumes, music, dance, crafts, and food that represent the rich variety in our heritage. Late June through early July.

202-357-2700

### National Capital Barbecue Battle

This is definitely the place for a hot time in town. Be sure to bring your taste buds to Pennsylvania Avenue between 9th and 12th Streets, NW, on the third weekend in June. Thanks to local restaurants, everything here is saucy, spicy, and finger-lickin' good. Cooking demonstrations and music. You could make a fortune here selling wet wipes. Admission fee. Check newspaper listings.

### ★ Independence Day Celebration

The best cakeless birthday party around begins with a 12:30 P.M. parade along Constitution Avenue, and ends with the spectacular fireworks display above the Washington Monument. The afternoon and early evening are filled with the sound of music—free concerts on the Monument grounds (popular music groups), jazz at Freedom Plaza (14th Street and Pennsylvania Avenue, NW), and the National Symphony on the Capitol's West Lawn (8 P.M.). Join the crowd to celebrate the birthday of the U.S.A.

202-619-7222

### Virginia Scottish Games

Maybe there's a reason they celebrate the Virginia Scottish Games in July: It's a good time of year not to wear pants—kilts are the uniform of the day. Highland dancing, sporting events, fiddling competitions, and plenty of bagpipe music entertain visitors at one of the largest Scottish festivals in the country (Episcopal High School, 3901 W. Braddock Road, Alexandria, Virginia).

703-838-4200

### Greater Washington Soap Box Derby

A capital race without ballots: Nine- to sixteen-year-olds zoom down Constitution Avenue, between New Jersey and Louisiana Avenues, NW, on Capitol Hill, in their homemade chariots. An exciting summer event for all ages. Check newspaper for listing; usually runs during the second week in July.

### Latin American Festival

¡Ole! If you're in town in July, don't miss out on this colorful annual event, with entertainment, international food, arts and crafts, and even a parade. While it's traditionally centered somewhere near the Washington Monument area, check the *Washington Post* for this year's exact location and time. Late July.

### Civil War Living History Day

In mid-August, when it's too hot to fight, visitors can watch reenactments of battles, with valiant "soldiers" dressed in wool uniforms, in a living history program at the Fort Ward Museum and Historic Site

(near Old Town, Alexandria). We're impressed with their willingness to sacrifice personal comfort for historic accuracy. One of the original Civil War forts ringing the city of Washington, parts of Fort Ward have been restored, complete with six mounted guns. Civil War artifacts in the museum here bring this period of history to life. Call for details.

703-838-4848

## Fall

Colorful foliage mixes with colorful events in this delightful season in the nation's capital.

### National Frisbee Festival

Come see the "flying saucers," and the dogs and people who catch them, at the largest noncompetitive Frisbee Festival in the U.S. Labor Day weekend on the grounds of the Washington Monument. Check the newspaper for details.

### International Children's Festival

**For Tikes...** It's a small world after all, at this annual festival for children, with dance and arts workshops, crafts, music, and numerous performances. Kids can get their faces painted, talk to clowns, watch puppet shows, sing, hula-hoop, and enjoy this beautiful setting in the Virginia countryside. Labor Day weekend at **Wolf Trap Farm Park.** Admission fee.

703-642-0862

### Adams Morgan Day

Foods, crafts, and music from Central America, Africa, and Europe take over this incredibly diverse neighborhood in early September. Treats for the eyes, ears, and tummy. Call for details.

202-789-7000

### Kennedy Center Open House Arts Festival

The halls are alive with the sounds of music. A day-long festival in September celebrates the performing arts, inside and outside of this Washington landmark. Local and national artists perform on a multitude of stages, and the National Symphony Orchestra provides an "instrument petting zoo," where children get to try out a favorite instrument. Check the *Washington Post* for details.

202-467-4600 or 1-800-444-1324

### Black Family Reunion

It's like one big happy family on the National Mall when gospel music, ethnic foods, dancing, and crafts help celebrate African American heritage. Mid-September. Check newspaper listings.

202-737-0120 or 202-619-7222

### Greek Fall Festival

On the third weekend in September, the Greek Orthodox Church of Saints Constantine and Helen hosts a Greek Festival to delight the eye and tummy (4115 16th Street, NW).

202-829-2910

### Renaissance Festival

Don your armor. From late August into mid-October, a rural setting in Crownsville, Maryland, becomes a Renaissance village, complete with jousters, magicians, wandering minstrels, medieval food, performances, and crafts. A long ride from D.C., but a whole day's worth of fun. Just remind the kids that only in medieval times did people use their fingers for silverware. Admission fee.

1-800-296-7304

### Rock Creek Park Day

A day at the park without hitting the swings. Rock Creek Park celebrates its birthday on the Saturday closest to September 25. You're invited. Environmental exhibits, crafts, food, music, and recreational activities for children highlight this event.

202-426-6829

### Washington National Cathedral's Open House

Rise to the top. On this very special day at the Cathedral, visitors are allowed to ascend to see the bells at the top of the central tower—a huge climb to an extraordinary view. Below, demonstrations of stone-carving and other crafts used in building the cathedral, carillon and organ-playing; and jugglers, puppeteers, dancers, and strolling musicians all entertain visitors. A Saturday in late September or October; check local listings.

202-537-6200

### Washington International Horse Show

A horse of a different color, this event is a draw for all ages—look at those horses, horses, horses. International teams compete in jumping events, World Cup Dressage, and polo and western reining exhibitions. Food, specialty boutiques, and a family day when kids can watch horse shoeing and learn about riding equipment and how to care for their mounts, round out the offerings. Admission fee; group discount rates. Late October at the MCI Center (6th and F Streets, NW).

301-840-0281

### Seafaring Celebration at the Navy Museum

Yo ho! The Navy Museum's Seafaring Celebration in early November features demonstrations of boat-building, in addition to model making, scrimshaw, music (a chance to hear sea chanteys), storytelling, and other crafts activities. A-vast celebration.

202-433-4882

### *Veterans' Day Ceremonies*

**For Teens…** The Tomb of the Unknowns in Arlington National Cemetery is the setting for this most somber holiday, November 11. A high-ranking government official (often the president) lays a wreath at the tomb. A service takes place at the Memorial Amphitheater, nearby in the cemetery. The Vietnam Veterans' Memorial, Mount Vernon, and the U.S. Navy Memorial are some other sites for Veterans' Day observances.

202-619-7222

## Winter

While everyone else is at home by the fire, this is a really good time to visit Washington, since everywhere you go will be less crowded (and usually heated, if you stay inside).

### *Annual Scottish Christmas Walk*

The guys in the pleated skirts are at it again, but this time it's a parade, with whole clans (not to mention horses and dogs), Highland dancers, kilted bagpipers, storytelling, caroling, craft booths, delicious seasonal food, and children's activities. A wonderful way to start a festive season. First Saturday in December.

703-549-0111

### *Smithsonian's National Museum of American History Holiday Celebration*

A big dose of good cheer comes with this annual celebration of ethnic holidays. From Chanukah, to Christmas, to Kwanzaa, to the New Year, craftspeople, musicians, storytellers, and other performers, as well as decorated Christmas trees, enchant youngsters *and* oldsters. Ethnic foods available.

202-357-2700

### *Pageant of Peace/Lighting of National Christmas Tree*

The first family's lighting of the national Christmas tree in early December inaugurates the three-week-long Pageant of Peace. Along with the fifty-seven additional decorated trees (for each state, the District of Columbia, and the six U.S. territories), there are live reindeer, musical performances (6–9 P.M.), a burning Yule log, a Nativity scene, and caroling. Wear mittens, a hat, earmuffs, wool socks, a muffler, boots—well, you get the idea. Ho ho ho.

    202-619-7222

### Woodlawn Plantation Christmas

These December festivities will carry you back to ol' Virginnie and the days of gracious living. Musicians and carolers stroll the grounds while visitors enjoy wagon rides and refreshments. See how the gentry decorated for the holidays. Call for details.

    703-780-4000

### B'nai B'rith Klutznick National Jewish Museum's Holiday Festival

A lighthearted look at a festive December holiday, this museum offers entertainment, music, games (your chance to learn to play with a dreidel, or small holiday top), and ethnic food for Chanukah, the Festival of Lights. Admission fee. The D.C. Jewish Community Center (1529 16th Street, NW) also celebrates with activities for all ages, including puppet shows, music, stories, and dreidel games. Admission fee.

    Klutznick: 202-857-6583
    D.C. J.C.C.: 202-518-9400

### Festival of Music and Lights

A delightful display of over 300,000 lights decorates the trees at the Washington Temple and Visitors Center of the Church of Jesus Christ of Latter-Day Saints in Kensington, Maryland, in December. A live nativity pageant (6–9 P.M.) outside and a Visitors' Center with seventeen Christmas trees inside inspire holiday spirit. Particularly striking are the trees decorated with ornaments from four different embassies each year. Drama, dance, and musical programs are featured through the holiday season.

    301-587-0144

## *Anacostia Museum's Kwanzaa Holiday Celebration*

December welcomes the Kwanzaa celebration at this museum with African-inspired music, dance, games, and folk-tales. A holiday workshop for families is held the first Saturday in December.

202-287-2061

## *Martin Luther King Jr. Day*

Fittingly, at the Lincoln Memorial, and also at the Martin Luther King Memorial Library (901 G Street, NW), the birthday of this famous civil rights leader is celebrated with wreath-laying, guest speakers, military color guard, choral music, prayer vigils, dance, and theater. Third Monday in January. Check the local paper.

202-619-7222

## *Presidents' Day*

Although many Americans consider Presidents' Day (third Monday in February) as bargain time for purchasing big sale items, here in D.C. we take these things so seriously that there are also separate celebrations for Abraham Lincoln's (February 12) and George Washington's (February 22) birthdays. The usual speeches, ceremonies, and parades abound. The Gettysburg Address is read at the Lincoln Memorial, and a wreath is laid, in Lincoln's memory. In Washington's case, Alexandria celebrates its native son with a weekend-long celebration. Check the local newspapers for all the details.

## *Inauguration Day*

A monumental event in itself, Inauguration Day occurs every four years on January 20, two months following the presidential election. A swearing-in ceremony on the Capitol steps is followed by speeches, a lengthy parade along Pennsylvania Avenue, and the gala round of inaugural balls. Crowds and cold weather are the only sure things you can plan for. Try to know someone important by the next Inauguration Day, so you can watch the festivities from somewhere warm.

202-619-7222

### *Chinese New Year Festival*

While tikes might not get a bang out of the firecrackers at this celebration, they will love the colorful dragons, lions, dancers, and
music-makers in the parade. Passing under the elaborate Friendship
Archway (H Street between 5th and 7th Streets, NW), the revelers
wind up and down the street several times, so onlookers can enjoy
their performance. February or early March; check local papers.

# Sports

Especially if you've been standing in lines and shuffling in and out
of important exhibits all morning, your body is probably ready for
some liberation. Here are some suggestions.

## Bike Rentals

Spring and fall in Washington are absolutely glorious for bike riding; even some winter days are mild enough for an invigorating out-
ing. We don't recommend hitting the city streets (you might just do
that, literally, with all the traffic); we do suggest finding out about
the wonderful trails you can explore. ADC publishes a *Greater
Washington Area Bike Map,* available in bookstores, or call 703-750-
0510. You can also contact the Washington Area Bicyclist Association (202-628-2500) for trail information. The National Park
Service (202-619-7222) has free maps of some of the trails. The
most popular bike paths are along the C & O Canal Towpath,
through Rock Creek Park, the Capital Crescent Trail, the Mount
Vernon Trail, and the Washington and Old Dominion Bike Trail.

### *Better Bikes*

Bikes and equipment delivered to your hotel; daily or multiple day
rentals available.

   202-293-2080

### *Big Wheel Bikes*

Four locations: Georgetown—1034 33rd Street, NW (202-337-
0254); Alexandria, Virginia—2 Prince Street (703-739-2300); Ar-

lington—3119 Lee Hwy. (703-522-1110); and Bethesda, Maryland— 6917 Arlington Road (301-652-0192).

### City Bikes
Located in Adams Morgan—2501 Champlain Street, NW

202-265-1564

### Fletcher's Boat House
Yes, they also rent bikes. 4940 Canal Road, NW

202-244-0461

### Thompson's Boat Center
Bikes, too. Rock Creek Parkway and Virginia Avenue.

202-333-4861

## Boating
The beauty of the Washington waterfront in almost all seasons will really float your boat. Come give it a try; everyone will sleep better tonight. Wear rubber-soled shoes and slather on that sun block. The Potomac River can be treacherous; call the U.S. Geological Survey River Line (703-260-0305) for river conditions information.

### Pedal Boats in the Tidal Basin
Everyone except the tiniest of tots can get into the act here: pedal boats. Tidal Basin Boat House, 1501 Maine Avenue, SW, off 15th Street can be very busy on weekends and in nice weather; call first.

202-479-2426

### Fletcher's Boat House
Canoes, rowing shells, small sailboats, and rowboats. 4940 Canal Road, NW (at Reservoir Road) Gentle water for the younger set. Snack bar.

202-244-0461

### *Jack's Boats*
Canoes, kayaks, and rowboats. 3500 K Street, NW in Georgetown, under the Key Bridge.

202-337-9642

### *Thompson's Boat Center*
For the serious as well as amateur paddlers. Canoes, rowboats, shells, double shells, and sunfish. Rock Creek Parkway and Virginia Avenue, NW.

202-333-4681

## Fishing
You shoulda seen the one that got away. You'll need to check on fishing regulations in D.C., and bring your own equipment. Fletcher's Boat House (above) sells bait and tackle.

202-244-0461

### *Chain Bridge*
Anywhere along the Potomac near Chain Bridge you can drop a line.

### *Fletcher's Cove on the Potomac*
This popular place to cast off is a mile above Key Bridge (in Georgetown).

### *Hains Point*
Near East Potomac Park, the wall along the Washington Channel here is a good place to perch.

## Golf
There are certainly enough choices for duffers in the Washington area to suit you to a tee.

### *East Potomac Park*
Ohio Drive at Hains Point. Renovated practice facility, even with covered and heated stalls. Two nine-hole courses and one eighteen-

hole course. Also, a **miniature golf** course (even for full-sized people); Circus Mini Golf Putt-4-Fun, Ohio Drive, SW

202-554-7660

### Langston, North East
2600 Benning Road, NE (Metro: Stadium–Armory), across from RFK Stadium; eighteen holes. Club rentals, pull carts, and riding carts.

202-397-8638

### Rock Creek Park
16th and Rittenhouse Streets, NW. Eighteen holes.

202-882-7332

## Hiking
A perfect response if someone tells you to go take a hike would be to explore some of the beautiful trails in the D.C. area. Bring your water bottle and insect repellent.

### Billy Goat Trail
On the Maryland side of Great Falls Park, 11710 MacArthur Boulevard, Potomac; remember the *name;* a four-mile climb.

301-299-3613

### C & O Canal Towpath
A favorite with locals, you have a choice along a 184-mile trail. From Georgetown to Glen Echo Park, seven miles; to Old Angler's Inn, 12.5 miles; to Great Falls, fourteen miles; or to Violette's Lock, twenty-two miles.

301-299-3613 or 202-653-5190

### Great Falls Park
This Virginia park offers sixteen miles of footpaths.

703-285-2965

### Rock Creek Park

A whole network of hiking trails. Guided tours with U.S. park rangers; call for details.

202-426-6829

### Theodore Roosevelt Island

Walk across the footbridge from the parking area on the Virginia side of the Potomac, and enjoy the 2.5 miles of paths through woods, marshland, and swamp.

703-289-2500

## Horseback Riding

Tired of exhaust fumes? Get a horse!

### Rock Creek Park Horse Center

Military and Glover Roads, NW. Guided rides on the equestrian trails in Rock Creek Park are offered at this center; minimum age is twelve. Reserve at least one week in advance; fee. Call for details. **Pony rides** for the younger set on a special pony trail.

202-362-0117

## Ice Skating

In the winter in Washington, ice is nice. If we're having one of our more wintry seasons, you can skate free on the **Reflecting Pool** (between the Lincoln Memorial and Washington Monument), on the pond in **Constitution Gardens** (near the Vietnam War Veterans Memorial), or on the **C & O Canal;** for conditions and details, call the U.S. Park Service.

202-619-7222

### Cabin John Ice Rink

In Bethesda, Maryland, at 10610 Westlake Drive, there's an all-year-round, indoor rink; rental skates; snack bar; pro shop. Suggestion: This is a good way to keep those kids busy in the *evening.* Call for schedule.

301-365-0585

### National Sculpture Garden Ice Rink

At 7th Street and Constitution Avenue, NW (Metro: Smithsonian) on the Mall, across from the Archives. Rental skates; snacks.

202-289-3360

### Pershing Park

At 14th Street and Pennsylvania Avenue, NW; skate rentals.

202-737-6938

## Swimming

Swimming is a great evening activity, where kids can unwind, but if you're here when the weather during the day is really hot, read on. If you try to swim in the Canal or the Potomac, you'll be in hot water; they are *not* safe for swimming.

### D.C. Department of Recreation Aquatic Program

To locate the nearest public outdoor or indoor pool, call the Aquatics Division of the D.C. Department of Recreation; ask also for advice about the neighborhood where the pool is located.

202-576-8884

### Montgomery Aquatic Center

In Bethesda, Maryland, you'll find this spiffy new indoor facility at 5900 Executive Boulevard N. (Metro: White Flint); another great evening activity.

301-468-4211

## Tennis

Tennis enthusiasts will *love* the selection of playing sites available in the nation's capital. To locate the courts nearest you, call the D.C. Department of Recreation (202-673-7646) or Rock Creek Tennis (202-722-5949).

### East Potomac Park

Located at 1090 Ohio Drive, SW; twenty-four courts, indoor, outdoor, lighted, and clay; reservations needed up to a week in advance.

202-554-5962

*Washington Tennis Center*
In Rock Creek Park, at 16th and Kennedy Streets, NW; indoor, outdoor, lighted, and clay; reservations needed up to a week in advance.

202-722-5949

# Spectator Sports

If you'd rather watch *other* people sweat, there are plenty of spectator sports to choose from. You can root for teams from around the world (embassy teams) as well as locals, and watch polo, rugby, cricket, and soccer—and you don't even need an accent to cheer. Call the National Park Service (202-619-7222) for the schedule at West Potomac Park. Now, if you don't mind paying to watch other people work, here are the Washington area highlights.

## Camden Yards

The Washington Senators deserted us in 1971, so if you really want to see a professional baseball game while you're in town, head for Baltimore (202-432-SEAT—Ticketmaster—or 410-481-SEAT), about an hour from D.C. You can visit the **Orioles Baseball Store** at 914 17th Street, NW, in D.C., for tickets or baseball souvenirs (202-296-BIRD). For bus information to the stadium, check with Metrobus (202-637-7000); also try the MARC train that goes from Union Station to Camden Yards (1-800-325-7245).

## Fed-Ex Field

Here's an attraction you don't even have to get to; it's the **Washington Redskins** football team stadium, and the only kinds of tickets they sell, season tickets, are always sold out. If you're football fans, keep on good terms with your Washington area friends and relatives; even if *they* don't have tickets, you can be sure they know someone who does. (Redskins Road and Stadium Drive, Landover, Maryland). As for everybody else, turn on your local TV set, grab some popcorn, and join the excitement.

301-276-6000

## George Mason University Patriot Center

The big events at this 10,000-seat college arena (4400 University Drive, Fairfax, Virginia) bring spectators to their feet to cheer. Check local sports listings.

703-993-3000 or 1-800-551-SEAT (Ticketmaster)

## MCI Center

At this huge, state-of-the-art, spectator sports and entertainment facility (601 F Street, NW; Metro: Gallery Place–Chinatown), visitors can enjoy the high tech interactive National Sports Gallery, the American Sportscasters Association Hall of Fame, the Discovery Channel Store, the film *Destination DC,* and several restaurants. Also, of course, you come here to see the Washington Wizards play NBA basketball, the Washington Mystics play WNBA basketball, the Georgetown Hoyas play NCAA basketball, and the Washington Capitals play NHL hockey.

202-628-3200

## Robert F. Kennedy (RFK) Stadium

For professional soccer, head for RFK Stadium to see the DC United, Washington's Major League Soccer team. For tickets, call Ticketmaster (202-432-SEAT or 1-800-551-SEAT); for a group of twenty or more, call 703-478-6600.

202-547-9077

# Entertainment/The Arts

While much of the politics in Washington is quite entertaining, this city has a sophisticated cultural scene of its own. If you're interested in backstage tours of any of the theaters, call the theater to ask for details. In addition to purchasing tickets directly from a specific venue, they are available through several outlets:

**TICKETplace** (202-TICKETS) is Washington's only discount day-of-show source, at the Old Post Office Pavilion (1100 Pennsylvania Avenue, NW; Metro: Federal Triangle).

**Ticketmaster** (202-432-SEAT), at the Hecht's Department Store (12th and G Streets, NW), and at the Marvin Center at GW University, across from Lisner Auditorium, (21st and H Streets, NW). Charges a fee.

**Tickets.com** (703-218-6500 or 1-800-955-5566; www.tickets.com) is a nationwide phone charge service, also requiring a fee for ticketing.

## American Film Institute

**For Tweens and Teens...** The American Film Institute (AFI) is the place for celluloid aficionados to go for classic and art films, as well as the popular variety, domestic and foreign. However, the AFI is moving to headquarters in a newly renovated art deco theater in downtown Silver Spring, Maryland, probably in 2003. We can all look forward to the return of this resource in its new location. For now, though, there's no address or phone number; rent a video.

## Arena Stage

**For Tweens and Teens...** Washington's first professional resident theater, the Arena is the place to go for topnotch dramatic productions (Sixth Street and Maine Avenue, SW; Metro: Waterfront). Both shows and performers from this outstanding theater have moved on into commercial success on Broadway, including James Earl Jones, Robert Prosky, Ned Beatty, George Grizzard, and Jane Alexander. Three different theaters are actually housed at the Arena, the large (827-seat) theater in the round (a type of performance setting that might be a new experience for many young people), the smaller Kreeger (500 seats), and the 180-seat Old Vat Room. New plays and playwrights have always been welcomed. Shows here will generally have appropriate language, but you might want to call regarding subject matter, for most kids.

202-488-3300
www.arenastage.org

## Carter Barron Amphitheater

A warm weather cultural mecca for the District (16th Street at Colorado Avenue, NW), the Carter Barron is the site for performances sponsored by the National Symphony Orchestra, the D.C. Blues Society, the Shakespeare Free for All, the District Curators, Inc. (popular music and jazz), and the National Park Service, running throughout the summer. Some concerts are free, while others have ticket charges. Check the *Washington Post* for schedule and details.

202-619-7222

## Comedy

**For Teens…** As for comedy in Washington *outside* Congress, check local listings for the most up-to-date information and appropriateness of content to the audience you have in mind. Some of the most popular are:

**Capitol Steps** (202-312-1555 or 202-432-SEAT)
**ComedySportz** (703-486-4242)
**Gross National Product** (202-783-7212 or 202-432-SEAT)
**Evening at the Improv** (202-296-7008)
**Headliners** (301-942-4242)

## D.A.R. Constitution Hall

An elegant building with an auditorium seating over 3,500 people, Constitution Hall (18th and D Streets, NW) hosts a variety of musical performances, from the Boston Symphony to Ray Charles. Housed in this same building are the headquarters for the Daughters of the American Revolution and a museum (discussed in chapter 4).

202-628-4780 or 1-800-432-SEAT

## D.C. Armory

Located at 2001 East Capitol Street, SE, this venerable capital landmark frequently houses the Ringling Brothers Barnum & Bailey Circus when it comes to town, as well as the National Christmas Show, and other special programs like trade shows and antique shows. The Armory is the headquarters for the National Guard, which uses it most of the time. Call for schedule and details.

202-547-9077

## Folger Shakespeare Theater

**For Teens...** The Elizabethan-style theater at the Folger Shakespeare Library is the setting for plays, lectures, readings, and musical performances (202 E. Capitol Street, SE; Metro: Capitol South); discussed in chapter 2. The Folger Consort, performing madrigals, troubadour songs, renaissance, medieval and baroque music has been wowing audiences for over twenty years, seasonally, October through May. The annual PEN/Faulkner fiction readings by major authors also take place here. Yea, verily.

202-544-7077
www.folger.edu

## Ford's Theater

**For Tweens and Teens...** "Other than *that*, Mrs. Lincoln, how did you like the show?" goes the old joke. Without the same risk to life and limb, you, too, can enjoy musical and dramatic performances, some even bound for Broadway (511 10th Street, NW; Metro: Metro Center). True to its period restoration, Ford's seats are actually chairs, and *not* scaled to certain relevant anatomical parts of today's theater-goers (bring cushions); see also chapter 8. Ford's Theatre's production of Charles Dickens' *A Christmas Carol* is a highlight of the D.C. Christmas season.

202-347-4833 or 1-800-955-5566 (Tickets.com)
www.fordstheatre.org

## GALA Hispanic Theater

A celebration in itself, the GALA Theater (1625 Park Road, NW) presents shows that are bilingual, Spanish and English, highlighting the Hispanic heritage of many D.C. residents. In addition to community-based theater, the GALA hosts programs of music, poetry, dance, and contemporary and classic plays. Check newspaper listings.

202-234-7174

## Gallaudet Theater

Spotlight this one if any members of your group are deaf, as performances are all in American Sign Language. The drama department at Gallaudet (800 Florida Avenue, NE) stages three productions a year in American Sign Language. In an appropriate twist, voice interpretation devices are available for the *hearing*. Call for details.

202-651-5000; TDD: 202-651-5050
www.gallaudet.edu

## George Mason University Patriot Center

**For Tweens and Teens...** Big-name country performers and major rock concerts are staples of this huge 10,000-seat arena (4400 University Drive, Fairfax, Virginia. Check local listings well in advance.

1-800-432-SEAT

Adjacent to the Patriot Center is the new **George Mason University Center for the Arts,** for performances of jazz and classical music, as well as drama.

703-993-8888

## Glen Echo Adventure Theater

**For Tikes and Tweens...** Housed in one of the historic buildings of Glen Echo Park (7300 MacArthur Boulevard; see chapter 9), Adventure Theater provides a kid-friendly experience where children and grownups nestle on carpeted steps to watch a live production on Saturday and Sunday afternoons. Afterward, the actors are often available to sign autographs and answer questions; admission fee.

301-320-5331

## The Puppet Company Playhouse

Also at Glen Echo, The Puppet Company Playhouse features professional puppeteers producing a variety of creative productions geared to specific ages of children. After the performances (Wednesday through Friday mornings and Saturday and Sunday mornings and afternoons), the puppeteers frequently demonstrate how the puppets work and talk with their young audience members; admission fee.

301-320-6668

## Hartke Theatre

The consistently high-quality dramatic productions at Catholic University's Hartke (Main Campus Entrance at 620 Michigan Avenue at 4th Street, NE) have turned out Academy Award-winning superstars as well as talented undergraduate actors. Performances here are a D.C. delight.

202-319-4000

## Horizons Theatre

**For Teens...** This theater concentrates on women's works and issues (4350 North Fairfax Drive, Suite 127, Arlington, Virginia). Many original plays are produced here first, and move on to larger venues. Some choices appropriate for teens; call for details.

703-243-8550
www.horizonstheatre.org

## Kennedy Center

This modern palace devoted to the performing arts (2700 F Street, NW; New Hampshire Avenue and Rock Creek Pkwy.; Metro: Foggy Bottom–GWU) offers productions on four different major stages, as well as smaller venues within the building. While a num-

## Helpful hint

While it's sometimes possible to get same-day tickets to performances at the Kennedy Center, it is best to check well in advance if you want tickets to a specific performance for a specific date; inquire about Pay-What-You-Can tickets, SPTs (specially priced tickets), and Rush SPTs.

ber of family-friendly events are scheduled around holiday seasons (Christmas, Easter, Labor Day Weekend, etc.), the Kennedy Center hosts regular performances of opera, classical music concerts, Broadway and pre-Broadway musicals, dance, and drama, which are often appealing to young people. The Theater Lab is famous for children's theater by day, with a special long-running comedy/mystery *(Shear Madness)* in the evenings. The Millennium Stage offers *free* daily 6 P.M. programs especially for families. Check local newspaper listings.

202-467-4600

## Library of Congress

**For Teens...** Concerts (fall through spring) in the Library's Auditorium (1st Street, SE, on Capitol Hill) might require tickets; many are even free. The Mary Pickford Theater also screens films.

202-707-5000
www.loc.gov/rr/perform/concert

## Lincoln Theater

Located in the " U Street Corridor," which years ago was known as "Black Broadway," the Lincoln (1215 U Street, NW; Metro: U Street–Cardozo) is restored to its former elegance. After years of decline, this area is undergoing a revival, with some new rock and contemporary music nightclubs and restaurants. At the Lincoln Theater, audiences again enjoy jazz, rhythm and blues, gospel, and comedy performances (see chapter 8). Especially at night, go to this area only with a group.

202-328-6000 or 1-800-432-SEAT

## Lisner Auditorium

Inexpensive or free tickets are available at the Lisner (21st and H Streets, NW, at George Washington University) for shows from rock to opera, plays to ballets. Not for college students only.

202-994-1500

## Marine Barracks

A one-and-a-half-hour parade featuring a color guard, marching Marines, the U.S. Marine Drum and Bugle Corps, and the U.S. Marine Corps Silent Drill Platoon follows the Friday evening summer concerts here (8th and I Streets, SE). Three weeks notice required for reservations; two months notice for group reservations. Free shuttle bus from parking at the Navy Yard to and from the Barracks. A colorful event for kids.

202-433-6060

## Merriweather Post Pavilion

An outdoor summer venue, Merriweather Post (Off Route 29, Columbia Pike, Columbia, Maryland) has both pavilion and lawn seating (at different prices), for acts as varied as Joan Rivers, James Taylor, Liza Minnelli, Elton John, and the most currently popular rock bands. Check local listings. Travel here by car.

301-982-1800
www.mppconcerts.com

## Movie Theaters

As in other cities, consult major local newspapers and visitor magazines for movie listings.

## National Theatre

Giving new meaning to "off-off-Broadway," productions bound for the Great White Way are often booked here (1321 Pennsylvania Avenue, NW; Metro: Federal Triangle or Metro Center), as are touring companies of current Broadway shows. This venerable Washington landmark has recently been restored, and offers backstage tours by appointment (202-783-3370). October through April, the National offers two free shows for kids on Saturday mornings; call for details.

202-628-6161 or 1-800-447-7400

## Nissan Pavilion

At this outdoor theater, 10,000 can fill the covered pavilion, while another 15,000 can spread out on the lawn (off Route 29, Columbia Pike, Columbia, Maryland); perhaps the Nissan could elect its own representative to Congress with these numbers. Summer highlights here have included such performers as Phish, The Cranberries, The Dave Matthews Band, Rush, REM, and Jimmy Buffett. The giant video screens assure you of a view. Car needed for this one.

> 7800 Cellar Door Drive, Manassas, Virginia
> 202-432-SEAT or 1-800-455-8999

## Round House Theatre

An all-around popular resident theater company in suburban Maryland, the Round House Theatre (12210 Bushey Drive, Silver Spring, Maryland) presents musical and dramatic productions from late August to mid-June. A kid-friendly way to see some well-done productions, though, of course, not all productions are suitable for kids; call first. Sometime during 2002, the Round House will move its house to Bethesda, Maryland, so check before you go.

> 301-933-9530

## Shakespeare Theatre at the Lansburgh

**For Tweens and Teens...** In a beautifully renovated old building, the Bard lives on (450 7th Street, NW; Metro: Archives–Navy Memorial). Stars such as Kelly McGillis, Richard Thomas, and Stacy Keach have lent their talents to this high-caliber outfit. In addition to its Shakespeare repertoire, the Lansburgh also offers works by other well known playwrights. A wonderful opportunity for kids to see first-class theater, if you can

**Helpful hint**
Tickets sometimes sell out months in advance; call way ahead to make your arrangements.

get tickets. Definitely a midsummer night's dream (or midwinter, or midfall, or midspring. . .). Forsooth.

202-547-1122

## Source Theater

**For Teens...** With its strong commitment to showcase works of new and unknown playwrights, Source Theater has established itself as an important part of the Washington theater scene (1835 14th Street, between S and T Streets, NW; Metro: U Street–Cardozo). In addition to Off-Broadway-style plays by established authors, this theater sponsors the Washington Theater Festival each summer, showcasing dozens of new shows in various D.C. locations.

202-462-1073

## Studio Theater

**For Teens...** A completely renovated two-stage theater, the Studio offers contemporary drama on its Mainstage; its Second Stage produces the works of up-and-coming new talent (1333 P Street at 14th, NW; Metro: Dupont Circle). Recipient of numerous Helen Hayes awards for outstanding dramatic achievement. Call for schedule.

202-332-3300

## Warner Theatre

A glamorous older cousin of the Kennedy Center, the Warner opened in 1924 as a combination movie and vaudeville palace (13th Street and Pennsylvania Avenue, NW; Metro: Metro Center or Federal Triangle). Now restored to its original glory, complete with crystal chandeliers and velvet draperies, it is also home to Broadway, off-Broadway, big star entertainment, and the annual performance of *The Nut-*

### Helpful hint

Tickets for this theater often sell out; it's best to ask for the schedule and order tickets way in advance of your trip to D.C.

*cracker* by the Washington Ballet. Going here is a real evening on the town.

202-783-4000
www.warnertheatre.com

## West Garden Court of the National Gallery of Art

On Sunday evenings, October through June, the National Gallery hosts free concerts in this beautiful space (north side of the Mall, between 3rd and 7th Streets, NW; Metro: Archives or Judiciary Square). Many different guest artists participate, as well as the National Gallery Orchestra. DAR Constitution Hall, various galleries, and area universities also offer free concerts. Check local newspapers and visitor magazines for listings.

202-737-4215

## Wolf Trap Farm Park for the Performing Arts

Metropolitan Washington's most popular outdoor theater, offering entertainment almost every night of the summer at its Filene Center amphitheater, Wolf Trap brings to the area pop, folk, rock and roll, jazz, R&B, classical, opera, and country music, as well as all kinds of dance and Broadway tours (1551 Trap Road, off Route 7, Vienna, Virginia—about 45 minutes from D.C.). As an alternative to the seats in the pavilion, there are less expensive lawn tickets available (a good place to bring a blanket and dine alfresco); plenty of picnic tables are also available. Children's Theatre in the Woods (July and August; 703-255-1827; reservations required) offers puppet shows, stories, clown acts, and plays, all for no charge. In the winter, performances take place in the Barns (actually two rebuilt barns) here, a smaller setting with wonderful acoustics. The Barnstorm Series, for children (fall/winter/spring weekends; 703-938-2404), includes puppetry, mime, story theater, dance, and folk music programs.

Education Department: 703-255-1933
703-255-1900 or 703-218-6500 (Tickets.com)
Call Metro Information regarding shuttle service from Metro:
    West Falls Church station and specific hours; 202-637-7000

## Woolly Mammoth Theater

**For Teens...** Aspiring playwrights should definitely discover Woolly Mammoth, which is an "alternative" theater that welcomes manuscripts from new authors (at the Kennedy Center until 2003; Metro: Foggy Bottom–GWU, with a long walk). Recognized for its work by numerous Helen Hayes awards for excellence in theater and regularly reviewed by the *New York Times,* the Woolly Mammoth strives to involve its audience in the issues it presents. Call to check appropriateness of specific performances for your group.

202-393-3939

# APPENDIX II
# Tours: Washington, D.C., Inside and Out

Any way you get around, Washington, D.C., can be inviting, and there are lots of organizations ready to welcome you. Especially if you're totally overwhelmed by all the choice sites we've been describing, you just might want to take a tour. Tantalizing tours range from bikes to boats, from trolleys to ghost walks. Here's a sampling to help you take your pick.

## Bike

For outdoor types who must get their exercise on tour, this is a good workout.

### Bike the Sites, Inc.

For guided bike tours on 21-speed Treks, look into the ten-mile Capital Sites Ride, beginning at the Freer Gallery of Art (March through November). The fee covers your helmet, water, and snacks. Adults must accompany kids under age fourteen.

> 202-966-8662
> www.bikethesites.com

# Boat

Because it's right on the water, D.C. offers a wealth of tour choices by boat.

## Capitol River Cruises

This 50-minute narrated tour leaves the Washington Harbour in Georgetown every hour on the hour (April through October). Travel along the Potomac River on this 65-foot steel riverboat, past Washington's major memorials and monuments; snack bar. Call for reservations.

> 301-460-7447 or 1-800-405-5511

## C & O Canal Boat Rides

Kids are fascinated by these boats with no engines; they are mule-drawn barges. Guides in period costume sing and story-tell their way through the ninety-minute voyage along the C & O Canal (April through October). Reserve in advance.

> 301-299-3613 (Great Falls, Maryland) or 202-653-5190
> (Georgetown)

## DC Ducks Land and Sea Tours

Can't decide whether to walk or swim? Here's your big chance! Take the ninety-minute guided tours aboard these amphibious open-air army vehicles all decked out in red, white, and blue (Union Station, March through October; Metro: Union Station). On land you'll bump along past some of D.C.'s major sites, and then—splash!— you'll cruise the Potomac for a half-hour.

> 202-966-3825

## Potomac Riverboat Company

Three different ships can take you sightseeing along the river, in-cluding one that drops you off to visit Mount Vernon (board at the Torpedo Factory in Old Town, Alexandria, at the end of King

Street, or at Georgetown Harbour; specific dates April through October); concession stand. Call for details to make your choice.

703-684-0580

## Potomac Spirit Narrated Cruise

This narrated cruise along the Potomac (Pier 4, 6th and Water Streets, SW; March through October) stops off at Mount Vernon for a two-hour visit; food available.

202-554-8000

## The Spirit of Mount Vernon

Here's another option for a visit to George Washington's gracious home and grounds along the Potomac: a cruise down the river, part of the day on the water and part at Mount Vernon (Pier 4, 6th and Water Streets, SW; January through October); concession stand. Remember, there's a restaurant at Mount Vernon; admission fee to Mount Vernon is included.

202-554-8000

# Bus, Limousine, Trolley

If you'd like a faster track, jump on one of the many tour vehicles circulating throughout the city every day. How, when, where:

## African American Heritage Tour

This two- or three-day program guides visitors through Washington's many attractions of special significance to African American heritage. Call to request the very helpful African American Heritage and Multicultural Guide, check the Web site, or just pick up the materials at the D.C. Visitors Center.

202-588-5535 or 202-789-7000
www.washington.org/tour/afroamer.html

## Capitol Entertainment Services

Minibus sightseeing packages include Monuments and Memorials, African American Heritage, and Student Discovery. Call for details.

202-636-9203

## Gold Line/Gray Line of Washington

Offering a wide variety of tours, this bus company can also provide multilingual guides (in many languages). Tour packages include: Washington After Dark; Li'l Red Trolley All Day Tours; Mount Vernon/Alexandria Tour; Washington, Embassy Row, and Arlington National Cemetery Tour; and the Interiors of Public Buildings Tour. Seasonally, there are also tours available to Williamsburg, Monticello, and Gettysburg.

301-386-8300 or 1-800-862-1400

## Old Town Trolley Tours of Washington

Board this replica of a Victorian streetcar for a narrated tour past major sites throughout Washington, including Embassy Row, Georgetown, the Mall, the Smithsonian museums, Union Station, the White House, Arlington National Cemetery, and some of the city's well-known neighborhoods (Union Station; Metro: Union Station). Free re-boarding at eighteen stops (one loop), so you can get off and explore further if you'd like. Evening tours, too, but reservations required.

202-966-3825

## Scandal Tours

Can you do justice to the scandals of Washington in only seventy-five minutes? Well, you can try. These tours employ actors from the comedy troupe Gross National Product to impersonate some major perpetrators, as this mobile comedy show steers you from one infamous site to the next (April through September). Reservations required.

1-800-758-8687

## Tech Tours

Aboard a multimedia minibus, you can settle back and enjoy a six-hour guided exploration of Washington, D.C. Includes escorted stops at major sites. Check the Web site for a virtual tour, and call for a brochure.

301-261-2486
www.TechTours.org

## Tourmobile Sightseeing, Inc.

All over Washington you will see Tourmobiles as they pick up and drop off visitors at twenty-one sites in the city and three at Arlington National Cemetery, guide-narrated spiels continuing along the way. Tourmobile also has tours to Mount Vernon and the Frederick Douglass National Historic Site, as well as some seasonal twilight tours. Tickets are available at Tourmobile Ticket/Information booths around the city, through Ticketmaster, or directly from Tourmobile drivers.

202-554-5100

# Self-Guided Tours

The advantage of a self-guided tour is that your guide never leaves you. The disadvantage is that your guide is as ill-informed as you are, so be sure to take along the appropriate materials to help him/her out. Enjoy the company.

## AAA Walking Tours

If you belong to AAA, you are probably already familiar with the Tour Books for different parts of the country. The Mid-Atlantic Tour Book offers Walking Tour suggestions, maps, and information for different parts of the city, in addition to Alexandria, Virginia. Check your phone book for your local office for the American Automobile Association.

703-222-9000

## Arlington National Cemetery Tour

Private cars are not permitted in the Cemetery, so you will notice that everyone is either walking or riding the Tourmobile. Pick up a map at the visitor center when you enter, and spend a few minutes selecting those sites you most want to visit here and planning your self-guided tour; this is a huge place, so you won't want to just wander.

703-979-0690

## Black History National Recreation Trail

To visit African American history sites in historic neighborhoods, call for the brochure, with details of sites, locations, and photos. Included are: the Frederick Douglass National Historic Site, Lincoln Park, Metropolitan A.M.E. Church, Howard University, Mary McLeod Bethune Council House National Historic Site, and the Mt. Zion Cemetery and Female Union Band Cemetery.

202-619-7222

## D.C. Heritage Tourism Coalition

This group of ninety "heritage organizations" shares with visitors Washington's beautiful historic and ethnic neighborhoods, parks and gardens, house museums, architecture, and places of worship. At the D.C. Visitors Center, pick up the map, welcome brochure, and convenient cards for specific areas of the city you plan to visit—each card describes major sites and has a small map for visitors to follow for that part of D.C.

For guided walking tours, call 202-828-WALK or check the
    Web
202-661-7581
www.dcheritage.org

## Mount Vernon

However you get to Mount Vernon and for however long you plan to stay, you will need an Adventure Map to follow while you visit (so pick one up when you arrive). Tours are self-guided, but along the way, both inside and out, you will meet docents in eighteenth-

century garb; these are the folks who can enrich your tourin
swering your questions.

703-780-2000

# Tape Tours

Driving your own car in Washington, D.C.? Here's an opportunity to bring along a "virtual guide"—a three-hour-long cassette tape tour through the city, Mount Vernon, and Old Town Alexandria. Produced by CCInc. in New Jersey, audiotapes are available at some hotels and gift shops; call for details.

201-236-1666

# Walking

Perhaps the most dependable source of transportation at your disposal, walking is a wonderful way to explore Washington.

## Anecdotal History Walks

Customized tours for groups or individuals are available, through specific areas, including Georgetown, Adams Morgan, or political Washington. Call for specific details and arrangements.

301-294-9514
www.dcsightseeing.com

## Doorways to Old Virginia

Truly a last minute treat (buy your ticket at least twenty minutes in advance), this guided walking tour, complete with costumed docents, is a fair-weather friend. You can get tickets next to the Ramsay House in Old Town,

### Helpful hint

Choose from the Ghosts and Graveyards Tour, a History Tour, or the Mostly Ghostly Tour, all complete with folklore, legends, and bizarre and strange tales of goings-on in colonial days. Groups should call in advance: 703-548-0100.

Alexandria, for these one-hour, six-block walking tours (April through November).

703-548-0100

## TourDC

Ninety-minute walking tours through Georgetown on Saturdays and Thursdays; book well in advance.

301-588-8999

## Tour de Force

Tour de Force customizes guided tours of Washington for groups; both walking tours and bus tours are offered.

703-525-2948

# Television and Radio Station Tours

Kids often find media of special interest. It's always exciting to see some familiar voices and faces, and to discover that their work is facilitated by real, life-size people doing their jobs here in Washington, D.C. Some television and radio stations offer regular tours; others require pre-scheduling, so call for details.

## Voice of America

**For Teens...** This is the world's largest radio station, broadcasting on twenty-six channels in forty-two languages around the world. Regular tours; call for reservations. No children under eighth grade.

202-619-3919

## Washington's major commercial television stations (tours):

WJLA, Channel 7: 202-364-7777

WTTG, Channel 5: 202-244-5151

WUSA, Channel 9: 202-895-5999

## Washington's major commercial radio stations (tours):

WTOP, 1500 AM: 202-895-5040

WRC, 980 AM: 301-587-7100

WGMS, 103.5 FM: 202-895-5040

If you have a crew genuinely interested in the world of the airwaves, check the Yellow Pages for more listings. Take a look at www.yellow pages.com.

# APPENDIX III
## Now What?

For months, we've been collecting ideas from parents, teachers, and kids who have visited Washington, D.C. As the answer to the inevitable question after your visit—"Now what?"—here are some follow-up suggestions to build on your travel experiences. These do not preclude getting your photographs developed, however, so get moving!

## The Capital Scavenger Hunt

Patience is a virtue. If you stuck with the scavenger hunt, you're in luck. The **answers** appear at the end of this appendix, and someone in your group will need to be in charge of the prizes for the most correctly answered questions. We suggest a Washington, D.C., sweatshirt or T-shirt or baseball cap or snow-scene paperweight (the kind with lots of little white sprinkles coming down over a famous Washington site) or a mug or a pen (containing shredded money, from the Bureau of Engraving and Printing). You name it, and send us *your* ideas.

## Sharing Your
## Washington, D.C., Experiences

You will want to reunite with those who shared your delayed plane flights, your missed connections, your weather joys or miseries, and your waits in the long line for the White House tour or the Bureau of Engraving and Printing. So, schedule a **REUNION.**

We hope at least some of you kept **JOURNALS,** as per our suggestion early in the book. This is the time to get together and compare notes; who wrote what about where and whom? How differently did people experience the same events? Taking turns reading sections aloud is sometimes hilarious or poignant; enjoy those shared memories.

And those **PHOTOGRAPHS.** Some groups have told us about **PICTURE PARTIES,** where all members bring their photos to display and share. Kids can help each other organize what they've got, and round out their own collections. Sometimes it's hard to identify everything you've seen all by yourself; putting heads together should help. At this event, participants can work on the labeling, to protect those memories for good. Some folks will take **SLIDES** or **VIDEOS** instead of prints. Individually or in groups, travelers can put together slide shows to share at a reunion, and everyone loves to watch videos of themselves and their friends.

One teacher posts the photos from each year's trip all over his classroom, so parents and students can enjoy looking at them all through the next year. They're quite an enticement for the next group of kids who hope to participate in this kind of trip, and wonderful fun for those who are looking back at what they've done.

No trip is complete without its **AWARDS.** These, of course, are *funny* awards; everyone can make suggestions for the categories and the recipients. If you talk about possibilities *before* the trip, lots of ideas will occur along the way. The *Turtle Award* will, of course, go to the one who has been consistently late for everything. The *Major Gifts Award* goes to the one who, by misplacing his jacket, shoe, backpack, ticket stubs, etc. has unwittingly contributed the most to the city of Washington. And the *Good Housekeeping Award* is for the ones whose hotel room(s) needed a backhoe just to clear away the rubble. Everyone can use creativity to come up with the categories, and have a secret ballot vote to choose the "winners." We're sitting by the mailbox waiting to hear what you think up.

# Individual and Group Project Ideas

So you thought you were finished learning about Washington, D.C.? Wrong. Here are some suggestions to keep those brain cells thriving.

## Tikes

If you could be the president for a day, what would you want to accomplish?

Make a flag for your room (or classroom) out of materials from a scrap bag and some glue.

## Tikes and Tweens

Make an original "native" mask like some you saw in the museums. Read about some of the uses of masks. How do styles vary from country to country?

Young children will enjoy creating their own original stamp designs. They can focus on a specific theme, such as a holiday, special event, or famous person. They might even want to commemorate their visit to Washington, D.C.

Gather some photos or artwork about your favorite spot in Washington, D.C. What makes that place significant for you?

## Tweens

The Washington Monument is a building that has no mortar to hold its stones together. See whether you can duplicate it (in miniature) using uniform wood blocks, sugar cubes, or other materials.

## Tweens and Teens

If you had to reestablish a capital city for the U.S. today, where would you locate it, and why? Draw its new location on a map of the U.S. (Teams of students could work on this issue and then present their plans to the class.)

For an imaginary country, you and some classmates can write an original constitution. What rights would you want to give to the citizens? What would be the obligations of the government?

Design a museum for an imaginary city. What purpose would your museum serve for the city's population and its visitors?

Washington, D.C., has a large percentage of its land devoted to "public spaces." What is the importance of public spaces in a city? What kinds of public spaces would you advocate in an "ideal" city?

## Teens

Of the government activities you witnessed on your trip to Washington, D.C., what was most impressive? Most disappointing?

There's a controversy over the rights and responsibilities of District of Columbia residents, since they have no voting representation in Congress and no state to provide a base for the city's financial support. What rights and responsibilities would *you* give to the capital's citizens? Should D.C. be granted "statehood" status? Why or why not?

Look at the public buildings that are the work of architects from the nineteenth and twentieth centuries. What public buildings are most impressive to you? Why?

After visiting the Kennedy Center and other performing arts facilities, and some of Washington's art galleries, what recommendation would you make about national support for the arts? What part of our national budget would you want to allocate to support art spaces and artists? Who should decide which projects and people get federal funds?

Research the work of James McNeill Whistler, contrasting his different styles—from the ornate oriental "Peacock Room" in the Freer to his "Arrangement in Black and Gray: the Artist's Mother" in the Louvre (Paris). Where can you find the largest collection of Whistler's work?

[Surprise! It's in the Freer Gallery, right here in Washington, D.C.]

Research African music. Trace its use as roots for American music: jazz, blues, R&B, rock.

Adults pay local, state, and federal taxes. Find out where your area's tax dollars go. If you were in charge of the federal budget, what categories would you want funded? (Think about interstate highways, defense, school lunches for impoverished children, medical research, NASA, etc.) Make a chart to show what percent of the national budget should go to each category you choose.

Write a letter to an elected official (from your city, county, state, or national government), discussing a problem you would like to see addressed and your suggestions for correcting it.

Every four years, our country goes through a national presidential election, and often there is great controversy about the process. What changes would *you* like to see for the next presidential election? (You might want to consider the following questions:

Should there be a uniform time when all polls close across the U.S.? Should radio and T.V. commentators not be allowed to predict individual states' outcomes using "exit polls"? Should "live" media in zones where the polls are already closed be accessible in areas where the polls are still open? Should states go to a mail-in or e-mail voting system? How can jurisdictions guard against voter fraud?

## All Ages

Write a letter to your local newspaper telling your impressions of Washington, D.C., from your trip.

Of all the magnificent artwork in the Basilica of the Shrine of the Immaculate Conception, perhaps the most impressive is the use of mosaic tiles. Try your hand at this medium, using a piece of cardboard for your pencil design, with rubber cement as a base coat. Cut up fabric or paper, broken eggshells, bits of ribbon or colored foil, to use for your creative project.

# A Few More Ideas to Think About

After seeing Washington, D.C., build a model of a capital city of a fictitious country. What kinds of monuments and public buildings would you want it to contain?

After seeing artifacts in the Smithsonian museums, construct a time capsule (in a shoebox or similar container). What kinds of items would you include to give future generations an idea of what life in the early twenty-first century was like?

# Scavenger Hunt Answers

1. The ornately carved Columbus Doors, at the main entrance to the Capitol, stand 17 feet high and weigh 20,000 pounds.

2. The lady is Justice, at the U.S. Supreme Court, where we hope she is hard at work.

3. These bronze cranes struggle to break free of their barbed wire bonds as the central figures of the National Japanese American Memorial.

4. A. Philip Randolph was the founder of the Sleeping Car Porters Union, and his statue stands appropriately in Union Station.

5. This clock is also in Union Station, over the doorway to the East Hall on the main floor.

6. The Hirschhorn, of course.

7. The *Enola Gay,* still the object of controversy as the plane that dropped the first atomic bomb on Hiroshima at the end of World War II, is suspended from the ceiling in the National Air and Space Museum.

8. Mercury, the Messenger of the Gods, stands poised over a beautiful fountain in the rotunda of the West Building of the National Gallery of Art.

9. A baseball autographed by the legendary Babe Ruth rests in a glass case at the National Museum of American History.

10. A statue of Alexander Hamilton, first Secretary of the Treasury, stands on the south plaza of the Treasury Building, at 15th Street and Pennsylvania Avenue, NW.

11. The Albert Einstein Memorial, outside the SW corner of the National Academy of Sciences Building at 2101 Constitution Avenue, NW, is a 12-foot bronze sculpture of this famous physicist. The universe is depicted at his feet. You can sit in his lap and pose for a photo (but it still won't make you a genius).

12. At the bottom of the enormous stairway is a plaque adding the names of Alaska and Hawaii, the forty-ninth and fiftieth states.

13. Corn and tobacco, the cash crops of Virginia in Thomas Jefferson's day, peek from beneath his coat as he stands in the Jefferson Memorial.

14. A $100,000 bill is on display in the Bureau of Engraving and Printing; for official use only, so don't get excited.

15. On Massachusetts Avenue, NW, near the Embassy of India, of course, is a larger-than-life sculpture of Gandhi, India's most revered national leader.

16. A sentence from George Washington's letter to the congregation of the historic Touro Synagogue in Newport, Rhode Island, after his visit there. The letter is on display in the B'nai B'rith Klutznick National Jewish Museum.

17. Rung for the opening of Congress and on national holidays (and practiced from 6:30–9:30 P.M. on Thursdays) in the clock tower of the Old Post Office Pavilion, the Ten Congress Bells are replicas of those at Westminster Abbey.

18. This quotation from William Shakespeare's *The Tempest* is inscribed on the pedestal under the female figure outside the Pennsylvania Avenue entrance of the National Archives.

19. There are four of these statues at the National Law Enforcement Officers Memorial.

20. A piece of moon rock is embedded in a stained glass window commemorating the flight of Apollo 11 in the Washington National Cathedral.

21. In the National Arboretum, there are twenty-two columns that once adorned the east portico of the U.S. Capitol building. Removed in 1958, they were set in rows (reminiscent of an ancient Greek temple) at the Arboretum in 1984.

22. The *Turtle,* America's first submarine, was invented in 1776. You can see it at the Navy Museum.

23. P.T.109 was the patrol boat that carried young Navy Lt. John F. Kennedy to safety after his ship was destroyed in World War II. It's featured in a Navy Museum exhibit.

24. "The Growlery" was Frederick Douglass's name for a small, one-room building behind his home that was off-limits to his household while he was working.

25. The mast of the USS *Maine* rests in Arlington National Cemetery, across Memorial Drive from the Amphitheater. The battle cry, "Remember the *Maine!*" commemorated the sinking of the *Maine* in Havana harbor in 1898, helping to provoke the Spanish–American War.

26. The Confederate Monument, "Appomattox," stands at the intersection of Washington and Prince Streets in Old Town, Alexandria, Virginia. Erected in 1889, the statue commemorates Alexandria's Confederate dead.

# Selected References

*AAA Mid-Atlantic Tour Book.* Heathrow: AAA Publishing, 2000.

*A Kid's Guide To Washington, D.C.* San Diego: Harcourt Brace & Company, 1989.

Bass, Holly and Ann Berta. *Frommer's Irreverent Guide to Washington, D.C.,* 2nd Edition. New York: Macmillan, 1999.

Baydush, Lisa, Editor. *Going Places With Children in Washington, D.C.,* 15th Edition. Rockville: Green Acres School, 1998.

Berkheim, Laura. *The Washington Historical Atlas: Who Did What When and Where in the Nation's Capital.* Rockville: Woodbine House, 1992.

Billings, Erin, Editor. *Let's Go Washington, D.C. 2000.* New York: St. Martin's Press, 2000.

Blum, John M., Bruce Catton, Edmund S. Morgan, Arthur M. Schlesinger, Jr., Kenneth M. Stampp, and C. Vann Woodward, *The National Experience.* New York: Harcourt, Brace & World, Inc., 1963.

Boikess, Olga, Editor. *Zagat Survey, 2000 Update: Washington, D.C., Baltimore Restaurants.* New York: Zagat Survey, LLC, 1999.

Brauer, Jeff and Veronica Wiles. *Out & About In Washington, DC.* Portland: On Your Own Publications, 1998.

Butler, Brian. *DC For Free: Hundreds of Free Things to Do in Washington, DC,* 3rd Revised Edition. Memphis: Mustang Publishing,1997.

Chapman, Abraham, Editor. *Black Voices: An Anthology of Afro-American Literature.* New York: The New American Library, 1968.

Colbert, Judy. *Fun Places to Go with Children in Washington, D.C.* San Francisco: Chronicle Books, 1998.

Division of Publications, National Park Service. *Washington DC: A Traveler's Guide to the District of Columbia and Nearby Attractions.* Washington, D.C.: U.S. Department of the Interior, 1989.

Evelyn, Douglas and Paul Dickson. *On This Spot: Pinpointing the Past in Washington, D.C.* Washington, D.C.: National Geographic Society, 1999.

Fogle, Jeanne. *Two Hundred Years: Stories of the Nation's Capital.* Arlington: Vandamere Press, 1991.

Ford, Elise Hartman. *Frommer's Memorable Walks in Washington, D.C.,* 3rd Edition. New York: Macmillan, 1999.

Ford, Elise Hartman. *Frommer's Washington, D.C. from $70 a Day,* 10th Edition. Foster City: IDG Books Worldwide, Inc., 2000.

Hathorn, Guy B., Howard R. Penniman, and Howard Zink, *Government and Politics in the United States.* New York: D. Van Nostrand Co., Inc., 1961.

Kelly, C. Brian. *Best Little Stories from the White House.* Nashville: Cumberland House, 1999.

McCormick, Patricia S. and Steve Cohen. *The Parents Guide to the Best Family Videos.* New York: St. Martin's Griffin, 1999.

McKay, Kathryn. *Around Washington, DC with Kids.* New York: Fodor's Travel Publications, 2000.

Minow, Nell. *The Movie Mom's Guide to Family Movies.* New York: Avon Books, 1999.

Nilsson, Dex. *The Names of Washington, D.C.* Rockville: Twinbrook Communications, 1998.

Pitch, Anthony S. *Exclusively Washington Trivia.* Potomac: Mino Publications, 2000.

Rubin, Beth. *The Complete Idiot's Travel Guide to Washington, D.C.* New York: Macmillan, 1999.

Rubin, Beth. *Frommer's Washington, D.C. with Kids.* New York: Macmillan, 1998.

Russell, Elizabeth F. *Our Nation's Capital: Activities and Projects for Learning About Washington, D.C.* New York: Scholastic Professional Books, 1996.

Stann, Kap, Jeff Williams, Randall Peffer, and Eric Wakin. *Washington, DC & the Capital Region: A Lonely Planet Travel Survival Kit.* Australia: Lonely Planet Publications, 1997.

Surkiewicz, Joe, Bob Sehlinger, with Eve Zibart. *The Unofficial Guide to Washington, D.C.,* 5th Edition. New York: Macmillan, 1999.

*The First Ladies.* Washington, D.C.: White House Historical Association, 1989.

Truman, Margaret. *White House Pets.* New York: David McKay Company, Inc., 1969.

Waldstein, Mark. *Mr. Cheap's Washington, D.C.* Holbrook: Adams Media Corporation, 1996.

*Washington, D.C. Tourist Guide,* 4th Edition. Greenville: Michelin Travel Publications, 1999.

www.digitalcity.com

www.smarterkids.com

www.turnoffthetv.com

www.washington.org

# Index